OXFORD

On Course for IELTS

Student's Book

On Course for

IELTS

Student's Book

Darren Conway & Brett Shirreffs

OXFORD
UNIVERSITY PRESS

253 Normanby Road, South Melbourne, Victoria 3205, Australia

Oxford University Press is a department of the University of Oxford.
It furthers the University's objective of excellence in research,
scholarship, and education by publishing worldwide in

Oxford New York
Auckland Cape Town Dar es Salaam Hong Kong Karachi
Kuala Lumpur Madrid Melbourne Mexico City Nairobi
New Delhi Shanghai Taipei Toronto

With offices in

Argentina Austria Brazil Chile Czech Republic France Greece
Guatemala Hungary Italy Japan Poland Portugal Singapore
South Korea Switzerland Thailand Turkey Ukraine Vietnam

OXFORD is a trade mark of Oxford University Press
in the UK and in certain other countries

National Library of Australia
Cataloguing-in-Publication data:

Darren Conway & Brett Shirreffs
On Course for IELTs Student's Book

ISBN 978 0 19 551663 0
ISBN 0 19 551663 X

1. International English Language Testing System. 2.
English language - Textbook for foreign speakers. 3.
English language - Examinations. 1. Shirreffs, Brett,
1968-. II. Title.

428

Typeset by OUPANZS

Printed in Hong Kong through Sheck Wah Tong Printing Press Ltd

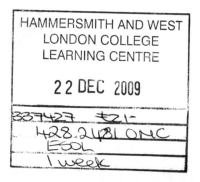

Acknowledgements

The authors and publisher wish to thank the following authors and copyright holders for granting permission to reproduce their material:

Sally Morgan, extract from *My Place*, 1987, published by Fremantle Arts Centre Press; Heather Shea-Schultz and John Fogarty, *Online Learning Today: Strategies that work*, 2002, reprinted with permission of the publisher Berrett-Koehler Publishers Inc., San Francisco, CA. All rights reserved, www.bkconnection.com; Fred Luthans, *Organisational Behavior*, 1985, published by McGraw Hill Singapore, reproduced with the permission of the McGraw-Hill companies; Larry Elliot, *Job satisfaction falls for public workers*, 22 March 2001, The Guardian, Guardian Newspapers Ltd; *Aventis Triangle Forum presentation*, 1999, presented by Michio Kaku, for the Center for Applied Policy Research (C.A.P.), University of Munich; *The New Yorker Collection*, 1976, James Stevenson from Cartoonbank.com. All rights reserved; *The UK 2000 Time Use Survey – When we do the things we do*, 2000, British National Statistics Department, Crown copyright material is reproduced with the permission of the Controller of the HMSO and the Queen's Printer for Scotland; 'Population change and People's Choices' from *6 Billion: A Time for Choices*, 1999, United Nations Population Fund, www.unfpa.org; *The Third World Debt* and *Spend A Few Minutes Learning the Facts of Life*, 2003, Christian Aid, UK; *In Contrast: Smart Growth versus Sprawl*, 8 September 2000, National Resources Defense Council, www.nrdc.org; Florence Sakade, extract from 'Peach Boy' 1958, from *Japanese Children's Favorite Stories*, published by Charles E. Tuttle Co. Inc. of Boston, Massachusetts and Tokyo, Japan; Chris Slane and Robert Sullivan, *Maui: Legends of the Outcast*, 1996, published by Slane Cartoons Ltd; Todd Dvorak *Illustrative Literature Catches On*, 22 July 2002, reprinted with permission of The Associated Press; Chris Turner, extract from *The Simpsons Generation*, 2001, Shift Magazine; Jean-Paul Rodrigue, *Changes in Global Trade Flows*, 1999–2002, Dept. of Economics and Geography, Hofstra University; Elliot Aronson, 'What is Social Psychology', 1995, from *The Social Animal*, published by W H Freeman & Company; *Whale population estimates*, 1997, published by Greenpeace International; Maggie Fox, *Smoking, drug use drop in US teens*, 18 December 2002, Reuters; Visa International *Heads or Tails* advertisement, 2003, by Colenso BBDO, Auckland, New Zealand reprinted with permission from Visa International; 'The Road Not Taken' from *The Poetry of Robert Frost*, edited by Edward Connery Lathem and published by Jonathan Cape, used by permission of the Estate of Robert Frost and the Random House Group Limited; Julie Middleton, *Optimists are better performers than pessimists*, 8 June 2002, New Zealand Herald, W&H Newspapers Ltd; Carla Trujillo, *Test Anxiety Reduction*, 1999, published by Carla Trujillo Ph.D., Director, Graduate Opportunities Program, University of California, Berkeley; Averil Coxhead, *Academic Word List*, Victoria University of Wellington; International Bottled Water Association *How is bottled water different from tap water?*, www.bottledwater.org, 2004; *Psychological Testing for managers and employers*, 15 January 2003, copyright held by Duane Lakin, Ph.D., management psychologist and author, The Unfair Advantage: Sell with NLP!; Jeremy Laurance, extract from *Experts split on branding for kids*, 10 October 2002, The Independent; Tony Halpin, *Girls must do even better – schools chief*, 25 November 2002, timesonline.co.uk, Times Online; *Labour Force Statistics*, 1981-2001, 2002 Edition, (table title, p.36) and (table title p.38). Copyright OECD, 2002; Noel O'Hare, 'Boys just wanna have fun', from *The Game of Our Lives*, 26 October 2002, New Zealand Listener, Auckland, New Zealand; Jonathan Fowler, 'Why Bottled Water is Fake? Study Shows Bottled Water Not Better', 3 May 2001, reprinted with the permission of The Associated Press.

The authors and publishers would also like to acknowledge these sources:

James Freeman, *To improve schools, forget computers*, 10 September 1999, USA Today; Tamara Henry, 'How Computers are used is key to learning', from *Computers no guarantee of higher test scores*, 30 September 1998, USA Today; extract from *Tourism in Bhutan*, 2002, Department of Tourism, Thimpu, Bhutan; Jody Reagor, Susan Ferguson, Dillia Salinas, Craig Gilchrist and Adam Jacob, extract from *Music, television and video games and their effect on children!*, University of Texas; David Jon Wiener, *interview with The Simpsons creator and its producer*, 2000, Empire Productions and Publishing, All rights reserved; Marie Karma Khayat and Margaret Clark Keating, extract from *Food from the Arab World*, 1959, Naufal Press; extract from *Nature vs. Nurture*, National Centre for Genome Resources (NCGR); Sally Cranfield and Max Glaskin, extract from *On the Desire of Wings*, 6 April 2002, New Scientist, vol 174, issue 2337, Reed Business Information, p43.

Every effort has been made to trace the original source of copyright material contained in this book. The publisher would be pleased to hear from copyright holders to rectify any errors or omissions.

The publishers and authors would like to thank the following for permission to reproduce copyright photographs:

Australian Picture Library/Corbis, p2 top left and bottom right, p20 right, p29, p30 left, p33, p43, p46 bottom left, p46 top, p86 bottom right, p98 top left, top middle, bottom left, bottom right, p101, p110 centre right, p111, p119, p129; Doc White/naturepl.com, p110 centre; p38 left, image courtesy of NASA/JPL/Caltech, Pasadena, California; Magnum Photos, p68; New Zealand Birds www.newzealandbirds.co.nz, p110 top left; Office of Film & Literature Classification, p120 bottom; Photolibrary.com, p 46 centre left, p58, p86 bottom right; Peter Menzel Photography, p103; Sanitarium Water Plus, p20 left; Science Museum/Science & Society Picture Library, p38 right.

The publishers and authors would like to thank the following people and institutions for their help in the development of this course:

Aspect ILA, Auckland; Aspect ILA, Christchurch; Paul Bress; Christchurch Language Centre; Crown English Language Academy, Auckland; EF International Language School, Sydney; Sarah Greatorex; Lisa Hale; Andrew Thomas, Sydney English Language Centre.

Special thanks to the staff and students at Languages International Ltd, Auckland, for their help in the development of this course.

Introduction

This is a course to help you prepare for the academic module of the IELTS exam. You will be able to use this material if your level is around IELTS 5 but if your level is higher you should still find it challenging and useful.

Content

The course consists of 12 units, each one based on a topic relevant to the IELTS exam. Each unit will provide around 10–12 hours of class work and so a typical course will last around 12 weeks. You will practise skills for all four IELTS subtests—reading, writing, speaking and listening—as well as related grammar (in the light blue boxes) and vocabulary (in the green boxes) in every unit.

How the course works

Clearly, the overall aim of the course is to help you maximise your IELTS score, which is why you have bought this book. However, we believe that the best way to do well in IELTS is to develop your overall ability to communicate in English: just doing practice IELTS tests is not the best way to prepare for the exam.

So, although there are many tasks in the book which are closely modelled on IELTS exam tasks, this is not a test practice book. The tasks in this book are designed to improve your ability to communicate in English and therefore do well in the exam.

Nevertheless, practising for the exam is of course still useful and you can practise individual IELTS test tasks by paying special attention to the tasks in this book marked *e*.

To practise doing full tests, use an exam practice book such as *IELTS Preparation and Practice: Practice Tests* (OUP, 2002), or visit the *On Course for IELTS* website.

Suggestions

To do well in IELTS you need to:

- speak and write confidently, fluently, and accurately on a wide range of topics.
- understand information quickly and accurately in different types of reading and listening texts on a wide range of topics.
- have confident control of a wide range of grammar and vocabulary.

To achieve these goals you should:

- read and listen to as much English as you can in your spare time.
- take the opportunity to speak with and write to English speakers whenever possible.
- keep your own vocabulary records and continue to build your vocabulary both inside and outside this course.
- pay attention to your own grammar and pronunciation: accuracy is important.
- Use this course!

Finally, we hope that you enjoy using this book and that it will enable you to communicate better in English. Good luck in the IELTS exam and in whatever you use your English for in the future!

First class

Tuning in

1 Make a list of the similarities and differences between these learning situations.

For example

Similarities

Everyone is learning sth

Differences

Some talking, some listening

2 Which situation:

a is most like your own experience?

My primary school was like this one. We had to ...

This reminds me of my ...

b would you prefer?

I like learning like this because ...

Reading

Before you read

1 Tell your partner what you remember about your first day at school.

· Was it:

exciting?	terrifying?	boring?
fun?	confusing?	memorable?

· What sights, sounds and people can you remember?

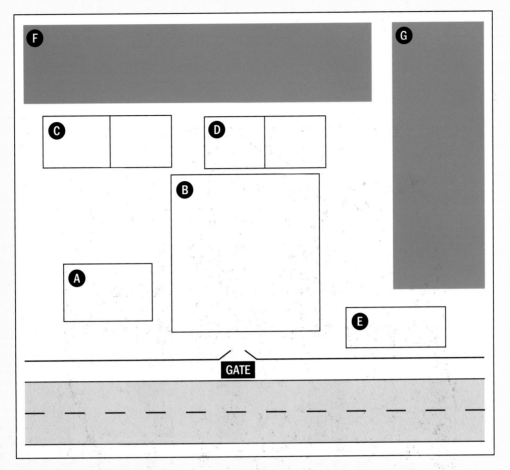

Listening

2 [cassette] **1.1** You will hear someone describing his primary school. Label the map.

First year classroom	Clinic	Field	Office
Playground	Gymnasium	Second year classroom	

Grammar focus

3 What word goes in the following gaps?   **4** [cassette] **1.2** Listen and check.

There ___ an office block on the left.

There _____ a couple of fields.

5 Now draw a rough map of your school and/or classroom as you remember it. Describe the map to a partner.

As you read

The text below is from *My Place,* the autobiography of Sally Morgan, an Australian woman. You are going to read the beginning of Chapter 2. It is about her first day at school.

6 Read through the whole text quickly, and answer these questions.
  a Is the feeling generally positive, or negative?
  b In what ways is it similar to your first day?
  c In what ways is it different?

7 Three key people are mentioned in the text. They are:
  · Sally
  · Her _____
  · And _____

Chapter 2
THE FACTORY

Mum chattered cheerfully as she led me down the path, through the main entrance to the grey weatherboard and asbestos buildings. One look and I was convinced that, like The Hospital, it was a place dedicated to taking the spirit out of life.

After touring the toilets, we sat down on the bottom step of the verandah. I was certain Mum
5   would never leave me in such a dreadful place, so I sat patiently, waiting for her to take me home.
'Have you got your sandwich?' she asked nervously when she realised I was staring at her.
'Yeah.'
'And a clean hankie?'
I nodded.
10   'What about your toilet-bag?'
'I've got it.'
'Oh.' Mum paused. Then, looking off into the distance, she said brightly, 'I'm sure you're going to love it here.'
Alarm bells. I knew that tone of voice, it was the one she always used whenever she spoke
15   about Dad getting better. I knew there was no hope.
'You're gunna leave me here, aren't ya?'
Mum smiled guiltily. 'You'll love it here. Look at all the kids the same age as you. You'll make friends. All children have to go to school someday. You're growing up.'
'So what?'
20   'So, when you turn six, you have to go to school, that's the law. I couldn't keep you home even if I wanted to. Now don't be silly, Sally, I'll stay with you till the bell goes.'
'What bell?'
'Oh ... they ring a bell when it's time for you to line up to go into your class. And later on, they ring a bell when it's time for you to leave.'

25 'So I'm gunna spend all day listenin' for bells?'

'Sally', Mum reasoned in an exasperated kind of way, 'don't be like that. You'll learn here, and they'll teach you how to add up. You love stories don't you? They'll tell you stories.'

Just then, a tall, middle-aged lady, with hair the colour and shape of macaroni, emerged from the first class-room in the block.

30 'May I have your attention please?' she said loudly. Everyone immediately stopped talking. 'My name is Miss Glazberg.'

'The bell will be going shortly', the tall lady informed the mothers, 'and when that happens I want you to instruct your children to line up in a straight line on the playground. I hope you heard that too, children, I will be checking to see who is the straightest. And I would appreciate it if the 35 mothers would all move off quickly and quietly after the children have lined up. That way, I will have plenty of time to settle them down and get to know them.'

I glared at Mum.

'I'll come with you to the line', she whispered.

The bell rang suddenly, loudly, terrifyingly. I clutched Mum's arm.

40 Slowly, she led me to where the other children were beginning to gather. She removed my hands from her arm but I grabbed onto the skirt of her dress. Some of the other mothers began moving off as instructed, waving as they went. One little boy in front of me started to cry. Suddenly, I wanted to cry, too.

'Come now, we can't have this', said Miss Glazberg as she freed Mum's dress from my clutches. 45 I kept my eyes down and grabbed onto another part of Mum.

'I have to go now, dear', Mum said desperately.

Miss Glazberg wrenched my fingers from around Mum's thigh and said, 'Say goodbye to your mother'. It was too late, Mum had turned and fled to the safety of the verandah.

'*Mum*', I called as she mounted the last wooden step, '*Mum!*'.

50 She turned quickly and waved, falling badly on the top step as she did so. I had no sympathy for her wounded ankle, or for the tears in her eyes.

'*Mum!*' I screamed as she hobbled off. '*Come back!*'

Despite the urgings of Miss Glazberg to follow the rest of the children inside, I stood firmly rooted to the playground, screaming and clutching for security my spotted, plastic toilet-bag and 55 a Vegemite sandwich.

Read again

8 Read the story again. Put the adjectives from the boxes in the correct order to show how the characters' feelings change.

angry	confused	afraid	worried

Sally is _____, then becomes _____, then _____, and finally she feels _____.

guilty	happy	upset

At first Sally's mum is _____, but then seems to feel _____, and finally she's _____.

9 This text describes a school building, but it also mentions 'The Factory' (the title of the chapter) and 'The Hospital' (line 3). Why?

10 Do you think a school is like a factory?

11 Were your teachers like Miss Glazberg? Describe a memorable teacher to your partner.

Listening: Ways of learning

Before you listen

You are going to hear a short lecture about ways of learning. According to the lecture, learning is more important than teaching.

1 What do you think this means? Do you agree?

The lecture describes two ways of learning:
- the 'deep approach'
- the 'surface approach'

2 What do you think these terms mean?

A _____ Approach

Learners whose main aim is to pass an exam
* *try to learn in order to repeat what they have learned*
* *memorise information needed for assessments*
* *make use of rote learning*
* *take a narrow view and concentrate on detail*
* *fail to distinguish principles from examples*
* *tend to stick closely to the course requirements*
* *are motivated by fear of failure.*

B _____ Approach

Learners whose main aim is to understand the subject
* *actively seek to understand the material/the subject*
* *make use of evidence, inquiry and evaluation*
* *take a broad view and relate ideas to one another*
* *are motivated by interest*
* *relate new ideas to previous knowledge*
* *relate concepts to everyday experience*
* *tend to read and study beyond the course requirements.*

As you listen

1.3 The lecture notes above are divided into two sections.

3 Label the sections as *Deep* and *Surface*.

4 Which approach is more successful? Which approach is more common?

Listen again

5 One point in the 'deep approach' section is not mentioned, and one point in the 'surface approach' section is not mentioned. Which ones?

After you listen

6 Which subjects were you interested in at school? Tell a partner.

7 Do you agree that a deep approach is generally more successful?

Text organisation

8 Complete this diagram with words from the box above it to show how the lecture is organised. Listen again if you are not sure. You will need to use two of the words twice.

Characteristics	Introduction
Evaluation	Definition

```
           ┌─────────┐
           │    1    │
           └────┬────┘
        ┌───────┴───────┐
   ┌─────────┐     ┌─────────┐
   │  2.1    │     │  3.1    │
   │  2.2    │     │  3.2    │
   └────┬────┘     └────┬────┘
        └───────┬───────┘
           ┌─────────┐
           │    4    │
           └─────────┘
```

Vocabulary focus

Here are two of the entries for the word *approach* in the *Oxford Advanced Learner's Dictionary*.

ap·proach /əˈprəʊtʃ; AmE əˈprəʊtʃ/ *verb, noun*
■ *verb*
MOVE NEAR| **1** to come near to sb/sth in distance or time: [V] *We heard the sound of an approaching car / a car approaching.* ◇ *Winter is approaching.* ◇ [VN] *As you approach the town, you'll see the college on the left.*

■ *noun*
TO PROBLEM/TASK| **1** [C] ~ (**to sth**) a way of dealing with sb/sth; a way of doing or thinking about sth such as a problem or a task: *The school has decided to adopt a different approach to discipline.* ◇ *She took the wrong approach in her dealings with them.*

1 Which meaning (the verb or the noun) matches the phrase *approach to learning*?

2 Which meaning did you learn first?

3 Which meaning (the verb or the noun) seems more concrete and which is more abstract?

4 Which one do you think is more common for an examination of 'academic' English like IELTS?

5 Find words in the lecture notes which you can put into each of these definitons (a–g). Then use your dictionary to check your answers.

a An _____ is when someone such as a teacher, makes a judgment about how good someone such as a student is at something, especially by giving them a test.

b If you _____ on a thing or an activity that you are doing, you think very carefully about it.

c If you can _____ between two things, or one thing from another, you can see the difference between them.

d A _____ is a general rule that helps to explain how things work.

e A _____ is something that you must do.

f _____ is when you think about how good something is.

g A _____ is an idea about how something is.

6 Write noun, verb, or adjective after each definition.

7 Which words in this exercise are mainly used to talk about education?

8 Make a list of the other members of these word families and mark the stress on each word.

For example

asˈsessment · asˈsess · asˈsessor

Putting it all together: knowing a word

In the diagram below are *some* of the things you need to know in order to know a word.

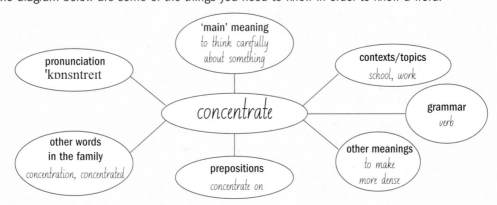

9 Choose two or three of the words from the lecture and make a chart for them like the one above.

Writing

Look at the graphs below. They all give information about computers in education.

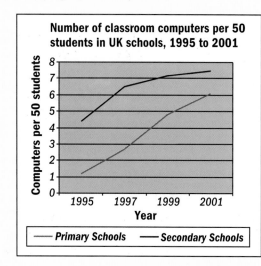

Number of classroom computers per 50 students in UK schools, 1995 to 2001

Computers per 50 students (y-axis: 0 to 8)
Year (x-axis: 1995, 1997, 1999, 2001)

—— Primary Schools   —— Secondary Schools

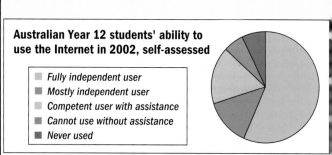

Australian Year 12 students' ability to use the Internet in 2002, self-assessed

- Fully independent user
- Mostly independent user
- Competent user with assistance
- Cannot use without assistance
- Never used

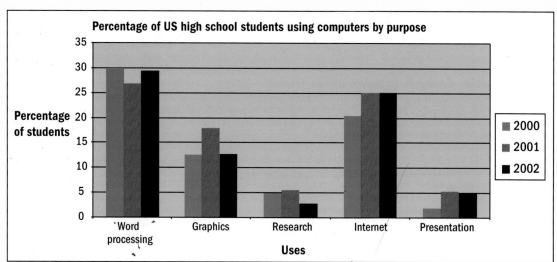

Percentage of US high school students using computers by purpose

Percentage of students (y-axis: 0 to 35)

Uses: Word processing, Graphics, Research, Internet, Presentation

- 2000
- 2001
- 2002

1 Would the situation be similar in your country?

2 Different graphs are used to show different kinds of information. Make three sentences from the box below and then match one sentence to each graph.

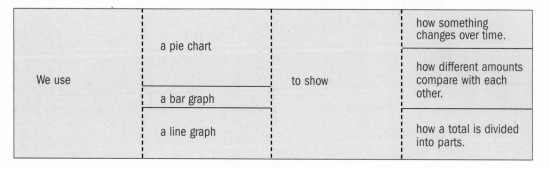

We use	a pie chart	to show	how something changes over time.
	a bar graph		how different amounts compare with each other.
	a line graph		how a total is divided into parts.

When you look at a graph, you need to focus on the most important information—the **main points**—rather than on the less important information—the **subordinate points**.

3 In the pie chart on page 8, which is the main point?

  a Most Australian students are good at using the Internet.

  b Some Australian students need a lot of help when using the Internet.

4 What is the main point in:

  a the line graph?

  b the bar graph?

5 What are the subordinate points for the bar graph?

Below are the reports that two students have written to describe the bar graph.

6 Read the reports. Which report describes the main points of the graph better? Why is the other report not as good?

Report A

Recently, high school students of developed countries would use the computers in their classrooms. It could help the teachers and students teaching or studying better. This report I will talk about the American high school students what they would computer to do from 2000 year to 2002 year.

In 2000, 30% high school students would use computer to find the word processing; 14% of them would use it to get the information of graphics; 5% used to research something; 20% students used it to the Internet such as send e-mail or chat with the other countries people. One 2% students used it to do the presentation.

In 2001, 27% students used it to find word processing that it was a small slightly than 2002; 18% students used it get the information of graphics; used it to research same as 2000; 25% used it to go to Internet; 5.5% students used it to do the presentation.

In 2002, 29% students used it to find the word processing; get the information of graphics same as 2000; only 3% students used it to research; used it to Internet same as 2001; 5% students used it to do the presentation.

Report B

The graph shows the percentage of American high school students who used computers for different reasons in their classrooms from 2000 to 2002.

The biggest usage of computers in schools is word processing. There are 30% of the students use computer as word processing, and the number dropped slightly to nearly 27% in 2001, then increased to just under 30% in 2002.

The second usage is Internet. In 2000, only 20% of the total use computers for Internet and this number went up rapidly to 25% in 2001 and is stable in 2002.

The biggest changing is in graphics: in 2000, about 12.5% of whole use computer as graphics and it increased dramatically in 2001 then decreased rapidly in 2002 to 12.5%.

We can see it is a little growth in Research in 2000 and 2001, and fell from 5% to nearly 3% in 2002. While only 2% of the students use computers as presentation in 2000 and the number increased to 5% in 2001 and 2002.

To sum up, the most important use is for word processing, and the biggest loss is for Graphics.

Using *show* (1)

Report B on page 9 starts like this:

The graph shows the percentage of American high school students who used computers for different reasons in their classrooms from 2000 to 2002.

There are two important ways to use *show*:
1 *show* + noun phrase
2 *show* + (*that* +) clause

1 **Which one is used in the example above?**

Here are two more examples of these uses of *show*.

a *This example shows that the number of computers in New Zealand schools is still increasing.*

b *The diagram above shows the kinds of situations in which computers are very helpful in education.*

2 **In which sentence does *show* mean:**

i **what you can actually see?**

ii **what you can understand from the facts?**

3 **In the following sentences, cross out *that* if it is not possible to use it. The first one has been done as an example.**

a The map shows ~~that~~ the number of buildings in each part of the city.

b The number of students who fail the exam shows that the questions are too difficult.

c In this report, we will show that computers are not useful in all areas of education.

d As we can see, this picture shows that the effects of such large numbers of tourists on natural places.

e Numbers alone cannot show that the way computers have changed modern classrooms.

Reading

Before you read

1 **What are the pros and cons of computers in education?**

On page 11, there are three excerpts from texts (A, B, and C) about computers in education in the USA.

As you read

2 **Skim read the texts quickly. For each text, decide whether the attitude to computers is:**
   a positive,
   b negative, or
   c neutral/balanced.

3 **Now match each text with the most appropriate title below. You do not need to use two of the titles.**
   a How computers are used is the key to learning
   b To improve schools, forget computers
   c Schools go hi-tech
   d Online learning today
   e Will e-books replace textbooks?

Text A

Title: ___B___   **Attitude:** ___©___

If you're upset about the quality of your child's education, you should be. By any reasonable measurement, American schools are failing to educate our kids. In a 1998 international test, American high school students finished 18th out of 21 nations in math and science literacy, and the test didn't even include any Asian countries. In a separate test for those students taking advanced physics, our kids finished dead last. In a government survey of American teenagers, only 21% of the kids were aware that there are 100 members of the U.S. Senate, but 81% knew that there are three brothers in the musical group Hanson.

What to do about it? First of all, let's stop pretending that high-speed data lines will solve America's educational problems. While politicians talk about Internet access and computer programs as if they're the pillars of a core curriculum, the evidence suggests that investments in technology do not improve test scores.

Says David Gelernter, a Yale computer science professor, 'Access to the Internet is like drivers' education, except more trivial. It's something you can learn in an afternoon. It's something good. It's something everybody should be familiar with. But to put it at the heart of education is, it seems to me, a very bad policy.'

Text B

Title: ___C___   **Attitude:** ___+ve___

With the United States spending about $5.2 billion annually on education technology, how and if computers contribute to improved student performance is a crucial question. A new study by Educational Testing Service reveals that how computers are used determines their efficacy.

Higher scores are obtained when they are used for math simulations, learning games and software applications that ask students to address real-life situations. But more popular applications known as drill-and-practice are linked to lower test scores.

The study analyzed fourth- and eighth-grade math scores from the 1996 National Assessment of Educational Progress.

- Among fourth-graders, students whose teachers used computers mainly for 'math/learning games' scored up to 15% of a grade level higher than other students.
- Eighth-graders whose teachers used computers mainly for drill-and-practice performed nearly half a grade level worse than other students.
- Students who spent more time on computers in school performed slightly worse in math than those who spent less time on them.

Text C

Title: ___©___   **Attitude:** ___N___

Real learning starts with the learner, not the teacher. People learn by solving problems, by making mistakes and correcting them, by hearing stories, by engaging multiple senses, and by following their innate curiosity. Learning doesn't have to take place in a classroom, a class doesn't have to last an hour, and motivation doesn't have to come from the threat of a ruler applied to one's knuckles. Indeed, the strongest motivation of all comes from within.

Pages, documents, classes, and files (and rulers) are anachronisms, vestiges of a bygone era of factories and smokestacks. As Alvin Toffler put it so well in *Future Shock* and *The Third Wave*, the Industrial Age has indeed given way to the Information Age.

Also, realize that all learning is social. People learn what works by conversing with one another informally. E-learning gives them freedom, unstructured time, and encouragement to learn this way (rather than cramming their brains with repetitive exercises and tests).

4   Read each text again. How does the writer support his or her argument?

5   Which article do you personally agree with the most? Do you disagree with any of the opinions?

Speaking

1   Divide into two groups. Think of ten different, new ways to complete the following statements.

   a   *To improve education, …*

   b   *People learn by …*

Your statements do need to be about education, but they do not need to be about computers.

For example

To improve education, forget computers.
People learn by making mistakes.

2   Share your ideas with the other group.

Answering a yes/no question

3 What answer would you give to the following questions?

   a Do you think people learn by making mistakes?

   b Do you think teachers should be paid more?

4 Here are some different ways of responding to these questions. Put them in the categories below.

Yes, I do.	I'm not sure.	No, not really.
Definitely.	Of course they do.	No, I don't.
Maybe.	Well, maybe some people do, but ...	Of course they should.
Absolutely.	Perhaps.	Absolutely not.

Strong positive	Positive	Uncertain	Negative	Strong negative
Definitely	Yes, I do	Maybe	I'm not sure	No, not really
Absolutely	Of course they do	Well maybe some people do	No, I don't	Of course they should
		Perhaps		Absolutely not

5 Now ask and answer the questions in Exercise 3 with a partner. Remember: only the beginnings of an answer are given above—you still need to explain your answer.

6 Write two more yes/no questions on education topics. Go around the class asking other students for their opinion.

Writing

To improve schools, forget computers

Ontario Universities Say Crush Threatens Quality of Education

Greater Flexibility in Education for 14–19 Year Olds

Schools go hi-tech

University fees rise

You are going to write an essay about the question on the right. The speaking and listening activities on page 13 are to help you prepare to write.

'To improve education, forget computers.'
To what extent do you agree with this statement?

Taking a position and supporting it

In the IELTS exam, the aim of the task 2 writing question is to see if you can:

  a clearly state your position (your basic opinion), and

  b support your position with examples and/or reasons.

So before you start writing you have to:

  a decide what your position is

  b think of examples or reasons to support your position.

You cannot *express* what you think if you do not *know* what you think.

1 What are the three basic positions you can take on an issue? Write them in the three spaces on the line below.

  • _____   • _____   • _____

←————————————————————————————————→

2 Now mark your own position on the computer issue on this line.

  What reasons would you give to support your opinion? Spend five minutes making notes.

3 Now tell your partner what you think, and why.

Listening

4   ⊡ **1.4** Listen to two different pairs discussing the essay question. Each pair looks at the statement in different ways.

  The first pair focuses on ...

  The second pair focuses on ...

Complete each sentence with one of the endings in the box.

> *... whether computers are really useful.*
> *... other ways of improving education.*

Listen again

5 Do they agree with your position? What reasons do they give to support their opinions?

6 Now use your notes from this activity to write a 250-word essay.

It never rains but it pours

Tuning in

1 Think of a place connected with water that was important to you when you were younger, for example: a beach, a river, a lake, a swimming pool, a waterfall ...

2 Talk to a partner.
  a Describe the place.
  b Explain when you went there, and who with.
  c Explain why it was important to you.

Describing past habits

2.1 Listen to someone describing her summer holidays as a child and complete the gaps in the sentences below.

    When I was a kid, _____ to the Mediterranean coast every summer. _____ a couple of weeks and _____ to the beach every day to swim.

3 How are the verbs in the sentences below different to the verbs in the one above?

    When I was a kid, we went to the Mediterranean coast every summer. We usually stayed a couple of weeks and we went down to the beach every day to swim.

We can also use verbs in the Past Simple to describe actions that happened only once.

    When I was twelve years old, we went to Australia for a holiday.

4 Can we also use verbs with *used to* and *would* to describe actions that happened only once?

Reading

Before you read

1 Can you guess what each of these articles is about?

❷ **Thousands flee rising waters**

❺ **Many countries lack clean supply, study finds**

❸ **China's costly dam project**

❶ **The Long, Dry Season**

❹ **Early Asian Monsoon Causes Floods and Landslides**

❻ **World's drinking water running out**

As you read

2 Now quickly read the newspaper articles and match each one to a headline.

Read again

3 For each article:

a what is the issue?

b what do you know about each issue?

For example *flooding*

For example *cause? place? solution?*

a As many as 76 million people, mostly children in developing countries, could die from preventable water-related illnesses by 2020 if countries don't rethink drinking water delivery systems, a new study by an Oakland environmental research institute concludes.

b The Three Gorges project to harness power from the Yangtze River is one of the most expensive and controversial engineering projects the world has ever seen.

c Is the drought over or isn't it? The national weather office says the country is still in a precarious situation.

d PRAGUE: Surging floods threatening major central European cities have forced tens of thousands to flee their homes with hospital patients flown to safety and authorities desperately fighting to save national monuments and priceless works of art.

e The world's fresh water supply is dwindling every year, according to research in the United States. Within 25 years, half the world's population could have trouble finding enough fresh water for drinking and irrigation.

f NEW DELHI, India, August 14, 2000 (ENS)—This year's summer rainy season has begun earlier than usual, causing extensive flooding in several south and south-east Asian countries.

Listening

As you listen

2.2 You will hear three short extracts, each one dealing with one of the water issues.

1 Make brief notes to complete the table below. You will probably need to listen twice. The first time, listen for the topics, and the second time add the detail.

Topic 1: _____	Topic 2: _____	Topic 3: *hydroelectricity*
Definition: *Climate where wind changes direction with season*	Causes: · Direct: rubbish, factory waste	Advantages:
Area:	· Indirect:	Disadvantages:
Effects:	Solutions:	

Focus on signposting

2 📼 **2.3** Listen to the extract from the hydroelectricity lecture again. It is slightly different this time. What words does the speaker use that make it easier to understand? Write them down.

For example

First of all,...

One important drawback is...

3 How do signposts help you as a listener?

4 So, should you use them as a speaker?

Speaking

1 Every country in the world has issues to do with water. Plan a 3–5 minute talk explaining the key issues in your country, or your part of your country. Use the following structure to organise your talk.

> *Situation: e.g. We are surrounded by ocean, so we get plenty of rain, which means we have plenty of fresh water ...*
>
> *Problem(s): e.g. But ... This is because ...*
> *Solution(s): e.g. We probably need to ...*
> *The government is trying to ...*

Writing

Brainstorming

1 What do we use water for? See how many uses you can write down in two minutes.

> *Uses for water*
> *drinking ...*

Listening

📼 **2.4** Listen to another group doing the same task.

2 Put a tick next to the things you have on your list if the speakers mention them.

3 Note down any extra uses of water that they mention.

4 Can you complete the table below?

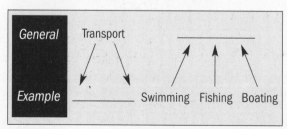

Organising ideas

Some of the ideas in the recording were very general, but some examples were more detailed.

For example

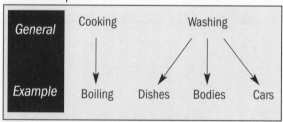

Now look at your own brainstorming list.

Sometimes only very general ideas were mentioned, and sometimes only examples were mentioned.

5 Can you think of more examples for each general point?

6 Can you think of a general description for each detailed example?

Expressing purpose

7 ▭ **2.5 Listen to an excerpt from the second recording and complete the sentences below.**

Water is used _____ _____ your house.

Water is used _____ _____ the car.

8 Which sentences have mistakes? Correct them.

a Water is used to generating electricity.
b It is used for transport goods.
c We use water in cooking.

Topic sentences

9 Read the introduction, topic sentences and conclusion of the text below and choose the best way to complete the following statement.

The main purpose of this text is to ...

a define water
b suggest how water should be used
c classify uses of water.

Water is one of the basic elements necessary for humans to survive. As the population of the world continues to grow, so does our need for water. It is therefore very important to analyse the main ways in which we use water, so that we can control how much we use and make sure that everyone has enough. Water use can be divided into four main categories.

One important use of water is ...

... is another major way that water is used.

The third main category of water use is ...

Perhaps the most important way that we use water, however, is ...

For a long time, people in industrialised countries have used water and damaged the sources of water without thinking about the long-term effects of their actions. It is clear, however, that in the future, we will all need to think carefully about the quantity and purpose of our water use so that everyone has a fair share of this essential element.

A *topic sentence* in a paragraph usually has these elements:

· the topic of the whole text
· the topic of the paragraph
· a word or some words that join the paragraph to the parts of the text before and after it.

10 Circle these three elements in the example topic sentence below.

First of all, a lot of water is used in the production of our food.

11 Use your notes from the listening section above and one of the topic sentences in the text to write one paragraph.

12 When you have finished and checked your paragraph, exchange your paragraph with another group's. Does your classmates' paragraph:

· have a good topic sentence?
· state the **general** points first and then support them with more **detailed** information?

Listening

This graph shows water use in these categories:

· Public supply
· Rural, livestock
· Electricity
· Irrigation
· Industry

1 Can you guess which colour on the graph represents each category?

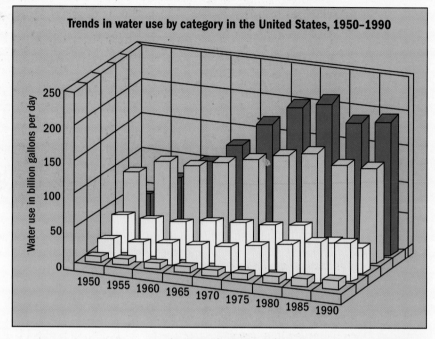

Trends in water use by category in the United States, 1950–1990

Water use in billion gallons per day

250
200
150
100
50
0

1950 1955 1960 1965 1970 1975 1980 1985 1990

2 🔲 **2.6** Listen and check your answers.

3 Listen again. Column A lists three categories. Column B lists three reasons why the water use has increased or decreased. Match the categories with the reasons.

4 Do you think the graph would be the same for your country?

A Categories of use	B Reasons for change
Public supply	Better technology
Irrigation	More intensive
Rural	Population pressure

Writing

1 Look at the diagram below, and try to explain to a partner how a hydroelectric dam works.

HYDROELECTRIC DAMS: How They Work

2 Now look at the sentences below. They describe how a hydroelectric dam works, but they are in the wrong order. Put them in the right order.

a On the upper side of the dam, a water gate is opened to let water surge through a tunnel leading to turbines.

b The electricity is carried through cables to wherever it is needed.

c Hydroelectric dams are very high-tech but simple machines.

d The water turns the turbines, which in turn spin generators to generate electricity.

e A dam holds back water, creating a reservoir of potential power.

Using *a* and *the*

3 Without looking back at the original paragraph, put *a*, *the*, or Ø (no article) in the gaps in the text.

__ hydroelectric dams are very high–tech but simple machines. __ dam holds back water, creating a reservoir of potential power. On the upper side of __ dam, __ water gate is opened to let water surge through __ tunnel leading to turbines. __ water turns the turbines, which in turn spin generators to generate electricity. __ electricity is carried through cables to wherever it is needed.

4 Now check the original text to see if you have filled the gaps in correctly. If any of your answers are different, check a grammar book to see if you can understand why.

Speaking

This map shows the site of a new dam. When the dam is finished, the river valley will be filled with water, flooding the town near the dam. Therefore, the town has to be moved to a new site.

1 Look carefully at the map, and then in groups, discuss the best site for the town. Think about these factors:
- amount of space
- transport routes
- conservation of natural areas
- kinds of landscape

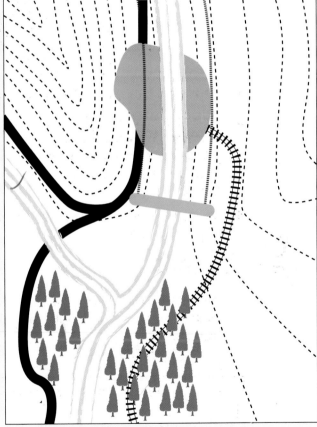

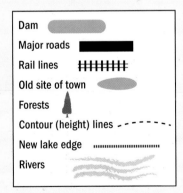

Dam	
Major roads	
Rail lines	┼┼┼┼┼┼
Old site of town	
Forests	
Contour (height) lines	- - - -
New lake edge	··············
Rivers	

2 You are going to present your recommendation, and the reasons for it, to another group. Make notes to help you plan your talk.

3 Organise your talk in this way:
- Decision
- Reason 1
- Reason 2

4 Listen to other groups, make notes and then decide as a class on the best site.

Reading

Before you read

Look carefully at these two bottled water labels, and spend a few minutes thinking about the questions before you discuss them with a partner.

1 Which one would you buy? Why?

2 Do you buy bottled water now? If yes, do you prefer any particular brand? Why?

3 Do you generally pay attention to labels when you buy things? Why, or why not?

As you read: interpreting statistics

4 Read the following text and choose the graph that you think illustrates the information.

Bottled water: A growth industry

Over half of all Americans (54 per cent) drink bottled water, and about 36 per cent of us imbibe regularly (more than once a week). Sales have nearly tripled in the last decade, to about $4 billion in 1997, rising from 17 litres per year for the average American in 1986 to 48 litres per year per person in 1997. Americans consumed a total of 12.98 billion litres of bottled water in 1997. Globally, the market was estimated in 1995 to be worth more than $14 billion annually in *wholesale* sales, and it has certainly grown since then. According to a 1992 inventory, there were already 700 brands of bottled water produced by about 430 bottling facilities in the United States, a number that most likely has grown since that time, because of the enormous expansion in bottled water sales.

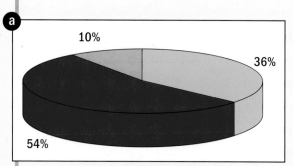

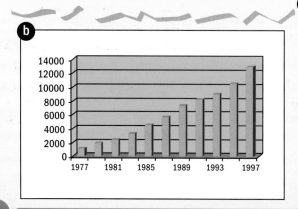

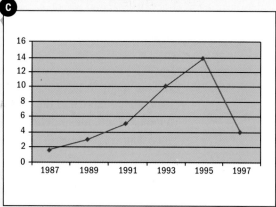

Reading skills: vocabulary in context

When you meet vocabulary in a text that you do not understand, the *context* (the parts of the text before and after the difficult word) can often help you to guess the meaning.

5 Try to guess the meaning of the following words in the text on page 20. *Do not use a dictionary.*
- imbibe
- tripled
- decade
- consumed
- inventory

6 Which of these words do you think you need to learn to use actively?

7 Read the following text and use the information in it to complete the graph.

What has driven this ever-greater consumer demand for bottled water? A 1993 poll of people who drink bottled water found that 35 per cent of bottled water drinkers used it primarily out of concern about tap water quality. Another 12 per cent chose bottled water because of both safety or health concerns and the desire for a substitute for other beverages (see Figure 2). Thus, as of 1993 at least, nearly half (47 per cent) of bottled water drinkers used it at least partially out of concern for their health and safety. Another 36 per cent drank it as a substitute for soft drinks and other beverages. Seventeen per cent said they chose bottled water for other reasons—such as 'taste' (7 per cent) or 'convenience.'

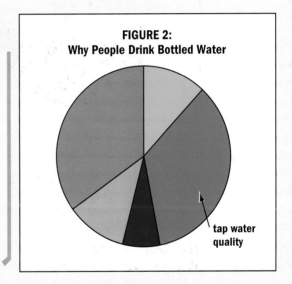

FIGURE 2:
Why People Drink Bottled Water

tap water quality

Speaking

To get the information for this article, the writers used the results of a survey. In this case, they asked a large number of people the same questions about bottled water so that they could find out about trends and make some general statements.

1 Think about something that you and other people around you buy or use often.

For example
- transport
- fast food
- newspapers

2 Write a short list of questions so that you can conduct a survey about people's choices.

For example

Transport
- *What kind of transport do you use most often?*
- *Why do you choose this form of transport?*
- *What are the disadvantages of this form of transport?*

3 Conduct the survey by asking your questions to a number of people around you—in your class, your school, your family, your neighbourhood, etc.

4 Look at the results of your survey. What are the main trends? Prepare a short spoken summary of the results and present them to other students. Try drawing some simple graphs to support your presentation.

Reading

Identifying the writer's point of view

Often we have a good idea what an article is going to say even before we read it.

You are going to read two short texts about bottled water. The first one was written by the International Bottled Water Association (IBWA). The second one expresses the view of the World Wide Fund for Nature (WWF).

Before you read

1 Try to predict what the texts will say. Complete the table using words from the box below.

	IBWA text	*WWF text*
Attitude to bottled water		
Reasons		

in favour	against	bad for the environment	taste
cost	quality	convenience	health	fashion

2 Now skim read the two texts *quickly* (three minutes only) to see if your predictions were correct.

3 Read the texts again, more slowly, to check:
a if you put the reasons in the correct column
b which reason in the box was not mentioned.

How is bottled water different from tap water?

Throughout much of the world, bottled water is produced and distributed as a packaged food product and made specifically for drinking. As a packaged food product, bottled water must adhere to U.S. Food and Drug Administration (FDA) Good Manufacturing Practices (GMPs) required of all FDA-regulated food products as well as specific GMPs unique to bottled water production and packaging. GMPs require that each container of bottled water is produced in a sanitary environment and packaged in sanitary, safety sealed containers that are approved by FDA for food contact. Bottled water is also subject to FDA food recall, misbranding and food adulteration provisions, which help ensure that consumers receive safe, high quality bottled water and protects consumers from substandard products.

Taste is another reason consumers choose bottled water. Chlorine is most often used to disinfect tap water and can leave an aftertaste. Some bottlers use ozonation, a form of supercharged oxygen and/or ultraviolet light as the final disinfecting agent, neither of which leaves an aftertaste.

Bottled water provides consumers with consistent safety, high quality, good taste and convenient portability. To help ensure that bottled water is safe and of the highest quality possible, all IBWA members use one or more of the following steps found in a multi-barrier approach: source protection and monitoring, reverse osmosis, distillation, filtration, ozonation and disinfection.

Study Shows Bottled Water Not Better

By JONATHAN FOWLER, Associated Press Writer

'Cheaper and better for the environment,'
says the WWF.

GENEVA (AP)—Despite perceptions that it's healthier, there is little difference between bottled water and tap water—apart from cost—a conservation group said on Thursday.

'Bottled water may be no safer, or healthier, than tap water in many countries while selling for up to 1,000 times the price,' the World Wildlife Fund said.

Bottled water is the fastest growing beverage industry in the world, worth up to $22 billion a year, according to the fund.

A study commissioned by the fund found the 'bottled water market is partly fueled by concerns over the safety of municipal water and by the marketing of many brands which portray them as being healthier than tap water.'

The fund also said bottled water sales were rising because people were worried about pollution.

'Our attitudes toward tap water are being shaped by the pollution which is choking the rivers and streams,' said the fund's water campaign director Richard Holland.

But the study—conducted by University of Geneva researcher Catherine Ferrier—said the only difference between some bottled water and tap water is that it is distributed in bottles rather than pipes.

While agreeing bottled water may be safer in areas where tap water may be contaminated, the fund said boiled or filtered tap water is still a better option for people on a lower income.

Buying bottled water is 'not a long term sustainable solution to securing access to healthy water. Protecting rivers will help ensure that tap water remains a service which delivers good quality drinking water for everyone at a fair price,' according to the fund.

The group added that 1.5 million tons of plastic are used to bottle water every year. 'Toxic chemicals can be released into the environment during the manufacture and disposal of bottles,' it said.

The bottled water market is booming

After reading

4   What is your personal view on bottled water? Have the texts influenced your opinion at all?

Topic words: the environment

When you choose to walk to work or school, rather than drive, you are being *environmentally friendly* (= helping to keep the environment clean and unpolluted).

1   What other environmentally friendly activities can you think of?

For example

recycling

2   Do you think that *you* are environmentally friendly?

3   From the second text, make a list of words to do with 'the environment'.

For example

nature, conservation

Qualifying a generalisation

1 Find the statements below in the texts on pages 22 and 23. They are slightly different. Rewrite the sentences so that they are the same as the original. The first one has been done for you.

a The quality is no better.
Original = *The quality is <u>often</u> no better.*

b Tap water is inconsistent.
Original =

c That leaves a bad taste in your mouth.
Original =

d Bottled water is no healthier or safer to drink than tap water.
Original =

e Bottled waters are exactly the same standard as tap water.
Original =

f Bottled water is safer in areas where tap water is contaminated.
Original =

2 How does the meaning change when you change the grammar in this way?

3 Choose a, b, or c to complete the following sentence.

> In writing, we use words like *can be, some, is generally* when we want our argument to sound:
>
> **a** strong and forceful
>
> **b** fair and reasonable
>
> **c** balanced and thoughtful.

Emphatic addition

1 Put these three sentences in order from the strongest in tone to the weakest.

a Bottled water is not only environmentally unfriendly but also a waste of money.

b Bottled water is environmentally unfriendly and a waste of money.

c Bottled water is both environmentally unfriendly and a waste of money.

2 Now try writing your own sentences with the following words, using emphatic forms.
· Bottled water: healthier, safer
· Hydroelectricity: cheap, clean

3 Do you actually agree with the sentences that you have written, or with the model sentences in Exercise 1?

Listening: discussion

2.7 You will hear two people—a man and a woman—discussing bottled water.

As you listen

1 Which speaker is more in favour of bottled water?

Listen again

2 Copy the table below and make notes. The first two points have been done for you.

Woman's opinion	Does the man agree or disagree?
Bottled water tastes better than tap water.	agrees
Bottled water is a healthy choice.	disagrees

Writing: structuring an argument

When you write an essay based on your opinion—like in task 2 IELTS—it is sometimes good to write about both sides of the issue: the one you do not personally support as well as the one you do support.

1   From the texts about bottled water—the reading texts and your notes from the listening—find three points *for* bottled water and three points *against* bottled water.

for	against
1 bottled water is pure because it comes from protected sources	1 bottled water costs up to 1000 times more than tap water
2	2
3	3

2   Now use these points to form the main body of a 250-word essay on the following statement.

> 'More and more people are buying and drinking bottled water rather than drinking tap water. There are many more drawbacks to this than there are benefits.'
>
> To what extent do you agree?

3   Finally, swap your essay with a partner.
 a   Can you clearly understand which side your partner supports?
 b   Does your partner use the same points that you do in your essay?

Cohesion: signposting in written language

Look at these excerpts from the topic sentences on page 17.

> ... is <u>another</u> major way that water is...
>
> The third main category of water use is...
>
> Perhaps the most important way that we use water, however, is ...

4   Underline the main linking—or signposting— words in each sentence. (The first one has been done for you).

Look at the text *How is bottled water different from tap water?* on page 22.

5   Underline the topic sentences in paragraph 2 and 3.

6   Underline the main linking word in the paragraph 3 topic sentence.

Finally, look at your essay on bottled water.

7   Do you need to make your topic sentences clearer?

8   Do you need to add any signposting words?

3 All work and no play

Tuning in

'All work and no play makes Jack a dull boy.'

1 What does this saying mean? Do you agree?

2 Do you have similar sayings about work and leisure in your culture?

Reading

1 Look at these job advertisements. For each one, try to write basic details in the table below.

Marketing Specialist

One of the world's largest airfreight companies is currently looking for a motivated marketing specialist to join their team.

In this position, you will be responsible for analysing the market, identifying opportunities and implementing effective strategies.

As well as tertiary qualifications, you will have at least 2 years' experience in a professional organisation. Your self-motivation, practical attitude and enthusiasm will enable you to move your career forward in this progressive environment. To apply, send your CV and covering letter to David Johnson, Recruitment Manager, at ...

Technical Manager

Would you like to work for a world-renowned global organisation with a record of innovation and growth?

As Technical Manager, you will lead a team of research and development professionals, ensuring that international standards are maintained.

You will hold a chemistry degree, and also have proven skills in project management and communication with clients. Working in a successful company with a team of skilled specialists, your career prospects in this position will be excellent.

Database Administrator

Did you make a New Year's resolution to advance your career? If you did, here is a great opportunity to do just that!

A leading software design company is looking for a database administrator to work with their software development and support teams.

Applicants will have significant experience in database and network administration, and skills in major software applications. Database certification is a prerequisite, and computer-related tertiary qualifications are preferred. An excellent attitude to work and good communications skills will complete the picture!

Accounts Officer

Our company is an international organisation working in an expanding industry sector, and we are looking for a bright, enthusiastic Accounts Officer. You will work in a large accounting team and be responsible for the account management of several key accounts.

You will have 2 to 3 years' experience in an accounting position, and have a strong customer service background. As the main contact for a number of important clients, you will have superior interpersonal and communication skills.

Job	Qualifications	Experience	Personality
Marketing Specialist			
Technical Manager			
Database Administrator			
Accounts Officer			

2 Which jobs would you be interested in doing? Why?

3 Which jobs would you not want to do? Why?

Vocabulary and grammar: Which preposition?

4   See if you know or can guess the prepositions that go in the gaps below, and then check the advertisements. Not all of the answers are in the advertisements, so you may need to check a dictionary.

· You are responsible _____ something.

· You apply _____ a job.

· You have experience _____ a particular job.

· You have a good attitude ____ work.

· You work ____ a company.

· You have skills ____ a particular activity.

· You specialise _____ a particular area of work.

Listening

Before you listen

1   Interview a partner to find out the following information.

Education

— past and present; plans

— likes and dislikes

Career

— past and present; plans

As you listen

2   **3.1** You will hear two interviews between students who have just finished secondary school and a careers advisor (a careers advisor is a person who helps you to plan your education and career). Listen and complete as much information as you can in the following table.

	Student A	*Student B*
Favourite subjects at school		
Interested in what career?		
Possible study paths		
What to do next		

Reading

Before you read

Some people have stressful jobs, some people find school stressful, and some people just have stressful lives.

1   What causes stress? Make a list of stressful situations.

Medical researchers and psychologists have identified a distinction between Type A and Type B personalities. People with Type A personalities typically suffer from higher levels of stress.

2   Do the self-test on page 28, to find out whether you have a Type A or Type B personality.

What type of person are you?

Type A—Type B self test

To determine your Type A or Type B profile, circle the number on the scales that best represents your behaviour.

Am casual about appointments	1 2 3 4 5 6 7 8	Am never late
Am not competitive	1 2 3 4 5 6 7 8	Am very competitive
Never feel rushed, even under pressure	1 2 3 4 5 6 7 8	Try to do many things at once; think about what I am going to do next
Do things slowly	1 2 3 4 5 6 7 8	Do things fast (eating, walking, etc.)
Express feelings	1 2 3 4 5 6 7 8	'Sit' on feelings
Have many interests	1 2 3 4 5 6 7 8	Have few interests outside work

Total your score: _____. Multiply it by three: _____.
The interpretation of your score is as follows:

Number of points	Type of personality
Less than 90	B
90 to 99	B+
100 to 105	A–
106 to 119	A
120 or more	A+

Speaking

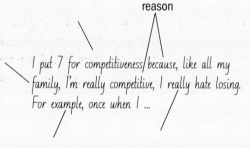

reason

I put 7 for competitiveness because, like all my family, I'm really competitive, I really hate losing. For example, once when I ...

3 Label the different parts of this explanation. The first one has been done for you:
- · Reason
- · Action
- · Comparison
- · Example
- · Paraphrase (= saying the same thing in a different way)

4 Explain your answers to a partner. Try to elaborate as in the example.

5 Tell your partner your overall score. Do you agree with this assessment of your personality?

Listening

3.2 Listen to an American professor of management, talking about the personality types introduced above.

1 Is he describing Type A personalities or Type B personalities?

2 Do you think the behaviour he describes is:
a an aspect of societies all around the world (including yours)?
b a particular aspect of American culture?

3.3 Now listen to some more comments on these personality types.

3 In the speaker's view, which type performs better in business? Why?

Listening: alternative work arrangements

Before you listen

1 In your country, what is a typical working week?
  a When do people start and finish work?
  b How long do they get for lunch?
  c How many hours and days a week do they work?

2 In many countries, the typical working week is changing. People are working on different days, and starting and finishing at different times. Why do you think this is happening?

As you listen

3.4 You are going to hear the beginning of a management lecture on alternative work arrangements.

3 Listen and complete the notes by writing one, two or three words in each gap.

Background

Last two generations, little change or variation
  · _job for _____
  · _hours typically _____

Now
  · _more changes in _____
  · _not just _____

Reason for alternatives
Attracting staff who

_1 _____ work traditional hours_

_2 _____ work traditional hours_

e.g. those:
  · _returning from maternity _____
  · _caring for _____
  · _wanting to spend more time on _____
  · _or with _____

3.5 In the next section of the lecture, you will hear a description of the alternatives.

4 Write the name given to each alternative in the first column.

5 Make notes on further details in the final column. You may need to listen again to make these notes.

alternative	definition	detail
1 *job—sharing*	One job shared by two people	— *full-time job shared by 2 people* — *needs good communication*
2 _____	Working less than full-time	
3 _____	Flexible working hours, agreed with employer	
4 _____	Working from home for part or all of week, in constant communication with office by phone, fax, computer	
5 _____	Working from home, but without need to stay in constant contact with office	

After you listen

6 Are any of the alternatives to work common, or becoming more common, in your country? Do any of these alternatives appeal to you personally?

According to the lecture, changes in the way people work are part of a generational change.

7 What other generational changes can you think of in the way that we live, work, study, spend our free time, etc.? Copy the table below and make notes, then explain your ideas to a partner.

Previous generations/the previous generation	Our generation

Writing

The tables below provide information on patterns of part-time employment in seven OECD (Organisation for Economic Cooperation and Development) countries.

1 Before you look at the tables, do you think part-time employment increased or decreased during the 1990s? Why?

2 Do you expect that patterns of part-time employment will be similar in different parts of the world? Why, or why not?

3 Spend five minutes looking at the data with a partner. What information does each table provide? Do they support your expectations? Is there anything surprising?

Table 1: Part-time as percentage of employment

	1991	1995	1999
Canada	18.1	18.6	18.5
United States	14.4	14.1	13.3
Japan	20	20.1	24.1
Korea	4.7	4.4	7.8
United Kingdom	20.7	22.3	22.9
Germany	11.8	14.2	17.1
Australia	23.9	25	26.1

Table 2: Female share of part-time employment

	1991	1995	1999
Canada	69.4	68.8	69.6
United States	67.7	68.7	68.4
Japan	70	70.2	67
Korea	59	61.2	55.2
United Kingdom	85.1	81.8	79.6
Germany	89.4	86.3	84.1
Australia	70.1	69.2	68.9

Table 3: Female part-time as percentage of female employment

	1991	1995	1999
Canada	28	28.2	28
United States	20.5	20.3	19
Japan	34.3	34.9	39.7
Korea	6.8	6.7	10.5
United Kingdom	40.3	40.7	40.6
Germany	25.2	29.1	33.1
Australia	39.7	40.2	41.4

Table 4: Male part-time as percentage of male employment

	1991	1995	1999
Canada	10.1	10.6	10.3
United States	8.8	8.4	8.1
Japan	10.1	10	13.4
Korea	3.2	2.9	5.9
United Kingdom	5.5	7.3	8.5
Germany	2.2	3.4	4.8
Australia	12.4	13.5	14.3

Below is a list of five generalisations about the data.

4 Which one is not true?

5 Which one covers all of the tables?

During the 1990s:
  a most part-time workers were women.
  b relatively few men worked part-time.
  c there were fairly wide variations in patterns of part-time employment.
  d the majority of women worked part-time.
  e the percentage of workers in part-time employment generally rose.

6 Match a generalisation with a specific table (you will need to correct the one that is not true).

These generalisations cover the most important general points from all of the information. But for each table we can make other general points.

For example

Table 1:

In some countries, the rise was quite sharp.

There was a wide range in the percentage of part-time employment.

Table 2:

In some countries the female share was very similar and it remained very stable throughout the decade.

In other areas, the female share fell quite significantly.

7   Now write similar generalisations for tables 3 and 4.

Making generalisations is very important, but they must be true, and you still need to support them with detail. For example, the *italics* in the generalisations below give the detail.

Table 1:

In some countries, *such as Korea and Germany,* the rise was very sharp.

There was a wide range in the percentage of part-time employment, *ranging in 1999 from only 7.8% in Korea, to 17% in Germany, and over 26% in Australia.*

Table 2:

In *North America, Japan and Australia* the female share was very similar, *at around 70%,* and it remained very stable throughout the decade.

In other areas, the female share fell quite significantly. *For example, in Korea the share fell from 59% to just over 55%, while in the UK it fell from 85.1% to 79.6%.*

8   Add similar supporting detail to your generalisations for tables 3 and 4.

Non-finite dependent clauses

A and B, below, both express the same ideas, but the ideas are linked together differently.

A   There was a wide range in the percentage of part-time employment, ranging in 1999 from only 7.8% in Korea, to 17% in Germany, and over 26% in Australia.

B   There was a wide range in the percentage of part-time employment. In 1999, it ranged from only 7.8% in Korea, to 17% in Germany, and over 26% in Australia.

> A = one sentence, with two clauses, one independent / main clause and one dependent clause.
> B = two sentences, with one clause in each sentence.

Both versions are grammatically correct. We sometimes use type A:
· for variety, which keeps the reader interested
· to show that some information is less important than other information (the information in the main clause is usually more important)
· because it is more concise.

1   Rewrite the following, combining two sentences into one.
Part-time employment increased slightly in Canada. It rose from 18.1% in 1991, to 18.5% at the end of the 90s.

For example

Part-time employment increased slightly in Canada, rising ...

a   The percentage of part-time employees rose sharply in Japan over this period. It increased from 20% to over 24%.

b   The percentage of British women in part-time employment was very stable. It remained between 40% and 41% throughout the decade.

2   Write two more sentences like this, using the information in any of the tables.

Speaking

1 Is unemployment a problem in your country?

2 What, in your view, are the causes of unemployment?

3 What kind of support does the government, or any other organisation, provide for unemployed workers?

For example

> money, food, help finding a job, free medical care, job training, etc.

Vocabulary focus

4 Are the following words nouns, verbs, or adjectives?

| unemployed | rich | poor | sick | elderly | young |

In fact, they are all adjectives, but they are special. They can function like a noun, because we can use them with a definite article—and without a following noun—to talk about this group of people. We can say, for example:

> The unemployed should receive more help from the government. [Not: The unemployed people should...]
> Respect for the elderly is an important part of our culture.

5 Now write two or three more statements about the groups of people in the box above.

Accommodating other points of view

6 To what extent do you agree with the following statements? For each statement, write A if you agree fully, P if you agree in part, and D if you disagree. Think about reasons for your opinion.

  a It's obvious that the unemployed don't want to work, because everyone who really wants a job can find one.
  b Government support for the unemployed should continue for as long as they need it.

  c It is likely that in the future, most people will need to change their job many times.
  d The unemployment rate would definitely be lower if the retirement age were lower.

7 Work with two partners. Compare your opinions. Do you agree or disagree? Why?

8 3.6 If you disagree, modify (= change) each statement to make it stronger, or weaker so that everyone in your group can agree with it. First, listen to another group doing this for statement a.

Reading

Before you read

1 We spend a lot of time at work, so it is important that we enjoy it. What kinds of things make us happy in our job? Make a list.

The newspaper article you are going to read is about job satisfaction in the public sector in the UK.

2 In your own country, do you think job satisfaction is generally higher in the public sector, or in the private sector? Why?

Previewing

Titles, headings and headlines help us to predict what a text will say, which can help us to read and understand the text more quickly.

3 Look at the headline. It provides a lot of information. From it we know that:
· job satisfaction has _____
· the main reason is probably _____
· the article reports information from a
  _____
· it was written in _____

> ## Job satisfaction falls for public workers
>
> **Nurses, teachers and civil servants face more stress says survey**
>
> Larry Elliott, economics editor
> Thursday March 22, 2001
> The Guardian

Predicting

4 Look at the set of ten statements below. Decide for each one whether you think it is probably true, or probably false. Write T or F in the prediction column.

Statements	Your prediction (T or F)	According to the article (T, F, NG)	In paragraph
1 Public sector workers feel they are under pressure.	T		
2 Workers in the public sector used to be happier than those in the private sector.	T		
3 Workers in the private sector are now happier than those in the public sector.	NG		
4 The average public sector employee is unhappy.	NG		
5 University teachers have not been as unhappy as other workers.	T		
6 Private sector employees experience less stress.	NG		
7 Teenage workers are generally fairly happy.	F		
8 Older workers tend to be less satisfied.	F		
9 Satisfaction is related to the size of the organisation you work for.	T		
10 The more academically qualified you are, the more likely you are to feel satisfied with your job.	F		

Reading

5 Read the text quickly to check your predictions. Write T, F, or NG (if the information is **N**ot **G**iven) in the middle column. Also write the number of the paragraph in which you found the answer.

1   Job satisfaction among Britain's 6 m public sector workers has fallen sharply over the past decade as rising levels of stress have made work less enjoyable for doctors, nurses, teachers, lecturers and civil servants, said research published yesterday.

2   The study from Andrew Oswald and Jonathan Gardner of Warwick University found that an increase in depression, strain, sleep loss and unhappiness during the 1990s had made employment more pressurised and less enjoyable in the public realm.

3   While public sector workers began the 1990s with far higher levels of job satisfaction than those in the private sector, the Warwick University research showed that this gap had been virtually eroded by 1998, which was a year of stringent control of government spending.

4   'I think this is very serious for Britain,' Professor Oswald said. 'Job satisfaction has dropped dramatically in the public sector throughout the 90s. Stress has risen quite dramatically.'

5   Prof Oswald said his view was that the decline in job satisfaction was linked to rising stress. 'The very heavy increase in workloads in the public sector has made workers much less happy', he said.

6   All groups of public sector workers have become less satisfied at work over the past decade, a period in which they have faced extra bureaucracy, pressure to meet targets as well as the introduction of working practices from the private sector.

7   The steady decline in satisfaction was particularly evident in the National Health Service, higher education and those working for local government.

8   The sample of 5,000 workers was re-interviewed each year through the 1990s, with stress levels assessed by the answers to 12 standard questions used to measure mental distress and psychological ill health.

9   Overall, the researchers found that job satisfaction was u-shaped in age, with initial contentment at work during teenage years disappearing by the age of 25.

10 Job satisfaction was lowest when people were in their 20s and 30s—the period when people struggle to balance work with their family commitments—and highest among staff in their 50s and 60s.

11 Recorded job satisfaction was higher among women than among men, lower among blacks than whites, slightly lower in union workplaces than non-union ones, high in small workplaces, and highest of all in not-for-profit organisations.

12 The self-employed also said that they enjoyed their work, according to the Warwick University research.

13 Measured by educational attainment, the study found that those workers with no qualifications were most satisfied with their jobs.

14 'It is Britons with university degrees, surprisingly, who report the lowest levels of satisfaction at work', Prof Oswald said.

6   Do you think that the situation would be similar in your own country?

increase and *decrease*

1   Complete the following table, with verbs or nouns from the text meaning *increase* or *decrease.* Include any modifying adverb or adjective. Some have been done as an example.

2   Write (+) if the word means increase, and (−) if it means decrease.

Paragraph	Verb	Adverb	Adjective	Noun
1	has fallen (−)	sharply		
2			−	increase (+)
4				
5				decline (−)
		heavy		increase (+)
7				

Present Perfect and Past Simple

Both A and B below refer to the same period (the 1990s), and both could be grammatically correct, depending on the situation. So the difference between the two is not the time, but in the way that we look at—and think about—what happened.

A Job satisfaction **has dropped** dramatically in the public sector throughout the 90s while stress **has risen** quite dramatically.

B Job satisfaction **dropped** dramatically in the public sector throughout the 90s. Stress **rose** quite dramatically.

1 Complete the table below with the words and phrases from the box to show how they are different.

A	B

Past Simple	Present Perfect	about a period which is clearly finished
about a period which is considered to still be continuing or relevant		
probably said in or close to the 1990s		probably said much later
focus is on the action/event		focus is on the result

2 If you were writing this report now, about the same research, which form would you use (Past Simple or Present Perfect)? Why?

3 Write five sentences describing changes that have occurred in your country in the last few years. (They do not need to be about employment or work.)

For example

Unemployment has fallen quite dramatically.
Prices have risen sharply.

4 Explain the changes to a partner.

Listening

3.7 To measure the stress levels of public sector employees, Andrew Oswald and Jonathan Gardner used the 'General Health Questionnaire', which is widely used by British doctors, psychologists and social scientists. There are twelve questions in the questionnaire.

1 You will hear someone reading out the questions. Listen only once, and write down as much as you can. Focus on the key words.

2 Now work with a partner to figure out exactly what was said. The first one has been done for you.

For example

a *Have you recently been able to concentrate on whatever you're doing?*

After you listen

Each question is answered on a 0 to 3 scale, 0 being the highest level of well-being (you feel very good), 3 being the lowest (you feel very bad). These are then added up to give the overall score. An average person gets a score of about 10 or 12, meaning that they give 1s nearly all the time.

3   What is your score? Do you think it is accurate?

Pronunciation

4   Mark the stressed words in each question.

5   Which words are usually stressed, the big words or the little words?

6   Which words are easier to hear, the big words or the little words? Choose the best words to complete this sentence.

The big words/little words are easier to hear because they are usually pronounced:

·   more loudly/more quietly

·   longer/shorter

7   Practise saying some of the sentences with natural stress and at natural speed.

8   Which verb form (Present Simple, Past Simple, Present Perfect, etc.) is used in the questionnaire? Why?

Writing: structuring an argument

Write a 250-word essay, on the following topic.

> There are many reasons for our choice of career.
>   **a**   Outline some of the factors which influence our choice.
>   **b**   State what the most important reasons are or were for you.

Before you write

1   Brainstorm for five minutes with a partner. How many different factors can you think of?

For example

> *family pressure*

2   Can you group the factors together in any way?

For example

> *perhaps 'family pressure' goes together with 'culture'*

3   Put the factors in a logical order. There is not only one way to order your argument, but there has to be a logical order.

For example

Option 1

most important for you

↓

least important for you

Option 2

least important for you

↓

most important for you

Option 3

economic reasons

↓

social reasons

4   For each general factor, note an example or supporting point.

Writing

5   Now, finish writing your plan and write the essay.

4 Well connected

Tuning in

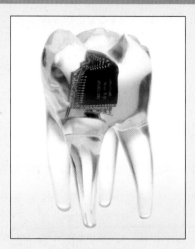

1 Look at the photographs above. Answer these questions for each object.
 a What do you think it is?
 b What is its purpose or function?
 c How does it work?

2 4.1 Listen to two people doing the same task. Do they have the same ideas as you? At the end of their discussion, you will hear the correct answers.

3 Do you think the second object would be useful? Would you buy one? Who *would* buy one?

Listening

4.2 Michio Kaku is a physicist. You will hear him giving a talk about the year 2020, when microchips will cost only one penny, or one cent.

Before you listen

1 With a partner, brainstorm a list of things that have a microchip in them now.

As you listen

2 Kaku is describing some of the things that will have a chip in them in the future, and what we could use them for. Match the things and their uses.

Box A lists the things.   Box B lists the uses.

A	B
a watch	**i** to monitor your diet
b tie clasp	**ii** to access the Internet
c earring	**iii** to access your cell phone or laptop
d glasses	**iv** to access GPS (the global positioning satellite system)
e clothes	**v** to access the earth's entire database
f toilet	**vi** to monitor your heartbeat

3 Which thing would be useful:
 · for parents? · at parties?
 · for meetings? · in the countryside?

After you listen

4 Does this sound like 'a wonderful future' to you?

Speaking

1   In groups, design a gadget that you think you can sell (maximum price $US 200).
   a   What would its purpose be?
   b   What are its features?
   c   Who would buy it?
   d   How much would it cost?
   e   What would you call it?

2   Draw your gadget, so that you can explain it to other students.

3   Now, move around the class trying to sell your gadget to other students. Everyone has $US 500 to spend. The winner is the person with the highest sales at the end of thirty minutes.

Word patterns

*The audio tooth **allows** useful information to be sent to you in secret, wherever you are and whenever you need it. For example, the tooth **enables** your manager to send you useful information during a meeting.*

The grammatical pattern for these verbs is:
   sth/sb *allows* sth/sb *to do* sth

4   What would your classmates' gadgets *allow* or *enable* you to do? Write five sentences to explain the gadgets' functions.

For example

Jean's device would allow you to learn a language while you are sleeping.

Communication

5   The box below contains a group of words, each in some way connected with *communication*. Put the words which you believe are related to each other into groups.

channel	canal	satellite	signal	message	route
path	receiver	transmitter	bridge	network	orbit
station	code	plane	ship	circuit	car
shuttle	airport	terminal	highway		

6   Explain to a partner the way in which you have grouped the words.

Speaking: Paraphrasing

When you cannot remember the right word for something, you can explain it using other words. This is *paraphrasing*.

For example

— *We walked beside this … oh, what do you call it? You know, like … like a river but it's not natural, people build it.*

— *Oh, you mean canal?*

— *Yeah, of course! Canal. So we walked beside this canal.*

1   Choose four or five other words from the box above. How would you paraphrase them?

It's like a …

It's a kind of …

It's a thing you use to …

It's a place that …

It's a way of …

It's a machine that …

Writing

Before you write

1 What does this diagram show?

2 Can you describe this satellite system and explain how it works? Use some of the words in the vocabulary exercise on page 39 to help you.

Passive (1)

Below, you can see part of a text explaining the satellite system.

3 Read the first sentence, then decide whether sentence 'a' or 'b' is the best way to continue the text. The first one has been done as an example.

1 Television programmes are prepared for broadcasting at the TV station.

	a	b
2	The material is then transmitted directly to an uplink centre.	The people at the TV station then transmit the material directly to an uplink centre.
3	Someone at the uplink centre beams these signals up to a near-earth orbiting satellite, which relays them back down to earth.	These signals are beamed to a near-earth orbiting satellite, and relayed back to earth.
4	Here, they are received by a repeater station.	A repeater station receives them here.

4 In this exercise, which sentences use the passive form of the verb?

5 In English, the topic—what we are talking about—comes at or near the beginning of the sentence. For example, what is the topic of sentence 1?

1 Television programmes are prepared for broadcasting at the TV station.

6 What is the topic of 2a and 2b?

2a is better than 2b because the topic flows more smoothly from 1 to 2a.

We choose the passive so that we can put the topic at the beginning of the sentence, rather than in the middle (as in 2b).

Writing

7 Now write a paragraph about the whole diagram. You will need to describe the diagram briefly, then explain all the parts of it. Be careful: you will not always need the passive.

Listening: Is there anyone out there?

Before you listen

1   What is the main point of the following passage?

   a   There must be life somewhere else in the universe.

   b   There are many stars in the universe.

   c   The universe is very beautiful.

   d   Intelligent beings on another planet must be watching us.

Alone in a Crowded Universe

The next time you are outdoors on a clear night away from city lights, look up at the sky and get a sense of the myriad of stars. Next, find a pair of binoculars, train them on the Milky Way, and appreciate how many more stars escaped your naked eye. Then look at a photo of the Andromeda Nebula as seen through a powerful telescope to realise how enormous is the number of stars that escaped your binoculars as well.

Once all those numbers have sunk in, you will finally be ready to ask how humans could possibly be unique in the universe. How many civilisations of intelligent beings like ourselves must be out there, looking back at us? How long before we are in communication with them, before we visit them, or before we are visited?

2   For the sentences below, circle the word or phrase that best indicates your personal opinion and give your reasons.

> *I think that it is **highly unlikely/unlikely/likely/highly likely** that there is intelligent life somewhere else in the universe.*

> *If intelligent life does exist elsewhere, I think that it is **highly unlikely/unlikely/likely/highly likely** that we will manage to communicate with them.*

Radio telescopes have been used in attempts to communicate with intelligent extra-terrestrials or intelligent alien life forms, elsewhere in the universe.

3   Each figure here is a message of some kind. How or what do you think each one is communicating?

4   Two of the messages were transmitted; one was received. Which ones do you think were transmitted?

5   What problems do you think we might face in making contact and communicating with aliens?

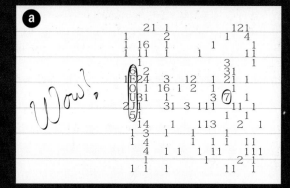

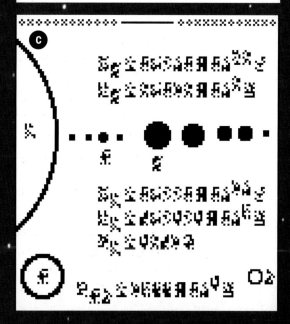

As you listen

🔊 **4.3** You will hear an interview with an astronomer about two organisations that have attempted to make contact with aliens: SETI (the Search for Extra-Terrestrial Intelligence) and Project Encounter.

6 In the first section, you will hear a list of the general problems that both groups face. Write one or two words for each problem.

7 In section 2, you will hear a comparison of the two groups. In the table below, underline the correct option for each organisation.

SETI	Project Encounter
Group of astronomers/Business	Group of astronomers/Business
Well established/Fairly new	Well established/Fairly new
Focus on transmitting/Focus on listening	Focus on transmitting/Focus on listening
Covering wide area of space/Covering narrow area	Covering wide area of space/Covering narrow area

Listen again

8 Match the three figures (on page 41) with the appropriate project. Which of the projects does the astronomer believe is more likely to succeed?

After you listen

9 Following this discussion, have you changed your opinion about the likelihood of making contact with extra-terrestrials?

10 Even if life elsewhere does exist, do you think it would be a good idea for us to make contact?

Probability

11 Here are some views on the likelihood of life elsewhere. Underline any language that indicates probability.

The chances of finding life elsewhere in the universe are incredibly small.

It's almost certain that we are not alone.

There must be life on other planets.

We may have to face the fact that primitive life is common in the Universe but that the development of intelligence is highly improbable.

I suppose there could be, but I don't think it's very likely.

Focus on form

12 What grammatical forms go with these expressions of probability? Write A, B or C in the gaps to complete the sentences.

A Infinitive
B Noun or -ing form
C that clause

The chances of + _____ + are good/poor/low/slim.

It's unlikely/possible/likely/certain + _____.

There must/could/can't + _____.

Speaking

1 Think of a famous road, bridge or tunnel. Prepare to talk to a partner about it for two minutes. Think about these questions.
- Where is it?
- What does it connect?
- When was it built?

- Who built it?
- Why is it important?
- Have you seen it/used it yourself?

Reading

Before you read

The two most important canals in the world are the Suez Canal and the Panama Canal.

1 Can you draw the two canals on the map below?

2 What parts of the world do they link?

3 Can you identify which canal is which in the photographs below?

4 What geographical differences are there between the two canals?

5 Which canal do you think was probably more difficult to build?

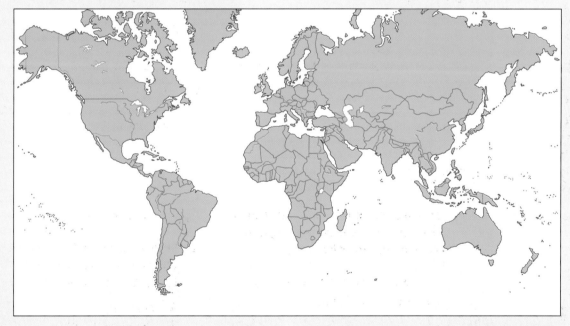

As you read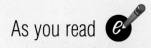

6 Complete the table below with answers from the texts on this page and page 45.

	Suez	**Panama**
Parts of the world they connect	_____	_____
Early history	First considered in *1000 BC or earlier*	First considered in _____
Final construction	Begun in _____	Begun in _____
Workforce	_____ workers	_____ workers
Total deaths	_____, 000 caused by _____	_____, 000 caused by _____
Completion	In _____	In _____
Control	Earlier foreign control by _____ but now controlled by _____	Earlier foreign control by _____, but now controlled by _____
Design: sea level or locks?	_____	_____
Canal length	_____	_____
Annual traffic	< _____ , 000 ships; _____ tonnes	< _____ , 000 ships; _____ tonnes

The Suez Canal

1   The 163-kilometre Suez Canal runs through the Sinai Peninsula in Egypt and links the Mediterranean and Red Seas. The canal has no locks, as the seas it connects are at essentially the same level. It can accommodate huge ships up to seventy metres wide and 500 metres long. Over 15 000 ships a year travel through the canal, carrying 300 to 400 million tonnes of cargo, which amounts to around 14% of world shipping trade, including 26% of oil exports.

2   The idea of a canal between the Red Sea and Mediterranean has a long history. By at least 1000 BC, the pharaohs had dug a canal between the Red Sea and the Nile, and boats could then travel down the Nile to the Mediterranean. The canal clogged up with sand, but was re-dug by the Greeks and then Romans, and later—in the 8th century AD—by the Arabs, before clogging up again. During his Egyptian campaign of 1798, Napoleon revived the idea of a direct link between the two seas, but his engineers thought it would be too difficult, having incorrectly calculated that the Red Sea was nine metres higher than the Mediterranean.

3   Ferdinand de Lesseps, a French diplomat to Egypt, again promoted the idea, and in 1854 he signed an agreement with the Egyptian government to construct the canal. Ownership was shared between the French and Egyptians. Digging started in April 1859. Over two million Egyptians worked on the construction of the canal, of whom at least 125 000 died due to accidents and diseases such as cholera. The canal opened to shipping in November 1869.

4   Due to the expense of canal construction, as well as the falling price of cotton, the Egyptian government ran up a large external debt during the 1860s. The British were able to take advantage of this situation by purchasing canal shares from Egypt in 1875. In this way they gained control of the canal, which they held until it was re-nationalised by Egypt in 1956.

The Panama Canal

1 As early as the 16th century, King Charles I of Spain, seeking a speedier passage between the Atlantic and the Pacific, ordered his Panamanian governor to survey the Panamanian Isthmus for a canal. The governor's report: it cannot be done. Well, maybe not in 1534. But both the Americans and the French had other ideas by the latter half of the 19th century.

2 The French made the first attempt at digging a trench from the Atlantic Ocean to the Pacific in 1878, when a committee of the Geographical Society of Paris signed a treaty with Colombia (of which Panama was then a province) to build a canal from Limon Bay to Panama City.

3 In retrospect, the French effort probably was doomed from the start because Ferdinand de Lesseps, builder of the Suez Canal in 1869, insisted on a sea-level canal requiring a massive 7 720-metre long tunnel through the mountains at Culebra. The builders also had no idea how to cope with the torrential rain and frequent horrific outbreaks of malaria and yellow fever. Ten years later, after at least 20 000 deaths from disease, the French gave up.

4 Theodore Roosevelt, who assumed the American presidency in 1901, was keen to see an American-built canal through the isthmus. When Colombia refused to sell the rights to dig the canal, Roosevelt threw U.S. power behind a Panamanian uprising and supported Panama's 1903 declaration of independence.

5 Roosevelt instigated a treaty with Panama that gave the United States the right to build the canal and created a 10-mile wide Canal Zone under American control surrounding the waterway. Construction of a lock canal, taking the canal over—rather than through—the geographical barriers, commenced in 1904.

6 The Americans took no chances. The army dispatched surgeon Col. William Gorgas to Panama to tackle malaria and yellow fever. Gorgas was fresh from Havana where he had helped eradicate yellow fever, following discoveries by his colleague Maj. Walter Reed and others that the disease was carried by a mosquito. Malaria also had recently been discovered to be transmitted by mosquito bites.

7 Once Gorgas's efforts had quickly eradicated yellow fever and reduced the incidence of malaria, two principal obstacles to the canal had been removed. The third obstacle was the terrain.

8 The lakes and locks proved to be the right idea at the right time. After ten years, during which 70 000 people worked on the project, $US400 million and 5 600 deaths, the Panama Canal officially opened on August 15, 1914, just as World War I was getting under way.

9 The canal returned to Panamanian control as the 20th century drew to a close. Considered by many engineers to be the century's greatest achievement in land-based engineering, the 80-kilometre canal now carries over 15 000 ships and 140 million tonnes of cargo a year.

After you read

7 Which project appears to have been more difficult?

8 The two canals have brought many benefits. We can trade more easily with other parts of the world, and we can travel more easily. But they cost many lives. Was it worth it?

Vocabulary

9 Find words in the texts which belong in the following categories. If you do not know exactly what the words mean, try to guess before you use your dictionary. One example has been done for you.

Geography	Politics	Disease	Canals
mountains			

Speaking

According to the American historian David McCullough, the Panama Canal 'ranks today, without any question, as one of the greatest achievements in American history'.

1   Make a list of the three greatest achievements in your own country's history. Plan a three- or four-minute talk, in which you:
    a   describe what happened in each event, and when
    b   explain why each one is important.

2   Before you give your talk, think about the way you have organised it. Are you organising by:
    a   time (most distant in time → most recent, or vice versa)?
    b   importance (most important → least, or vice versa)?

3   Do you have some other way of organising your points? What is most important is not *how* you organise, but that your talk shows some signs of organisation.

Reading

Before you read

1   Look at these photographs. For each picture, talk to a partner about these questions.
    ·   Where is it?
    ·   What sort of lifestyle do the people who live there have?
    ·   What would be the pros and cons of living there?

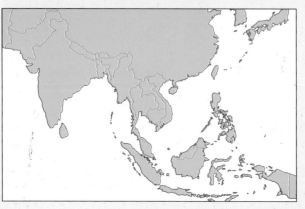

2   One of the photographs above was taken in Bhutan. Which one? What do you know about Bhutan? Can you find it on the map?

3   The text on page 47 explains the approach that the government of Bhutan has taken to tourism. The text mentions the impacts. First, brainstorm some of the impacts of tourism, both positive and negative on:
    ·   the environment
    ·   the culture of a country
    ·   the economy.

As you read

4 Choose words from the box to complete this summary of the text.

The tourism policy of the Government of Bhutan is to control _____ in order to minimise _____ and maximise _____.

problems	numbers	development
resources	benefits	culture

5 Which paragraph contains the following information?
A The general policy
B The benefits of tourism
C The current state of the tourism industry in Bhutan
D The negative impacts of tourism
E The basic principles of the policy
F How tourism is controlled

TOURISM IN BHUTAN

1 Tourism in Bhutan was privatised by the Royal Government of Bhutan in 1991. Today it is a vibrant business with eighty private operators at the helm of affairs.

2 There are, however, problems associated with tourism which, if not controlled, can have a devastating and irreversible impact on the local environment, culture and identity of the people. Realizing these problems and the fact that the resources on which tourism is based are limited, the Royal Government of Bhutan adheres strongly to a policy of low volume, high value tourism.

3 The tourism industry in Bhutan is founded on the principle of sustainability, meaning that tourism must be environmentally and ecologically friendly, socially and culturally acceptable and economically viable. The number of tourists visiting Bhutan is regulated to a manageable level because of the lack of infrastructure.

4 The Royal Government of Bhutan recognizes that tourism is a world-wide phenomenon and an important means of achieving socioeconomic development, particularly for developing countries like Bhutan. It also recognizes that tourism, in affording the opportunity to travel, can help in promoting understanding among peoples and building closer ties of friendship based on appreciation and respect for different cultures and lifestyles.

5 Towards achieving this objective, the Royal Government, since the inception of tourism in the year 1974, has adopted a very cautious approach to growth and development of the tourism industry in Bhutan. In order to minimize the problems, the number of tourists has been maintained at a manageable level and this control on number is exercised through a policy of government-regulated tourist tariffs and a set of administrative requirements.

After you read

6 Does it seem like a good idea to restrict the number of tourists in Bhutan?

7 Should more countries do the same?

Vocabulary

The article talks about the lack of *infrastructure* in Bhutan. Check the meaning of *infrastructure* in an English–English dictionary.

8 What kind of infrastructure is necessary for a country that receives a lot of tourists?

Collocations

9 Try to match up the following words from memory, then look back at the text to check:
a if you were correct
b the meaning.

Note that sometimes there is more than one possibility.

Adverb	+	Adjective
environmentally		acceptable
economically		friendly
culturally		viable

Adjective	+	Noun
low		volume
high		phenomenon
worldwide		level
manageable		value
devastating		impact

Verb	+	Noun
achieve		problem
minimise		understanding
promote		objective

Listening

📻 **4.4** You will hear a conversation between someone who has visited Bhutan and someone who would like to. The table below shows most of the items the speakers talk about.

10 Listen, and tick to show whether the woman had positive or negative feelings about each item. The first one has been done for you.

Item in the conversation	Positive feelings	Negative feelings
· Her overall impression of Bhutan	✓	
· The limited number of tourists allowed in Bhutan		
· The policy of having an official guide		
· The guide that she had on her visit		
· The policy of the Bhutanese having to wear national costume		
· Bhutan's policy of cultural isolation		

Speaking

11 Where in the world would you most like to visit? New York, Antarctica, Bhutan, Shanghai, ...?

12 When you think about places you would like to visit, what considerations are most important for you: the culture, the scenery, the people, the language, the environment, the economy, the history?

13 Exchange ideas with a partner.

Writing

You are going to write a 250–300 word essay on the following topic.

> The twentieth century was a period of great human progress. But this progress had many costs: financial, social, cultural, environmental, and even human.
>
> Is progress worth these costs?

Generating ideas

1 What do you, personally, think progress is? Is it more knowledge, better technology, better health, fewer wars?

2 Spend three minutes making a list. Then compare your list with a partner. Do you agree on the most important indications of progress?

Using supporting examples

3   Think of one or two real examples for each of the costs of progress mentioned in the essay topic.

·   Financial costs:
·   Social costs: e.g. *bigger cities → more crime ...*
·   Cultural costs: e.g. *McDonald's on every street corner ...*
·   Environmental costs:
·   Human casualties: e.g. *Panama Canal workers ...*

4   Explain your examples to a partner.

Taking a position

5   Weighing up the arguments—the benefits of progress against the costs of that progress— what is your personal position? Is it worth it?

Writing a plan: organising your essay

6   There are many ways you could organise your essay. Here are some of the options. Which one would you choose, or would you choose another way?

Option 1	*Option 2*	*Option 3*
Paragraph 1 Intro: Progress	Paragraph 1 Intro	Paragraph 1 Intro: Progress
Paragraph 2 Costs	Paragraph 2 Progress	Paragraph 2 Costs Example 1: Financial
Paragraph 3 Conclusion	Paragraph 3 Costs	Paragraph 2 Costs Example 2: Social
	Paragraph 4 Conclusion	Paragraph 3 Costs Example 3: Environmental
		Paragraph 5 Conclusion

For each of these options, there are both advantages and disadvantages:

·   With option 1, you can write more on each element, but you cannot give much detail on the examples of costs.
·   With option 2, you can give more weight to the topic of progress, but less to the costs.
·   With option 3, you can cover the examples in more detail, but you cannot cover them all.

7   Once you have chosen an overall structure for your essay, write the plan, then write the essay.

Tuning in

1   Do you know the name of each of these activities? Put them into categories.

2   **Add other activities that belong in each category.**

3   **Can you think of other categories of recreation? Make a list.**

For example

Attending sports events as a spectator

4   **Now explain your categories to a partner, then discuss these questions.**

a   What are your favourite leisure activities?

b   Why do you enjoy them?

c   How often do you do them, who with, where, etc.?

Comparison and contrast

5   **Write five sentences about the similarities between different activities on your lists.**

For example

Both backgammon and 'Go' are played on a board.

Like t'ai chi, karate is a martial art.

Football and basketball are both professional sports.

Neither hiking nor reading have rules.

6   **Write five sentences about the differences between activities.**

For example

Unlike 'Go', backgammon depends partly on luck.

Karate can be competitive, whereas t'ai chi generally isn't.

Chess has more complicated rules than 'Go'.

7   **Copy this table and make lists of the words we use to describe similarities and differences.**

Similarities	Differences
Both ... and ...	Unlike ...

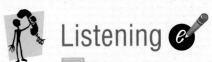

Listening 🎤

🔊 **5.1** You will hear a radio programme on the ancient game of *Go*.

As you listen

1 Write between one and three words in each gap.

History	Game invented in **1** _china_ in about **2** _11000_ First played in Japan in **3** _sunce the 6th_ Moved to Europe in **4** _19 century_
Name in other countries	The word 'Go' comes from **5** _Japanise_ Known as wei chi in **6** _chinese_ and baduk in **7** _chonea_
Board	Played with black and white stones on board with 19 x 19 **8** _intersecting line_
Aim	To surround opponent's stones and **9** _capture-territory_
Interesting because	Rules very **10** _very simple_, strategy very **11** _complicts_
Played by	More than **12** _15 million_ proj

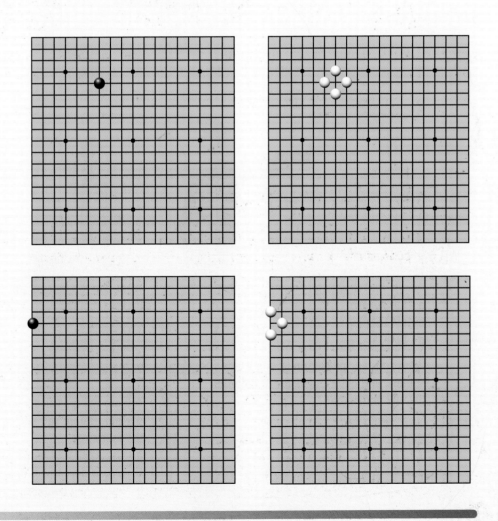

Passive (2)

Here are two sentences from the radio programme about *Go*.

   a *It has been played in Japan since 740 AD.*

   b *The game is played on a board with 19 by 19 intersecting lines.*

2 What does 'It' refer to here?

3 Put a circle around the topic of each sentence.

As we saw in the last unit, we often use the passive to keep the topic—the old, known information—at the beginning of the sentence.

But we also choose the passive so that we can control where we put important, new information.

4 Underline the new information in sentences 'a' and 'b'.

So now you can make a rule:

In English we usually put the topic at the _____ of the sentence, and important, new information at the _____ of the sentence.

5 Why would this active sentence not be OK in this radio talk about *Go*?

   'Millions of people play it.'

Speaking

1 What is the problem in this cartoon?

2 Who is responsible for solving this problem?
   a the speaker
   b the listener
   c both

3 What can the speaker do—using words, sounds, and body language—to help the listener understand?

For example

   – *'Have you got that?'*
   – *watching the listener's facial expressions*

4 What can the listener do to check his or her understanding?

For example

   – *'So, what you're saying is ...'*
   – *'What was that again?'*

5 You are going to describe a game to a partner. Before you speak, make notes on the following:
   a history (if you know)   **d** aim
   b played on/with ...   **e** rules
   c interesting because ...   **f** played by ...

Try to choose a game which your partner will not know. If you cannot think of an unfamiliar game, do the activity without naming the game, and see if your partner can guess what it is.

6   Read the rules for the game below. If there is anything you do not understand, talk about it with your classmates and teacher until you do understand.

7   Now play the game.

The Yes/No Game

Aim: to make your partner say *yes* or *no* and collect all of his or her counters
Played with: five counters each (coins, matchsticks or beans will do)
Number of players: two
Procedure:
Each player starts with five counters.
Start a conversation in which you try to make the other person say *yes* or *no*.
Each time someone says *yes* or *no,* they must give one counter to their partner.
Other rules:
You must also give up a counter if:
*   you pause for more than two seconds before answering;
*   you give the same answer twice in a row (e.g. you answer *'not much'* for one question and then again for the next question).
Winner: the first person to collect all of the other person's counters.

Grammar focus

There are many alternatives to *yes* and *no.* Some are listed below.

I think so.	Maybe.	Sometimes.	Not much.	Quite often.	Never.
I hope not.	Of course.	I do.	Naturally.	I have.	Quite a lot.
I used to.	Possibly.	I'd like to.	Definitely.	I love it.	Usually.
I'm not sure.	I might.	I don't.			

8   Complete the table below with the words and phrases from the box.

Form	Example
Auxiliary and modal verbs	*I have.*
Other verbs	*I think so.*
Adverbs of frequency	*Sometimes.*
Adverbs of degree	*Not much.*
Modal adverbs	*Definitely.*
Other adverbs	*Of course.*
Adjectives	*I'm not sure.*

9   **Can you think of any other forms that can be used to give short answers like this?**

You cannot use all of these in the same situation: it depends on the grammar and the meaning. You should always try to expand on your answer. In general, however, responding with an answer like this is:

a   more interesting than saying just *yes* or *no* all of the time

b   more precise: all of these answers give more information than just *yes* or *no.*

10   Play the Yes/No game again, with a new partner. This time, try to use a wider range of answers than you used the first time.

Speaking

1 Think about how you spend an average day. How much time do you spend, on average, on the following activities?

	Weekday	Weekend day
Sleep		
Employment (or Education)		
Travel (to or from work, school, etc.)		
Housework		
Eating/Personal care		
Free Time		

2 Compare your answers with a partner.

3 Then compare your answers with the information in the graphs below on the way that British people spent their time in the year 2000. How similar, or different, is your time use and British time use?

How the UK fills its day

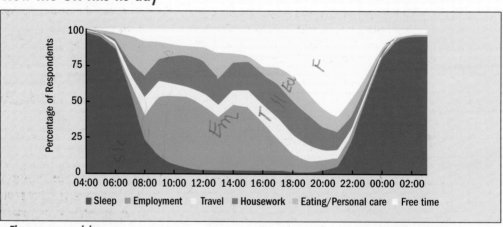

The average weekday

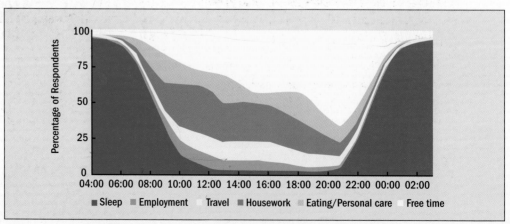

The average weekend day

Writing

1   With a partner, identify the key points from the British data in the graphs on page 54. Write a 150–200 word description of the data.

Organising text

2   Now compare your text with the original text, written by the British National Statistics Department. First you will need to put the original in the correct order. The first one has been done for you.

A   On average, adults go to bed an hour later at the weekend (89% by 1am).

B   On weekdays, 77% of adults are awake and up by 8am.

C   On weekend days, people tend to get up later (69% by 9am), work less and do more housework, travel and leisure activities during the day.

D   Beyond 4pm, people are then doing housework, eating or enjoying leisure time.

E   Main meal times fall between 8–9.30am; 1pm and 5–9pm.

F   The two charts show the percentage of adults that are participating in six activities (sleep, employment, travel, housework, eating/personal care and free time) every hour, across a 24-hour period.

G   By midnight, 81% of adults are asleep, while 12% are still enjoying free time and 4% are working or travelling.

H   The first chart maps time use on an average weekday and the second, time use on an average weekend day.

I   Most are then at work or studying until at least 4pm.

J   Peak meal times do not vary greatly compared with during the week, but longer is spent eating and on personal care at other times of the day at the weekend.

(1) The two charts above show the percentage of adults that are participating in six activities (sleep, employment, travel, housework, eating/personal care and free time) every hour, across a 24-hour period. (2) …

3   Decide with your classmates exactly what the correct order is.

4   Now compare your text with the original.
a   Does your text cover the same points?
b   Is it organised in a similar way?
c   Do you think your text is better in any way?

5   The original text has three paragraphs. Where do you think the second and third paragraphs begin?

6   What are the two main organising principles in this text?
a   General-Particular
b   Contrast
c   Time
d   Importance (e.g. biggest to smallest)

General vs. specific

Sometimes the original text gives exact figures.

For example

77% of adults are awake and up by 8am.

At other times, it is less precise or generalises, saying that a statement is generally but *not always* true.

For example

Most are then at work or studying until at least 4pm.

7   Find two other phrases in the text that are used to make generalisations. One is a verb, the other is a prepositional phrase.

Verb: _____ to …

Prepositional Phrase: on _____

Speaking

8   Describe a typical weekend where you live.

Reading *e*

Before you read

1 Would you prefer your children to spend their free time playing chess, playing the piano, or playing video games? Why?

2 Do you agree with the opinions in the following headlines?

> **Violent video games are turning our kids into killing machines**

> **Video games increase aggression, says new study**

3 From the following table, make a sentence that expresses your opinion.

Violent entertainment has	no effect little effect some effect a significant effect a major effect	on children's behaviour.

4 Where in the table could you insert the following modifiers: *very, quite, absolutely*?

5 What support do you have for your opinion?
- Personal experience
- Feeling
- Stories in the media
- What other people have told you
- Logic
- Research
- Other

6 Explain your opinion to a partner. Do you agree with each other?

As you read

This article reports the opinion of Geoffrey Goldstein, a psychologist who specialises in violent behaviour.

7 Skim the text very quickly (two minutes maximum), and choose the statement (a–d) that best reflects Goldstein's opinion.

Goldstein believes violent video games have:

a no effect on children's behaviour.

b little effect on children's behaviour.

c a significant effect on children's behaviour.

d a major effect on children's behaviour.

Boys just wanna have fun

1 'Violent video games are turning our kids into killing machines'; 'Video games increase aggression, says new study'. The headlines sell newspapers, but how accurate are they? Geoffrey Goldstein, author of *Why We Watch: the Attractions of Violent Entertainment* and a psychologist who specialises in violent behaviour, says that many of the studies are flawed because researchers into video-game violence make basic mistakes. Typically, a study is done by getting a class of school children to fill in a questionnaire on how long they play video games. The heavy gamers and the light gamers are then compared—and, inevitably, the heavy gamers have negative characteristics such as more aggressiveness and lower school performance.

2 'But when you make a study like this,' says Goldstein, 'dividing the class at the median in terms of how often they play video games, you end up comparing mainly boys with mainly girls because most of the heavy gamers are boys. What you find is that the heavy gamers in comparison with the light gamers reflect masculine characteristics. That is, they are more aggressive than girls. Their school performance is lower. They read fewer books and so on. So you end up with a study of sex differences that masks as a study of video games.'

3 Researchers also often fail to distinguish between aggressive play and aggressive behaviour, says Goldstein. Another typical

study method is to divide children into three groups, in which one group plays a violent video game such as Mortal Kombat, the second a non-violent game and the third plays no game at all. The children are then observed in the playground. Watching kids who played Mortal Kombat do martial arts moves, the researcher marks them down as showing aggressive behaviour.

4   However, Goldstein says that's nonsense. 'Violent games cause violent play. If we don't distinguish between aggressive play and aggressive behaviour, we lose the whole value of play which is to do in fantasy what you don't have to carry out in reality ... There is no intention to injure anyone and rarely do children get injured as a result of this kind of play.'

5   Goldstein says he could only find two studies that made a distinction between aggressive play and aggressive behaviour. When they do make that distinction, what they find is that aggressive media, video games, TV programmes, increase aggressive play and have no effect on aggressive behaviour.

6   Real violence is frightening to children and has emotional and physical effects on them, says Goldstein. Children don't become de-sensitised by video violence because it is not real. 'There is no victim that one intends to injure. There is only a digital enemy, a digital victim.'

7   Statistics seem to support Goldstein's view. In the US, youth violence fell dramatically in the 90s, over the same period that video-game use sky-rocketed.

Read again

8 For each of the statements below, write *A* if Goldstein agrees, *D* if he disagrees and *N* if there is no information in the text.

  a Researchers in this area typically use inappropriate methods.
  b Boys do better at school than girls.
  c Television is more violent than video games.
  d Violent play and violent behaviour are different.
  e Violent entertainment causes aggressive play to increase.
  f Fantasy is important.
  g Children try to hurt each other when they are playing.
  h Children recognise the difference between real and fantasy violence.

9 What are the two typical mistakes that researchers make, according to Goldstein?

After you read

10 Have you changed your opinion in any way after reading this article?

11 Do you agree that children can distinguish between reality and fantasy? At what age do you think they become able to do this?

12 Do you think the findings would be similar for your country?

Vocabulary

Word attack

13 What do you think the following two words mean? What clues are there?
  Paragraph 1: *flawed*
  Paragraph 7: *sky-rocketed*

Topics

14 Make a list of words from the text to do with *violence*.

Listening

5.2 You will hear a presentation of survey findings on video game use in the USA.

Before you listen

1   Here are the main reasons that people give for playing these games. Can you guess the order of importance of these reasons?

- [ ] Challenging
- [ ] Fun
- [ ] Can play with friends and family
- [ ] A way to keep up with technology
- [ ] Offer a lot of entertainment for the price

As you listen

2   Listen to section 1 and check your guesses.

3   Now listen to section 2. Make notes to complete the table below.

Most popular console games

(a) _____ games: 39%

action games: (b) _____%

sports games: (c) _____%

(d) _____ games: 31%

Most popular computer games

puzzle/board/card games: (e) _____%

(f) _____ games: 28%

(g) _____ games: 23%

simulations: (h) _____%

Demographics

(i) _____% of computer game players and

(j) _____% of console game players are male.

   96% of those purchasing console games are over the age of (k) _____; compared to

(l) _____% of those purchasing computer games.

Speaking

1   With a partner, design a survey which you can give to another class to find out:
   a   the most popular leisure activities
   b   who they do these activities with
   c   why they choose these activities: e.g. *to relieve stress.*

2   Draw a graph or graphs of your findings, and present them to another class.

Writing

Below you will find part of an essay written by a group of students at the University of Texas.

You will find:

· the introduction

· topic sentences for the body paragraphs

· the conclusion.

1 Read the introduction and conclusion. Are the authors positive, negative, or neutral? Do you agree with them or disagree?

2 If you agree, complete the body paragraphs. If you disagree, rewrite the introduction so that it reflects your own opinion, *then* complete the body paragraphs. (Do not rewrite the conclusion yet.)

Music, Television, and Video Games and Their Effect on Children!

The children of today are surrounded by technology and entertainment that is full of violence. It is estimated that the average child watches from three to five hours of television a day! Listening to music is also a time-consuming pastime among children. With all of that exposure, one might pose the question, 'How can seeing so much violence on television and video games and hearing about violence in music affect a child's behaviour?' Obviously these media have a big influence on childrens' behaviour: we can see it in the way they attempt to emulate their favourite rock stars by dressing in a similar style and the way children play games, imitating their favourite cartoon personalities or superheroes. Studies have shown that extensive television viewing may be associated with 'aggressive behaviour, poor academic performance, precocious sexuality, obesity, and the use of drugs or alcohol.' Television, video games, and music are very influential and if there is too much violence available for children to watch, play, or listen to, this can sway their attitudes in a negative direction.

Music is a big part of children's lives, especially as the children become older and enter adolescence. ...

Television is especially influential on the children of today. ...

Another form of entertainment that can have a strong influence on a child's behaviour is video games. ...

In conclusion, television, music, and video games are all things that are fun and sometimes educational for kids. However, these media can be a bad influence on children, depending on the content. Children are extremely impressionable and if they are exposed to violent television, music or video games then they will start to emulate that show, artist or song, or video game with their behaviour. These are all so powerful that they should be used to teach children how to problem solve and help them expand their minds, not show them how to kill someone or teach them other violent behaviour.

Focus on the conclusion

Conclusions often have a very typical structure, following these steps:

    a concede/admit that the opposing argument is partly true

    b repeat your own argument

    c and recommend future action.

3 In this conclusion, draw boxes around the parts that form steps a, b and c.

In conclusion, television, music, and video games are all things that are fun and sometimes educational for kids. However, these media can be a bad influence on children, depending on the content. Children are extremely impressionable and if they are exposed to violent television, music or video games then they will start to emulate that show, artist or song, or video game with their behaviour. These are all so powerful that they should be used to teach children how to problem solve and help them expand their minds, not show them how to kill someone or teach them other violent behaviour.

4 It is very important to distinguish the opposing opinion from your own opinion. Which linking word is used in this conclusion to show the separation between the two points of view?

5 Using the same organising structure, write the conclusion for a writer who has a more positive view of television, music and video games.

Because the conclusion gives the reader the final impression of our opinion, it is important to be very clear about how strongly we feel about a topic, or how sure we are about our opinion.

6 For each of the following issues, what is your personal position, black and white (= *This is very clear, I am sure about what is right*) or grey (= *I am not sure what is right in this case—there are very good arguments on both sides.*)? Decide on your position, then compare with a partner. You do not need to give your reasons at the moment.

Issue	black and white	grey
Physical punishment of children		
Sex education in schools		
Compulsory military service		
Capital punishment		

One way that you show your opinion is in your use of modal verbs, like *can, could, should, will*, etc., and qualifying adverbs like *sometimes, generally, always*, etc.

7 Underline all the words like this in the conclusion in the text.

8 Notice how the meaning—and strength of opinion—changes if you change, add, or leave out these words. For each group of sentences below, decide which sentence is strongest and most definite in meaning, and which is weakest and least definite. The first has been done as an example.

a
  i Video games can be fun and sometimes educational for kids.   *Less definite*
  ii Video games are fun and educational for kids.   *Strong*
  iii Video games are always fun and educational for kids.   *Very strong*

b
  i These media can be a bad influence on children.
  ii These media are a bad influence on children.
  iii These media are often a bad influence on children.

c
  i If children watch violent television, they will emulate that show.
  ii If children watch violent television, they emulate that show.
  iii If children watch violent television, they may emulate that show.

d
  i The media should be used to teach children.
  ii The media could be used to teach children.
  iii The media must be used to teach children.

9   Based on your position in the
black/white/grey activity, write a sentence
on each of the issues which reflects your
personal opinion.

For example

*No matter what the crime is, capital punishment is
never a fair punishment.*

Speaking: Public facilities

Your local government owns some land just
outside the central city which has a railway on it,
including the central train station. The rail
company has decided to move the train station
into the centre of the city, so that more people will
use the trains. They have also decided to change
the route, so they do not need the tracks. The
government has decided that it will use the land
for one of the following projects.

· a concert hall
· an information technology park
· a public swimming pool and gymnasium
· a new national art gallery
· a sports stadium
· a park
· a new national library

1   In groups, decide which of the projects
would be best for your town or city. Make a
poster, explaining your project and listing
the benefits.

2   Use your poster to present your proposal to
other groups.

3   As a class, decide which proposal is best.

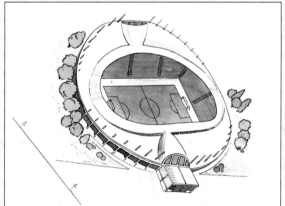

Listening

Before you listen

1   Do you belong to any clubs, or have you ever
belonged to any? Describe the activities of
the club(s) you belong to.

Photography Club	Film Society
Chess Club	Tennis Club
Tramping/Hiking Club	Gaming Club
Asian Students' Association	Diving Club

As you listen

2   **5.3** In the first part of this listening,
you will hear information about four
university clubs. Identify the name of each
club (1–4) from the list.

3   In the second part of the listening, you will
hear a student giving his personal details so
that he can join a club.

a   Before you listen, make a list of all the
kinds of information you think you will
hear. Compare these with a partner's
ideas.

b   As you listen, write down all the details.
Make sure you get the spelling exactly
right!

c   After you listen, check that you and your
partner have exactly the same
information.

After you listen

4   Would you be interested in joining any of
these clubs?

6 The first six billion

Tuning in

1 What do you know about world population? Decide with a partner whether the statements in the population quiz are true (T) or false (F). You must agree with your partner: if you disagree, give reasons for your opinion and discuss the statement until you both agree. Use the Useful language table below.

Population Quiz

1 The population of India is higher than the population of China.
2 The total world population reached 6 billion in 1999.
3 There are more than twenty cities around the world with a population over 10 million.
4 The Netherlands is the world's most densely populated country.
5 The population of Japan fell during the 1990s.
6 The world's population has doubled in the last twenty-five years.
7 Europe is the most heavily populated continent.
8 More than half of the world's population lives in a town or city.
9 One million people immigrate to the USA every year.

2 Now check your answers on page 63.

Useful language for discussing which sentences are true	
Adverbs	**Modal verbs**
This one's possibly true.	This one may/could be true.
This one's probably true.	
This one's definitely/certainly true.	This one must be true.
Or, you could just say:	
I don't really know.	
I have no idea.	

Expressing guesses

3 What is the difference between saying: *It is true* and *It must be true* or *It's definitely true*? **Clue:** which one did you say after you checked the answers?

4 What is the difference between saying: *It's definitely true* and *It must be true*? Which one feels more personal and subjective? Which one feels more impersonal and objective?

Note: you can, and speakers very often do, use both the adverb and the modal verb at the same time for emphasis.

It could possibly be true.

It definitely must be false.

In fact we often add a 'thinking' or 'saying' verb as well.

I think it could possibly be true.

I'd say it definitely must be false.

Listening

6.1 You will hear five different speakers discussing topics relating to population.

1   Match each speaker with one of the six diagrams below. One of the diagrams is not mentioned.

2   Which of the issues in the graphs apply to your country? Discuss this briefly with a partner.

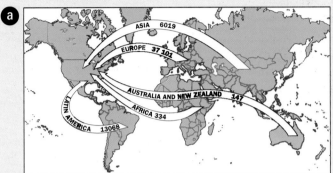

a   ASIA 6019 | EUROPE 37 101 | AUSTRALIA AND NEW ZEALAND 147 | AFRICA 334 | LATIN AMERICA 13068

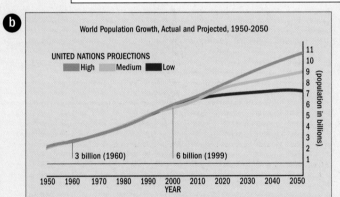

b   World Population Growth, Actual and Projected, 1950-2050

UNITED NATIONS PROJECTIONS
High   Medium   Low

3 billion (1960)   6 billion (1999)

(population in billions)

1950 1960 1970 1980 1990 2000 2010 2020 2030 2040 2050
YEAR

c

Age   **1999**
Males   Females
Percentage of population

Age   **2050**
Males   Females
Percentage of population

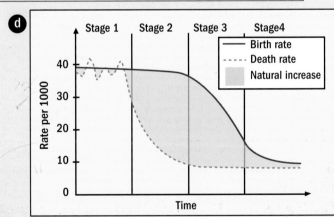

d   Stage 1   Stage 2   Stage 3   Stage4
Birth rate
Death rate
Natural increase
Rate per 1000
Time

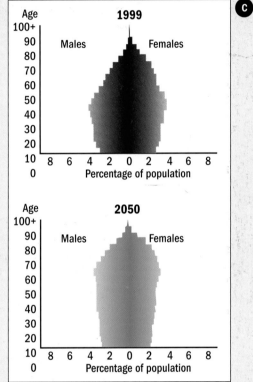

f   Per square mile
Over 500
100 – 499
50 – 99
10 – 49
under 10

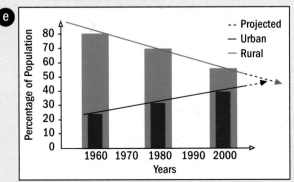

e   Projected
Urban
Rural
Percentage of Population
1960 1970 1980 1990 2000
Years

Using *show* (2)

As you saw in unit 1, the verb pattern *show* + noun phrase is very important when you describe graphs and diagrams, because this is how you describe what you can see before you start to explain it. There are several different kinds of phrases that you can use after *show* (and other similar verbs).

3 Look at these examples, and group them under the heading in the table that describes their structure.

This graph/diagram shows:

  a the countries with the greatest population density

b the way the population profile of the country is changing

c how many people are moving from the country to the cities

d world population projections for the next fifty years

e the regions that America's immigrants came from

f how birth and death rates change as a country develops

g the population densities of different countries

h where America's immigrants came from originally.

show + noun + prepositional phrase	*show* + noun + relative clause	*show* + question word + clause

4 Try to write one sentence of your own using each pattern to describe the graphs on page 63.

Reading

The text on page 65 has nine paragraphs (1–9) and the box below has eight headings (A–H).

Before you read

1 With a partner, look at the headings and see if you can predict what each paragraph says. If you do not understand the heading—especially the vocabulary—just leave it and move to the next one. Do not use a dictionary.

As you read

2 Match the headings with the correct paragraph (paragraph 1 has been done as an example).

3 Write a heading for the paragraph which does not have one.

A Regional Distribution Changing	**B** Fertility is Declining, but Unevenly
C Death Rate Cut by Half	**D** Education Leads to Smaller, Healthier Families
E International Migration	**F** Global Trend Towards Urbanisation
G Water, Land and Food	**H** Ageing Populations

Population Change and People's Choices

(C) Death Rate Cut by Half

1   Since 1950, the death rate has been cut in half, from about twenty to fewer than ten deaths per year per thousand people. At the same time, average global life expectancy has risen from forty-four to sixty-six years.

2   Asia's fertility fell sharply in the last fifty years, from 5.9 to 2.6 children per woman. Sub-Saharan Africa's has dropped much more slowly, from 6.5 to 5.5. Latin America and the Caribbean have seen a decline from 5.9 to 2.7, North Africa and Western Asia from 6.6 to 3.5. Europe's fertility rate fell from 2.6 to 1.4, well below replacement level. On the other hand, Northern America's fertility fell from 3.5 in 1950–1955 to 1.8 in the late 1970s, and then rebounded to the 1.9 to 2.0 range, where it has remained. It is projected to stay around 1.9 to the middle of the 21st century.

3   One of the strongest and most consistent relationships in demography is between mothers' education and infant mortality—the children of women with more years of schooling are much more likely to survive infancy. More-educated mothers have better health care, marry later and are significantly more likely to use contraception to space their children.

4   A gradual ageing of the global population in the decades to come is all but certain. The reasons for this trend reflect the substantial human progress of this century—lowered infant and child mortality; better nutrition, education, health care and access to family planning; and longer life expectancies.

5   Today, as a result of high fertility in the recent past, there are more young people than ever—over 1 billion between ages fifteen and twenty-four. They are entering their peak child-bearing years. In all developing countries, the proportion of the population aged 15–24 peaked around 1985 at 21 per cent. Between 1995 and 2050, it will decline from 19 to 14 per cent, but actual numbers will grow from 859 million to 1.06 billion.

6   As the global population has doubled over the past forty years, the shifts in geographical distribution of that population have been equally remarkable. In 1960, 2.1 billion of the world's 3 billion people lived in less-developed regions (70 per cent of the global population). By late 1999, the less-developed regions had grown to 4.8 billion (80 per cent); 98 per cent of the projected growth of the world population by 2025 will occur in these regions.

7   The proportion of people in developing countries who live in cities has almost doubled since 1960 (from less than 22 per cent to more than 40 per cent), while in more-developed regions the urban share has grown from 61 per cent to 76 per cent. There is a significant association between this population movement from rural to urban areas and declines in average family size.

8   Globally, the number of international migrants increased from 75 million to 120 million between 1965 and 1990, keeping pace with population growth. As a result, the proportion of migrants worldwide has remained around 2 per cent of the total population.

9   An estimated 1.1 billion people were without access to clean drinking water in 1996; 2.8 billion people lacked access to sanitation services. Each year an estimated 5 to 7 million hectares of agricultural land are lost to erosion. The world's absolute food supply is almost certainly sufficient for six billion or more people now and in the future: yet some 841 million people—nearly one sixth of the world's population—are chronically malnourished today.

4   Write 'good news' or 'bad news' next to each paragraph. Compare with a partner. Do you agree? Why, or why not?

5   Why do you think the title of the text is 'Population Change and People's Choices'? What choices does the text mention or imply?

For example

People choose to marry later

Working out meaning

Some of the vocabulary in this text is quite difficult. Quickly go through the text and underline all of the words that are unfamiliar to you.

6 Work with a partner.
   a see if your partner knows the word and can explain it to you; if not
   b use the context in the surrounding paragraph to see if you can figure out the meaning together; then
   c use a dictionary if you cannot figure out the meaning and you think the word is important.

7 What is the difference between ...?
   a *an estimated 1.1 billion people* (para 9)
   b *approximately 1.1 billion people*

   c *sufficient* (para 9)
   d *enough*

   e *It is projected to ...* (para 2)
   f *It is predicted to ...*

Cause and effect

8 According to the text, education leads to smaller, healthier families. Can you remember why this is so? (If not, check.)

9 Compare the following sentences:
   a Education leads to smaller, healthier families.
   b Education causes women to have smaller, healthier families.
   c Education is linked to smaller, healthier families.
   d Education contributes to smaller, healthier families.

10 Which sentence:
   i Means 'education is *one of* a group of causes'?

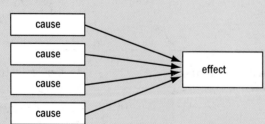

   ii Suggests education is a very direct cause?

   iii Does not say clearly whether education is the cause or the effect?

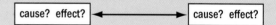

   iv Suggests education is the first cause, but it has an indirect effect?

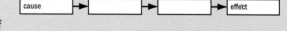

Listening

1 **6.2** and **6.3** Divide into two groups. Group A will listen to someone discussing population issues in Egypt. Group B will listen to someone discussing New Zealand. Each group should make brief notes.

2 Get together with someone from the other group and exchange information.

Speaking

1 Think about your own town, area, or country, or another country that you have lived in or visited. Make brief notes for a five-minute talk about population issues. Follow the structure: Situation–Problem(s). You can use the graphs and the listening texts for ideas.

2 Working with a partner, take turns to give your talk. Listen carefully to your partner, but do not interrupt them as they speak. As you listen, write three follow-up questions to ask when your partner has finished speaking.

3 Discuss with your partner what could be done to deal with the problems that you have described.

Writing: Analysing data

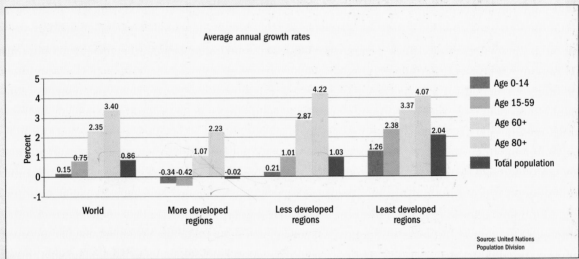

Average annual growth rates

Source: United Nations Population Division

1 Which of the following statements are true (T), which are false (F) and which cannot be confirmed (NI) according to the information in the graph above?

a Worldwide, the 15–59 year old group is growing faster than other age groups.

b The poorest parts of the world have the fastest growing populations.

c Overall population is declining in developed countries.

d There are now more people in developed countries over the age of forty than under.

e Population in developed countries will continue to decline.

f In all parts of the world, the largest part of the population is the 80+ age group.

Making comparisons and contrasts

2 Put the following sentences into the correct part of the table below.

a The population of the least developed countries is growing even faster than the population of the less developed countries.

b Populations are growing fast in poorer countries, whereas in the richer countries, populations are in fact shrinking.

c The part of the population aged between zero and fifty-nine is not growing as fast as the part aged sixty and over.

d Although the number of young and middle-aged people in developed countries is decreasing, the number of older people is still growing quite quickly.

e In the less developed countries, the part of the population aged between fifteen and fifty-nine is growing almost exactly as fast as the population as a whole.

positive comparison	negative comparison
expressing equality	contrast

3 Now look at the sentences again and underline the words that express the comparison or the contrast.

4 Finally, write sentences that are similar to the examples above, but use the following words to express the comparisons and contrasts.

less quickly	however	the same ... as	while	more quickly

Writing: Text organisation

1 Look at the headline and photograph on the right. Who and where do you think these people are? Working with a partner, complete the following sentence: *The Third World Debt has cost them two goats, a pig and a child because* ...

The Third World Debt has already cost them two goats, a pig and a child.

2   Read the text on the right quickly to check your explanation.

3   The text argues that wealthy countries and banks should not ask poor countries to pay their debts. Do you think this is reasonable? Make a list of reasons why and why not.

> They were farmers.
>
> They grew vegetables.
>
> They even had a few animals.
>
> Their government had to put up prices to help pay its debt.
>
> The price of seed went up ten times.
>
> They could not afford to grow enough to eat.
>
> They had to sell their animals.
>
> They had to sell their land.
>
> Their son became ill.
>
> They could not afford the medicine.
>
> They could not even afford a headstone for his grave.
>
> They suffer, like millions of others, because of the Third World Debt.
>
> They cannot change the situation on their own.
>
> They need you to write to your bank.
>
> They need you to write to your MP.
>
> They need your help a lot more than British banks need their money.
>
> **Christian Aid**
> We believe in life before death

Conditionals

4   Think of two or three ways to complete the following sentences.
  a   If they don't pay their debts, ...
  b   If the government reduced the price of seed, ...

5   Which sentence (a or b) means:
  · this probably won't happen, or it's not possible?
  · this might happen, it's possible?

6   Complete the following sentences.

> The structure of type A is usually If + present,
> _____ + _____
>
> The structure of type B is usually If +
> _____, would/could + infinitive

7   Both types of sentence are about (choose one):
  a   the past   **c**   the present
  b   the future   **d**   the present and future.

Logical connections

8   There are no linkers in the text on this page. Insert *and, but, then* and *so* to show the logical connections between ideas.

and	but	so

9   Here are alternative ways of expressing these ideas. Put them in the correct column in the table.

however	in addition
this means that	unfortunately
for this reason	finally
therefore	as a result
secondly	consequently
also	furthermore

10   This text, like many others, has the following structure.
  A   Situation
  B   Problem
  C   Solution

Find and mark these sections on the text above.

Writing

You are going to do the following task.

> Some people believe that the population explosion is not a serious problem, because the world has enough resources to support a large population.
>
> Do you agree or disagree?

1 Read the excerpts below. Do these writers agree or disagree with the statement in the writing question, or are you unsure?

2 Write a 250-word essay, giving reasons for your answer.

Excerpt A

OC ee ju

Many people believe that there is no need for concern over the rapidly rising world population. They claim that we already have enough resources, and in particular food, to meet the needs of everyone, and that it is simply a matter of distributing resources to those who need them. Furthermore, they claim, advances in technology such as genetic engineering mean that food supply is likely to increase even faster than the population, just as it has done for the last 200 years. There are a number of problems with these views, however.

Excerpt B

agree

It is also clear that new technology is being developed constantly, in many areas: agriculture, genetics, robotics and many others. All this new technology will make it easier not only to keep people alive, but also to allow them to live in places where they couldn't before. Soon, we will see people living in the deserts, under the sea and on the moon. This will of course relieve pressure on overcrowded cities and let us sustain an increasing population.

agr

3 Divide the class into two halves: those who agree, and those who disagree. Talk with other people in your group and make a list of arguments supporting your view.

4 Now talk with someone from the opposing group. Make a note of their arguments. If you do not understand their arguments, ask them to clarify.

5 Write a plan for your own essay. Make your own argument, but include the opposing views.

For example

Paragraph 1	Intro
Paragraph 2	Opposing view
Paragraph 3	My view: point 1
Paragraph 4	My view: point 2
Paragraph 5	Conclusion

6 Write your essay, allowing yourself forty minutes.

Useful language

Asking for clarification

Sorry, I don't follow. Could you explain that again?
What do you mean?

Checking whether you understood

So, are you saying that ...?
So, do you mean ...?
So, what you're saying is that ...

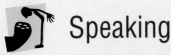

Speaking

1   The advertisement below comes from the same series as the text on page 69. Do you think it is an effective advertisement? What techniques does it (and the advertisement on page 69) use?

Spend a few minutes learning the facts of life.

1. The world produces enough food to feed all its inhabitants.

2. A child dies from starvation every two seconds.

3. In 1989, the West gave the Third World £30 billion in aid.

4. In 1989, the Third World gave the West £93 billion in debt repayments.

5. The average life expectancy in Britain is 75.

6. The average life expectancy in Ethiopia is 47.

7. 25% of the world's population uses 75% of the world's resources.

8. 50% of the world's population does not have access to clean water.

9. Christian Aid works with thousands of people in communities across the world.

10. We need your help to help them. Give now.

Christian **Aid**
We believe in life before death

---

2   Think of an advertisement that you like. It can be for any product or service, and from the television or radio or from print media. Spend three minutes making notes for a three-minute talk about the advertisement.
·   Describe the advertisement in detail.
·   Explain why it is effective or why you like it.

3   Work with a partner and take turns to give your talk.

4   When you have both given your talks, discuss the following questions together.
·   Does advertising have a significant effect on behaviour?
·   Does advertising have a useful purpose, or is it a waste of money?

Listening

6.4 You will hear two people discussing the same issues about advertising.

As you listen

1   Note down the main points that they make.

2   Which of their opinions do you agree with? Which ones do you disagree with?

After you listen

3   Compare your notes and ideas with a partner.

Reading

Before you read

1 Draw a rough map of the area around where you live, showing main roads, schools, shops, parks, offices, etc. Explain the map to a partner.

2 Why are cities growing in all countries? What are the problems caused by the rapid growth of cities?

As you read

3 This text is about city growth in the USA. Read the first three paragraphs quickly and decide which one:
· describes the problem that the USA needs to solve
· describes the situation in the USA now
· outlines the solution to the problem.

In Contrast:
Smart Growth versus Sprawl

Megastores surrounded by acres of asphalt. Cookie-cutter subdivisions. Traffic-clogged highways. Plowed-under farmland turned into strip malls. They're all part of sprawl—poorly planned, land-hungry development that eats up farms, meadows and forests, turning them into wasteful, sterile strips and subdivisions that serve cars better than people.

The alternative to sprawl isn't a halt to growth. The population of the United States is expected to increase by 50 per cent in the first half of the 21st century. Those additional 130 million people will need places to live, work, shop, and play. The question is not whether we will build new homes, offices, shops and movie theaters to accommodate them, but where we will build them and how. If we allow sprawl to continue, we can expect additional loss of open space as well as more dependence on cars and an increase in the pollution they produce.

'Smart growth' breaks this cycle. It means better planning, concentrating development where schools, roads, and sewer lines are already in place, and reinvesting in older communities instead of abandoning them. It places homes near major transit stations or within walking distance of shops, restaurants, and offices. Smart-growth communities not only help preserve natural, open spaces, but also are more livable and attractive than their sprawling counterparts.

Vocabulary

4 The text uses a lot of words that describe parts of the natural and man-made landscape. Try to group the words in the box according to these headings.

Countryside features	Transport features	Places for leisure and shopping	Places for work
farmland meadows	traffic-clogged highway transit station highway subdivision	stripmalls megastores movie theatres	subdivisions office school

megastores	subdivisions	highways	farmland
strip malls	meadows	forests	movie theatres
schools	transit stations	offices	

The rest of this text is on page 73. There are ten paragraphs which are not in the correct order: five describe problems and five describe the solutions to these problems.

5 Decide which paragraphs (A–J) describe problems, and which describe solutions.

6 Match each problem with its solution.

A In smart-growth neighborhoods, homes, shops, community services, public transit stops, and movie theaters all cluster within walking or biking distance of one another. Communities use less land, but don't feel crowded because homes, stores, and offices are built around public squares, parks, gardens, and tree-lined thoroughfares that lend a green and inviting feel to living and work spaces.

B People in spread-out locations drive more— much more. With no mass transit nearby, and stores clustered on highways far away, even a simple errand to pick up a loaf of bread requires a car. At least partly as a result of sprawl, a typical new household puts about 31 000 miles per year on its 2.3 cars, making roughly twelve trips each day. As a consequence, the number of trips taken on foot has dropped by 42 per cent in the last twenty years, with almost 70 per cent of children's trips taken in the back seat of a car.

C Rural preservation programs can save farmland and scenic landscapes from sprawling development. In Montgomery County, Maryland, a comprehensive preservation program has saved over 93 000 acres of working farmland and open space. In Oregon, farmland losses have been reduced from 30 000 acres annually to about 2 000 through smart-growth management measures, such as drawing development boundaries around urban areas and limiting development beyond them. Altogether, Oregon has protected more than 16 million acres of agricultural land from development.

D Smart-growth communities encourage walking and neighborhood activities. Walks are visually interesting because houses are closer to the street and different areas of the community are connected by networks of pleasant streets, parks and wide sidewalks. Streets are made more pleasant by the presence of gardens and inviting shops. Because smart-growth communities are designed for people, not cars, traffic-calming devices, such as traffic circles, speed bumps, and brick cross-walks, may be used to slow cars that pass through.

E Walkable, mixed-use areas, such as pedestrian plazas, increase social interactions and enhance a community's quality of life. People meet walking to and from restaurants, shops, and neighborhood parks, creating a sense of community. And people who can shop, run errands, visit the dentist and take the kids to soccer practice close to home save time— and reduce stress.

F Sprawling development often leapfrogs over established urban and suburban areas to place isolated new developments at the ends of long ribbons of highway. Community space is absent. Each home stands on its own bare lot—miles from shops, markets, restaurants, and civic centers. Rows of carbon-copy houses crowding treeless streets and cul-de-sacs give such areas a barren, sterile appearance.

G Strip malls create visual blight and dependence on cars, while discouraging face-to-face social encounters. People reach such retail areas—far from where they live and work—by traveling on crowded highways in closed vehicles, increasing a sense of isolation from other people and the natural environment.

H People who live and work in smart-growth communities are only a short walk away from a bus, light rail, or train stop. Because of clustered development and dedicated bicycle lanes and trails, smart growth communities are also bicycle friendly. Supporters of smart growth celebrated the fact that funding for public transportation, bike paths, and sidewalks increased during most of the 1990s. But in the last two years, funding to build new roads grew by 21 per cent while funds for transportation alternatives, such as this light rail line, fell by 19 per cent.

I Between 1960 and 1990, the U.S. population grew less than 50 per cent, while the amount of open land that fell under developers' bulldozers more than doubled. Each year, 3.2 million acres of open space are developed. This translates into 356 acres per hour. The result? Habitat loss and fragmentation that has pushed many species, such as the Florida panther, to the brink of extinction. The loss each year of thousands of acres of prime farmland that can never be recovered. And the destruction of forests in places like Washington's Puget Sound lowland, where the area covered by trees has declined 37 per cent in the last 24 years.

J The need for increased driving in sprawling areas requires a massive and expensive network of highways and causes serious air pollution problems. As sprawl intensified between 1970 and 1990, the number of miles Americans drive each year doubled from one trillion to two trillion. In spite of continuing improvement in emission controls, highway vehicles still emit some 60 million tons of carbon monoxide every year as well as up to 50 per cent of toxic air pollutants.

After you read

7 Which of these problems exist in your country? Are any of these solutions being used in cities in your country?

8 Can you think of any other solutions to city sprawl?

Vocabulary

9 Add words from paragraphs A–J to the table in the vocabulary exercise on page 72.

Telling tales

Tuning in

All cultures have their own traditional stories, and some of them become known all around the world.

1 Read these extracts from traditional stories and match the story to one of the pictures.

2 Do you know which culture or country each story comes from?

3 Can you tell a partner what else happens in these stories?

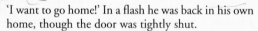

a

'I want to go home!' In a flash he was back in his own home, though the door was tightly shut.

'How did you get in?' called his mother from the kitchen stove, the minute she set eyes on him. Excitedly, her son told her of his adventures.

'Where's the silver coin?' his mother asked. Aladdin clapped a hand to his brow. For all he had brought home was the old oil lamp. 'Oh, mother! I'm so sorry. This is all I've got.'

'Well, let's hope it works. It's so dirty…' and the widow began to rub the lamp.

Suddenly out shot another genie, in a cloud of smoke.

'You've set me free, after centuries! I was a prisoner in the lamp, waiting to be freed by someone rubbing it. Now, I'm your obedient servant. Tell me your wishes.' And the genie bowed respectfully, awaiting Aladdin's orders.

b

The eleventh task was one of the most difficult. Hercules was required to fetch the Golden Apples of the Hesperides, who were the daughters of Atlas. Hercules went to ask Atlas if he would get the apples for him. Atlas offered to as long as Hercules would hold up the heavens until he returned. Hercules accepted. Atlas went to get the apples, and then returned and told Hercules that he would deliver the apples for him. Hercules saw through the trick and used his wits to outsmart Atlas. Hercules told Atlas that this was fine. He asked Atlas to hold the heavens up for just a minute while he adjusted the pad on his shoulders. When Atlas took the load, Hercules grabbed the apples and ran away laughing.

c

(2)

That night, freed from the nightmare of the rats, the citizens of Hamelin slept more soundly than ever. And when the strange sound of piping wafted through the streets at dawn, only the children heard it. Drawn as by magic, they hurried out of their homes. Again, the Pied Piper paced through the town, this time, it was children of all sizes that flocked at his heels to the sound of his strange piping. The long procession soon left the town and made its way through the wood and across the forest till it reached the foot of a huge mountain. When the piper came to the dark rock, he played his pipe even louder still and a great door creaked open. Beyond lay a cave. In trooped the children behind the Pied Piper, and when the last child had gone into the darkness, the door creaked shut. A great landslide came down the mountain blocking the entrance to the cave forever. Only one little lame boy escaped this fate. It was he who told the anxious citizens, searching for their children, what had happened.

d

Once upon a time an old man and woman lived in the mountains. Every day the old man went to the mountain and collected firewood, while the old woman went to the river and did the laundry. One day, she was doing the washing when a big peach came floating down the river towards her. As it was a big and juicy-looking fruit, she thought that her husband would be glad to eat it so she took it home. When the old man came back for lunch and saw the nice peach, he was really happy. The old woman cut the big peach open with a knife. What a surprise! A lovely little boy was in the peach.

The old man and woman had no children so they were really grateful the gods had sent them a boy in this peach. Since he was born in a peach, they decided to call him Momotaro, which means 'peach-boy'.

4 Now tell your partner a traditional story from your culture, or one that you know from another culture.

Vocabulary

As you can see from this dictionary definition, the Hercules story is an example of a myth.

> **myth** /mɪθ/ *noun* [C, U] **1** a story from ancient times, especially one that was told to explain natural events or to describe the early history of a people; this type of story: *ancient Greek myths* ◇ *a creation myth* (= that explains how the world began) ◇ *the heroes of myth and legend* **2** something that many people believe but that does not exist or is false [SYN] FALLACY. *It is a myth that women are worse drivers than men.* (= to show that it does not exist). ◇ *Contrary to popular myth women are not worse drivers than men.*

5 Do you know the difference between these other kinds of story?

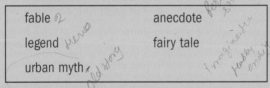

fable	anecdote
legend	fairy tale
urban myth	

6 Look in an English–English dictionary to check the meanings.

7 Now, working with a partner, think of an example of each one (including a myth).

8 Tell one or two of your stories to another group. Can they identify which sort of story you have just told them?

9 The second meaning of *myth* is very useful. Note that it is about beliefs and popular opinions, not stories. Can you think of any popular opinions that, in your opinion, are myths?

For example

> It's a myth that children are better language learners than adults.

Listening

Before you listen

When you look up *urban myth* or *urban legend* in the dictionary, you will probably find something like this:

'a well-known story that many people believe, about something strange or terrible that has happened to an ordinary person.'

As you listen

1   **7.1** Listen to four speakers telling urban legends or myths that they have heard. In the table, write down the basic information you hear about the myths.

Speaker	1	2	3	4
Who was involved in the myth?				
What was the main action?				
Is the story based on fact?				

Listen again

2   Look at these extracts from the urban myths. All four speakers use the word *anyway* in their story. Can you remember (or can you guess) where each speaker said *anyway*?

     a   there was supposed to be a problem with the alligators/no, maybe it was in Florida/there was apparently this problem with the alligators/they were getting into the sewerage system and causing trouble

     b   I went to a big swimming pool complex with water slides and all that/I was there with my older brother/he would have been 14 or so/in the water slides, the tunnels, apparently these guys had been stopping halfway down and like, putting razor blades into the slide

     c   and she was sitting there eating it/then she got this crunchy bit and thought it must just be a piece of crisp vegetable or something/she took another bite, and it was crunchy again and it also tasted pretty bad/so she opened the burger and took out the chicken fillet

     d   they feel it's safer than having money in the bank/they have all of these gold bracelets all the way up their arms/this guy I know/he'd been working in Cairo for years/said that this guy he knew had been driving through one of the poor parts of Cairo in a taxi, when the taxi stopped to let this woman all dressed in black

3   What does *anyway* mean in these extracts?
     a   I've just given some background detail; now here's the main point.
     b   I've just given the main point; now here's some background detail.

4   Now listen again and check whether you were right.

After you listen

5   Do you know any urban myths? If so, do you think they are based on fact?

Narrative tenses

6 📻 **7.2** Look at these extracts from the urban myths that you listened to. Try to complete the gaps with the verb in brackets in the tense that you think the speakers used. Listen to the urban myths again to check your answers.

> She _____(sit) there eating it, then she _____(get) this crunchy bit
>
> said that this guy he knew _____(drive) through one of the poor parts of Cairo in a taxi, when the taxi _____(stop)

7 Now look at the extracts again and draw circles around the verbs that are used to describe the *central action* of the story. Draw boxes around the verbs that are used to describe *background states or actions* of the story.

8 Write the following names of verb tenses in the correct places to complete the statements in the summary.

Past Simple	Past Continuous	Past Perfect Simple or Continuous

When telling stories:

· we use the _____ tense to describe the central actions of the story.

· we use the _____ and _____ tenses to describe states or actions that form the background to the story.

· the _____ tense describes states or actions that happened at around the time of the main actions; the _____ tense describes states or actions that happened before the main actions.

Speaking

1 Read these short urban myths. What do they all have in common? Why do you think the people involved needed to tell their stories?

'I had been shopping for a plant all day and was on my way home. As I reached an intersection a hedge sprang up, obscuring my vision and I did not see the other car.'

'I had been driving for forty years when I fell asleep at the wheel and had an accident.'

'As I approached the intersection a sign appeared in a place where no stop sign had ever appeared before. I was unable to stop in time to avoid the accident.'

2 Tell a partner an anecdote about an accident (any kind of accident—it does not have to be a car accident). Pay special attention to your grammar as you tell the story.

Listening

Before you listen

1 **What is animation? Do you enjoy animated films? Why, or why not?**

Elements of the movie that an animator needs to consider include:

- the storyline (or plot)
- the characters   *Alice*
- the set
- the 'look'

2 **What does each of the above words mean? Which, in your opinion, is the most important to a good movie?**

3 **What do you or your classmates know about the process of animation?**

   a What kind of people do you need to make an animated movie?

   b What steps do these people need to go through to make the movie?

For example

(b)   1   Think up a storyline

2

Pixar is a company that makes computer-animated films. They made *Toy Story*, for example. You are going to hear a description of the process that they use to create a computer-animated film.

4 **Read the introduction to the process.**

THE PIXAR PROCESS

There is a scene in *Toy Story 2* when the old man repairing Woody tells the impatient toy collector Al, 'You can't rush art.' This is especially true at Pixar, where films go through four stages: development, creating the storyline; pre-production, addressing technical challenges; production, making the film; and post-production, 'polishing' the final product.

As the introduction explains, there are four main stages in the creation of Pixar's films. Look at the list below on the right: these are sub-stages within the main stages.

5 **Try to match each sub-stage with a main stage.**

Main stages	Sub-stages
1 Development: creating the storyline	**a** Models are made
	b Voices are recorded
	c A story idea is pitched
	d The computer data is translated into pictures
2 Pre-production: addressing the technical challenges	**e** The art department creates the look and feel
	f The text outline is written
3 Production: making the film	**g** The sets are made
	h Lighting completes the look
	i The shot is animated
4 Post-production: 'polishing' the final product	**j** Final touches are added
	k The shots are laid out
	l Storyboards are drawn

As you listen

6 🎞 **7.3 Check and complete the matching of sub-stages to stages.**

After you listen

7 **Why do you think animated films are so popular, with adults as well as with children? What advantages do animated films have over films made with live actors?**

8 **In your opinion, will animated characters become more common than live actors in the future?**

Reading: Comics and graphic novels

1   These pictures are part of a comic book story. Work with a partner to put the frames into the correct order.

2   In this case, what was most helpful to you in deciding on the correct order, the pictures or the text? Why?

3   Do you enjoy reading stories in this format? Are comic books/graphic novels popular in your country? Why?

4   Do you think that comic books/graphic novels can be considered as 'serious' works of literature? Why, or why not?

As you read

5   Read the article on the next page about graphic novels quickly. Does the article:

a support the view that graphic novels are a serious literary form?

b reject the view that graphic novels are a serious literary form?

c give a balanced presentation of both views?

1   For a time, the business of comic books seemed limited to tales of costumed superheroes, gumshoe detectives or thwarted alien invasions, the clientele an assortment of adolescents, collectors and geeks. But the industry stereotype is undergoing a transformation of sorts thanks to a longer, more literary comic offshoot called the graphic novel.

2   Bolstered by comic writers and artists bent on telling more complex tales and by a string of Hollywood films adapted from graphic novels—including the new *Road to Perdition*—publishers, booksellers and readers are beginning to take note.

3   'This is an art form that is every bit as valid for telling stories and entertaining people as films or any other form,' Max Allan Collins, author of *Road to Perdition*, said in an interview from his home in this Mississippi River town.

4   'The thing about it is that everybody understands the vocabulary of comics ... The hope is that people who see and like the movie will be interested enough to begin to cross that perceived forbidden land into the world of comics and graphic novels,' said Collins, who for fifteen years wrote the Dick Tracy comic strip.

5   Cosmetically, the graphic novel resembles any other book on the shelf, covered with hardback or glossy trade paper, printed with standard paper and plastic-wrap free.

6   Between the covers is another matter, though. In the 300-page *Road to Perdition*, the black-and-white panels drawn by London-based cartoonist Richard Piers Rayner make visual the images and action of traditional literature.

7   The panels—which vary from one to four per page—give form and feature to characters, set scenes of homes, diners and downtowns in sharp detail and provide a sense of action and drama. Text balloons advance the plot and story line.

8   Publishers and comic connoisseurs use the term 'illustrative literature' to describe the books, which they say emerged from reader demand for more sophisticated comic-driven storytelling.

9   Calvin Reid, news editor for *Publisher's Weekly*, said it is simplistic to view the graphic novel as merely a glorified comic book.

10   'There is a whole new market that has grown up with comics in the last twenty years that is looking for more,' Reid said. 'And publishers have been adapting to a bigger share of their audience wanting longer, more sophisticated stories... without having to go into the comic store once a week.'

11   The 1987 publication of *Maus*, the Pulitzer Prize-winning book by Art Spiegelman about the holocaust, is credited by many for setting the graphic novel apart from traditional comic books. In the 1990s, publishers of all sizes—from giants like DC Comics to independents—devoted more resources to developing the graphic novel market.

12   In bookstores, graphic novel subject matter runs the gamut. Superhero stories still exist, but so do humor, mystery, erotica, biography, historical fiction and journalism, such as Joe Sacco's graphic novel *Gorazde: War in Eastern Bosnia 1992–1995*.

13   In recent years, more traditional publishing houses, such as Pantheon and Doubleday, have opened graphic novel divisions. Bookstores are giving graphic novels more shelf space. Book reviewers are devoting more space to graphic novels and treating them as serious literary works.

14   Hollywood has adapted films from many graphic novels, including last year's *Ghost World* and *From Hell*, the Jack the Ripper thriller, starring Johnny Depp. Dozens of other books have been optioned by various studios.

15   Sales are up over previous years, although it's unclear whether readers are new or comic veterans, or whether the increase is being driven by a handful of hot titles.

16   As of last week, 1.5 million books have sold so far this year, according to Neilsen BookScan, a company that tracks book sales. It is an increase of 700 000 over last year. A run of 25 000 to 50 000 copies per book is considered successful by current industry standards.

17   'I think they are really starting to catch on,' said Carl Lennertz of the American Booksellers Association. 'There are still a lot of issues to overcome, like distribution, prices, and the cost and time it takes to publish. But I see these slowly breaking into the mainstream.'

18   For Collins, 50, mainstream acceptance may be too long a wait. *Road to Perdition*, first published in 1998 as the first of a trilogy, took more than four years to write, he said. He plans to write his next book as traditional fiction.

19   'There is a part of me that wants to move faster with the next ones,' said Collins. 'There is also a need to reach out to a wider audience.'

Read again

6   **Find the part of the text that describes:**
· the opinion of a graphic novel author
Paragraph(s) _3_
· the design of graphic novels
Paragraph(s) _6, 7, 5_
· evidence that sales are increasing
Paragraph(s) _16_

· problems in selling more graphic novels
Paragraph(s) _17_

7   **How do we know that graphic novels are being taken more seriously now?**

For example

movie adaptations of graphic novels

Speaking: Role play

Read the following situation. A parent has asked to meet her 10-year-old child's teacher, because she is concerned about her child's teacher using graphic novels and comics in reading classes.

1 Before the meeting, divide the class into two groups.
- One group takes the role of parent.
- The other group takes the role of teacher.
- Look at your role card on the right, and plan together what you are going to say when you meet.

PARENT

Your child has brought a graphic novel home to read for her reading homework. You do not like this. You think that she should be reading traditional books.

TEACHER

The parent of one of your students has asked to meet you. You know that she wants to complain because you sometimes ask your students to read graphic novels. You think they are excellent for education.

---

2 Now form pairs of Teacher and Parent. You have a ten-minute meeting to discuss your problem. By the end of the meeting you need to reach an agreement about what will happen in the future.

3 After the meetings, check around the class. In how many meetings:
- did the teacher 'win'?
- did the parent 'win'?
- was there a compromise?

Present Perfect

A Have you read any good books recently?
B Have you seen any good films recently?
C What have you been reading recently?

1 Which answers from the box are possible for each question?

2 What would you personally answer to each of these questions?

3 Why can't we say (usually) 'have you been seeing any good films recently'?

Read the grammar notes in the box below before you answer.

> Sentences A and B are Present Perfect Simple. The activity is finished (the books are finished, the films are finished). The focus is on the completion.

> Sentence C is Present Perfect Continuous (or Progressive, as it is also known). The book or books may be finished—we do not know. The focus is on the activity, rather than the result. We could answer about one book that we have finished, or one that we have started but not finished, or many that we have finished or not finished.

4 Now tell a partner about any books or articles you have read recently, or any films that you have seen.

> Nothing much.
>
> I have, actually. I've seen …
>
> No, I haven't.
>
> Not really.
>
> I've read a couple of Hemingways and I'm halfway through a book about …
>
> Yes, I have. I read a great Australian novel last month and …
>
> I've just finished this great book called …

Speaking

Writers in English

1 The first column lists some well-known British and American writers. The other column lists their best known characters. Can you match them?

Writers	Characters
Agatha Christie	Tom Sawyer
William Shakespeare	Romeo and Juliet
Charles Dickens	James Bond
Ernest Hemingway	The Old Man
Ian Fleming	Poirot
Mark Twain	Oliver Twist

2 What else do you know about these writers?
- When did they live?
- What kinds of books did they write?
- Have you read any of their books?

Reading

1 These lines come from a famous play. Do you recognise the play?

> What's there? A cup, closed in my true love's hand?
>
> Poison, I see, hath been his timeless end:
>
> O churl! Drunk all, and left no friendly drop
>
> To help me after? I will kiss thy lips;
>
> Haply some poison yet doth hang on them,
>
> To make die with a restorative.
>
> [Kisses him]
>
> Thy lips are warm.

2 Talk to a partner. What happens in this play?

After you read

3 The play that you talked about was written more than 400 years ago. Is it still useful to read classic books?

4 Who is your favourite writer?

5 Describe one of his or her books.

Writing

> 'The traditional book, as a way of relating stories and communicating information and ideas, will not survive the 21st century.' Do you agree or disagree?

You are going to write a 250-word essay on this topic.

Generating ideas

1 **Build up a list of ideas with your classmates.**

Threats to the book (why it may not survive)	Advantages of the book (why it may survive)

Taking a position

2 **On balance, do you think the traditional book will survive the 21st century?**

Writing a plan

3 **Write a plan of the essay to express your view.**

The structure of the introduction

> Books have played a vital role in human civilisation. They have been central to religion, science, education, and entertainment. But many people believe that the book is a thing of the past not the future, and that it is unlikely to survive the century. My view, however, is that despite the many threats to its dominance, the book will remain as strong at the end of the century as it is at the beginning.

As in the example above, introductions typically have three steps in their structure. The first two steps almost always occur, while with step 3 there are more choices about whether you include it, and if you do include it, how you do it.

Step 1: Establish the importance and/or relevance of the topic. *Why is it worth writing and reading about this topic?*

Step 2: Raise an issue or problem related to the topic.

Step 3: State:
a the question that you intend to answer and/or
b what your essay covers and how it is organised and/or
c what your own position is.

4 **Identify these steps in the example introduction. Does this introduction include step 3? If so, is it 3a, 3b, or 3c, or a combination of these?**

5 **Below are some other ways of taking step 3. Which technique do they use?**

i In this essay, I will argue that the book is in fact not in any danger.

ii I outline some of the reasons why books have become less popular, before showing that it will nevertheless survive the century.

iii But is the book really in danger?

iv This essay sets out the threats to the book as well as some of the reasons why it may still survive the century.

The language of the introduction

6 **Look back at i–iv. What tense(s) do they use? Both are appropriate for academic writing.**

7 **Which sentences are:**
a personal in style?
b impersonal in style?

8 **Now write your own essay with:**
- a clearly stated view
- a clearly organised text
- a well structured introduction
- a well structured conclusion.

Speaking

Comic books are a relatively new way of telling stories. Traditional storytelling, first in spoken form and later in written form, is the oldest way of telling stories.

1 How many different ways, both old and new, can you think of for telling stories? Make a list below.

For example
  · *Spoken and written 'traditional' stories*
  · *Videos*
  · *Comic books*

2 Now do a survey to find out what sort of stories and story-telling methods people around you prefer.

You could ask your classmates, students in other classes, your friends, family or workmates.

You could ask people to put the methods in the order of their preferences, or just say which one or two are their favourites.

You could also ask people to say why they prefer their favourite method.

3 When you have enough information, show it in a graph. The kind of graph you use will depend on the kind of questions you asked and the kind of answers you received.

4 Finally, make a spoken presentation of the most important findings in your results to others.

Writing

5 Now write a text to describe your graph.

Listening

Before you listen

You are going to hear three groups of people making plans to go out for entertainment.

1 What expressions for suggesting and making arrangements do you expect to hear? Make a list.

For example
  Why don't we ...?

As you listen

2 ▭ 7.4 Complete the table with information from the conversations.

After you listen

3 Which expressions for suggesting and making arrangements did you hear? Were they the same as the expressions you predicted above?

	Conversation 1	*Conversation 2*	*Conversation 3*
Kind of entertainment			
Reasons			
Meeting time/place			

Page-85,
create your own superhero

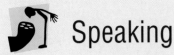
Speaking

1 Which of these two views of the relationship between TV and society do you believe is more accurate?

View A

TV reflects society. (= TV shows what society is like; society is the cause and TV is the effect)

View B

Society reflects TV. (= Society shows what TV is like; TV is the cause and society is the effect)

Text 1

> **IND:** Matt, I read somewhere you once said, 'I never understood why parents hated me until I had a seven-year old of my own.'
>
> **MG:** I was making a joke. I said, 'Now that I have kids, I understand why parents get annoyed.' My own kids say, 'Are we there yet, are we there yet, are we there yet?' *The Simpsons* didn't originate that annoying chant, but we definitely popularised it. If I apologise for something like that, I'm lying.
>
> **MS:** I know what Matt was talking about. Once in a while at my kid's school, I run into some parents who find out I work with the show, and they give me a lecture about what a bad influence it is on their kids. I think a lot of parents have a tendency to point the finger at TV for things their kids do wrong. If I heard my kids say 'damn' or 'hell,' as much as I would like to pin it on *The Simpsons*, chances are they picked it up from me in traffic. It's easier to blame TV than to look at your own behavior. Kids will pick stuff up from TV, without a doubt. But there's a lot of heart to the show; it's about a family that really does love each other and sticks together. We don't like to hit people over the head with messages, but if you look close enough, it's right in front of you. But the main purpose is to be funny, not to preach.

2 Talk to a partner, explaining which view you think is more accurate and why.

3 The two extracts below are about the American TV show *The Simpsons*.
   a What format is this show? (drama, comedy, cartoon ...?)
   b What is the show about?
   c Have you ever seen *The Simpsons*? Do you like it? Why, or why not?

Which one of the extracts below indicates that *The Simpsons* has a View A-type relationship with American society? And which one a View B-type relationship?

Text 2

> The very bedrock of the show—its recurring characters, its setting, the basic premise of the series—is satirical. The show builds from the founding idea that the Simpson family are an average American household; early raves about the show frequently pointed out that *The Simpsons* seemed much more realistic than the flesh-and-blood people populating live-action sitcoms. This 'realism' consisted of a world in which no authority was legitimate, no leader uncorrupted. The parents were all bumbling, the cops all corrupt. The celebrities—including guests from our world—were all grotesquely vain, the businesspeople veritably oozing pure evil. And yet it struck deep chords around the English-speaking world because—like all great satire—it rang true. We *did*—and do—live in a world of corrupt authorities, clueless leaders, rapacious business men. It wasn't just funny; it was true.

4 Are TV programmes like this good or bad for society? Or do you think they do not have much influence on society?

8 Sugar and spice

Tuning in

1 These are all important food commodities.
· Can you identify them?
· Do you know where they originally came from?

For example

That looks like chilli. I'm pretty sure it's from South America and it was brought to Europe by Columbus.

A

Rice

B

Sugarcane

C

Wheat

D

chilli

E

Coffee

Listening

8.1 You will hear another group doing the same task.

2 As part of the discussion you will hear the correct answers. Use them to complete the table below. **Note:** The order of the pictures above is the same as the order you will hear in the discussion.

3 Are any of these commodities important to you personally?

	Name	Origin	Important dates
A	Rice	Thailand/china Japan	4000BC.on
B	Sugarcan	Papua New Guinea	Australia 8000 years
C	Wheat	Middle East	califor
D	chilli	South America/Bolivia Columbus	"
E	Coffee beans	S. Africa/ Ethiopia	1500yrs ago

Speaking

4   A *commodity* is a product that can be traded. With a partner, make a list of what you believe to be the ten most important food (or drink) commodities. This list could be based on volume (i.e. which are the most traded commodities?), economic value, nutritional value (which are most important to health?), or a combination of these or any other factors. Your list may or may not include the commodities in the pictures.

5   Explain your list to another pair.

For example

> We think ... is by far the most important, because ...

6   Why is trade in general important in the modern world?

Speaking

1   Do you come from a coffee-drinking culture, or a tea-drinking culture? Or are both drunk equally?

2   When, where, and by whom are these drinks usually drunk in your country?

3   Which, if any, do you drink?

4   Coffee and tea have little nutritional value. Why do you think they are so popular?

Reading

This text is about a traditional Middle-Eastern coffee ceremony, rather than everyday coffee drinking. It has two paragraphs.

5   Write a brief summary (no more than ten words) of the topic of each paragraph.

6   Does anything similar occur in your culture?

7   Make notes on a food or drink ceremony in your country, or in another culture that you are familiar with. You could describe a formal ceremony, or you could just describe the everyday routine for serving a meal.

8   Describe the ceremony or routine to a partner.

Coffee serving is a ceremony. Rules of etiquette on this subject require the hostess to personally hand around the cups although a servant may assist by holding the tray. When only men are present the host will hand each cup to his guests. The eldest or the most important person in the room is served first. Age takes precedence, if there is some doubt as to rank. In former times a man was always served before a woman but that custom is usually reversed today.

Sugar is stirred into the beverage during its brewing and not when it is served, as with other styles of coffee. The amount of sugar which is added must be appropriate to the occasion. The more sugar, the happier the occasion, with the exception that coffee served after dinner at any time is usually only slightly sweetened. At weddings, betrothals, christenings or birthdays, sweet coffee is always prepared. At the time of death or other sorrow, it is always bitter. A guest has the privilege of saying how much sugar he prefers. His host or hostess will ask for a guest's preference before ordering the coffee to be made.

Reading

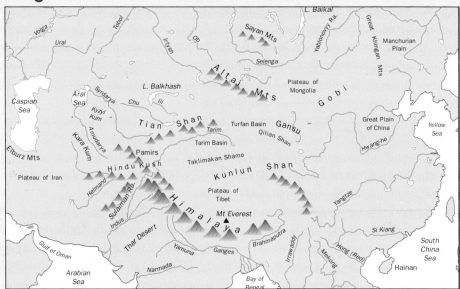

As you read

There is a lot of detail in this text, but the main point is very simple.

1   **Choose one from a–c to complete the summary of the main point of this text.**

The area around the Silk Road has an extreme environment and is:

a very difficult to travel through. *desert*

b very difficult to live in.

c very isolated. *oasis*

The Silk Road

The region separating China from Europe and Western Asia is not the most hospitable in the world. Much of it is taken up by the Taklimakan desert, one of the most hostile environments on our planet. There is very little vegetation, and almost no rainfall. The desert has claimed the lives of countless people. The locals have a very great respect for this 'Land of Death'; few travellers in the past have had anything good to say about it. It covers a vast area, through which few roads pass; caravans throughout history have travelled around its edges, from one isolated oasis to the next. The climate is harsh. In the summer the daytime temperatures are in the 40s, with temperatures greater than 50 degrees Celsius measured not infrequently in the sub-sea level basin of Turfan. In winter the temperatures dip below minus 20 degrees. Temperatures soar in the sun, but drop very rapidly at dusk. Sandstorms here are very common, and particularly dangerous due to the strength of the winds and the nature of the surface. Unlike the Gobi desert, where there is a relatively large number of oases, and water can be found not too far below the surface, the Taklimakan has much sparser resources.

The land surrounding the Taklimakan is equally hostile. To the northeast lies the Gobi desert, almost as harsh in climate as the Taklimakan itself; on the remaining three sides lie some of the highest mountains in the world. To the South are the Himalaya, Karakorum and Kunlun ranges, which provide an effective barrier separating Central Asia from the Indian sub-continent. Only a few icy passes cross these ranges, and they are some of the most difficult in the world; they are mostly over 5000 metres in altitude, and are dangerously narrow, with precipitous drops into deep ravines. To the north and west lie the Tianshan and Pamir ranges; though greener and less high, the passes crossing these have still provided more than enough problems for the travellers of the past. Approaching the area from the east, the least difficult entry is along the 'Gansu Corridor', a relatively fertile strip running along the base of the Qilian mountains, separating the great Mongolian plateau and the Gobi from the Tibetan High Plateau. Coming from the west or south, the only way in is over the passes.

2   Despite the detail, the structure of the text is also simple. Complete the diagram below with brief notes.

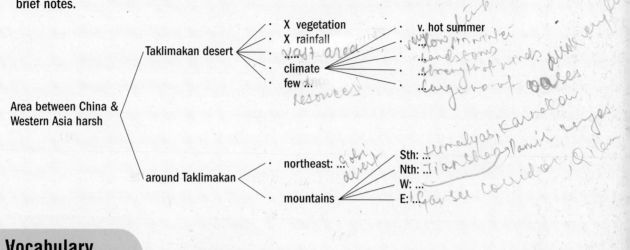

Taklimakan desert
· X vegetation
· X rainfall
· *vast area*
· climate
· few *resources*

· v. hot summer
· *very low rainfall*
· *sandstorms*
· *strength of winds*
· *large no. of oases*

Area between China & Western Asia harsh

around Taklimakan
· northeast: *Gobi desert*
· mountains

Sth: *Himalyas, Karakoran*
Nth: *Tianshan*
W: *Pamir ranges*
E: *Gansu corridor, Qilan*

Vocabulary

Word attack

3   What do you think the following words from paragraph 1 mean?
· *hospitable* (is it positive or negative?)
· *hostile* (is it positive or negative?)
· *vegetation* (what other word like this do you know?)
· *vast* (it covers a big/small area)
· *harsh* (the climate is ...?)
· *dip* (temperatures ... below 20 degrees)
· *dusk* (temperatures drop rapidly at ...)
· *sparse* (unlike the Gobi, where there are a lot of oases and water can be found)

4   Check your answers in a dictionary. Were you correct?

5   Make a list of words from the second paragraph that you do not know well. Can you guess their meaning? What clues are there in the context?

Dictionary skills

6   The word *nature* occurs in the first paragraph. What is its meaning in this context? Choose the correct sense (1–5) from this *Oxford Advanced Learner's Dictionary* entry.

7   The word *barrier* (paragraph 2) also has many senses. Use your dictionary to identify what *barrier* means in this context.

na·ture /ˈneɪtʃə(r)/ *noun*
PLANTS, ANIMALS 1 (often ·Nature) [U] all the plants, animals and things that exist in the universe that are not made by people: *the beauties of nature* ◇ *man-made substances not found in nature* ◇ *nature conservation* HELP You cannot use 'the nature' in this meaning: *the beauties of the nature*. It is often better to use another appropriate word, for example **the countryside, the scenery** or **wildlife**: *We stopped to admire the scenery.* ◇ *We stopped to admire the nature.*
2 (often **Nature**) [U] the way that things happen in the physical world when it is not controlled by people: *the forces/laws of nature* ◇ *Just let nature take its course.* ◇ *Her illness was Nature's way of telling her to do less.*—see also MOTHER NATURE
CHARACTER 3 [C, U] the usual way that a person or an animal behaves that is part of their character: *It's not in his nature to be unkind.* ◇ *She is very sensitive by nature.* ◇ *We appealed to his better nature* (= his kindness).—see also GOOD NATURE, HUMAN NATURE, SECOND NATURE
BASIC QUALITIES 4 [sing.] the basic qualities of a thing: *the changing nature of society* ◇ *It's difficult to define the exact nature of the problem.* ◇ *My work is very specialized in nature.*
TYPE/KIND 5 [sing.] a type or kind of sth: *books of a scientific nature* ◇ *Don't worry about things of that nature.*

Linking ideas

8   The relationship between the first sentence of paragraph 1, and the second sentence of paragraph 1 and the first sentence of paragraph 2 is one of General ➤ Particular.

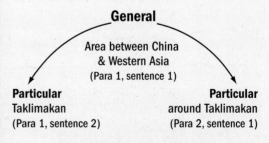

General

Area between China
& Western Asia
(Para 1, sentence 1)

Particular
Taklimakan
(Para 1, sentence 2)

Particular
around Taklimakan
(Para 2, sentence 1)

9   Find two parts (sentences or parts of sentences) of paragraph 1 which are linked by:
a   General ➤ Particular
b   Contrast
c   Cause and Effect

Speaking

1   Draw a rough map of a distinctive or important part of your country.

2   Make notes on the geography of the area, including the climate, and why the area is distinctive or important.

3   Organise your notes into a logical order, with brief supporting notes for the main points. Do not just list facts: make points using supporting detail.

4   Describe your map to a partner and explain your points.

Reading

The structure of the second part of the text on the Silk Road is very similar to the first, but the point is different. Here, the point is that the name of the route is 'misleading'.

1   Make notes to complete the diagram below.

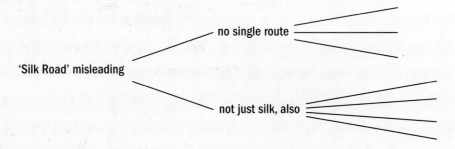

The Nature of the Route

The description of this route to the west as the 'Silk Road' is somewhat misleading. Firstly, no single route was taken; crossing Central Asia several different branches developed, passing through different oasis settlements. The routes all started from the capital in Changan, headed up the Gansu corridor, and reached Dunhuang on the edge of the Taklimakan. The northern route then passed through Yumen Guan (Jade Gate Pass) and crossed the neck of the Gobi desert to Hami (Kumul), before following the Tianshan mountains round the northern fringes of the Taklimakan. It passed through the major oases of Turfan and Kuqa before arriving at Kashgar, at the foot of the Pamirs. The southern route branched off at Dunhuang, passing through the Yang Guan and skirting the southern edges of the desert, via Miran, Hetian (Khotan) and Shache (Yarkand), finally turning north again to meet the other route at Kashgar. Numerous other routes were also used to a lesser extent.

Secondly, the Silk Road was not a trade route that existed solely for the purpose of trading in silk; many other commodities were also traded, from gold and ivory to exotic animals and plants. Of all the precious goods crossing this area, silk was perhaps the most remarkable for the people of the West. It is often thought that the Romans had first encountered silk in one of their campaigns against the Parthians in 53 BC, and realised that it could not have been produced by this relatively unsophisticated people. They reputedly learnt from Parthian prisoners that it came from a mysterious tribe in the east, who they came to refer to as the silk people, 'Seres'. In practice, it is likely that silk and other goods were beginning to filter into Europe before this time, though only in very small quantities. The Romans obtained samples of this new material, and it quickly became very popular in Rome, for its soft texture and attractiveness. The Parthians quickly realised that there was money to be made from trading the material, and sent trade missions towards the east. The Romans also sent their own agents out to explore the route, and to try to obtain silk at a lower price than that set by the Parthians. For this reason, the trade route to the East was seen by the Romans as a route for silk rather than the other goods that were traded. The name 'Silk Road' itself does not originate from the Romans, however, but is a nineteenth-century term, coined by the German scholar, von Richthofen.

After you read: Focus on text organisation

2   The second part of the Silk Road text is organised very much like the first part (on page 88). The main logical relationship in both cases is General ➤ Particular.

Part 1

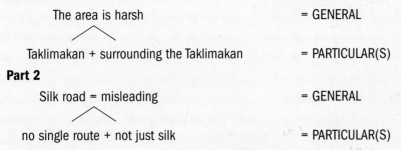

| The area is harsh | = GENERAL |
| Taklimakan + surrounding the Taklimakan | = PARTICULAR(S) |

Part 2

| Silk road = misleading | = GENERAL |
| no single route + not just silk | = PARTICULAR(S) |

So the organisation is the same, but the linking words are different.

· In part 2 the particular points are linked by *firstly* and _____.

· In part 1, the second point is linked by the word _____.

· In which case, part 1 or 2, could the linking word be replaced by *furthermore*? Part _____

· In which case, part 1 or 2, could the linking word be replaced by *also*? Part _____

Speaking

The most important mode of transport on the Silk Road was the camel. It was reliable, but slow.

3   What does the following graphic tell you?

4   What do the different sized globes illustrate?

5   With a partner, write four questions based on the graphic that you can ask another student.

For example

> *Do you think that it is good that the speed of communication has increased so much?*

6   Now get together with another student and ask and answer each other's questions.

1500–1840 Average speed of wagon and sailships: 16 km/hr

1850–1930 Average speed of trains: 100 km/hr
Average speed of steamships: 25 km/hr

1950 Average speed of airplanes: 480–640 km/hr

1970 Average speed of jet planes: 800–1120 km/hr

1990 Numeric transmission: instantaneous

Writing

7   Write a 350-word essay. In your essay:
   · describe the graphic
   · discuss the impact of this progress.

8   Which part of this task is like task 2 in the IELTS Writing test? Which part is like task 1?

Listening

The diagram below provides information on international trade between some parts of the world in 2001. It is missing some information, which you will hear in a mini-lecture.

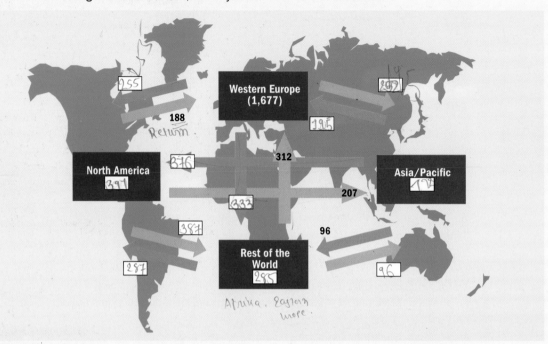

Before you listen

1 What do you think the numbers represent?

2 With a partner, write five predictions about the data.

For example

· *North America exports more to Western Europe than it imports.*
· *Western Europe has the largest internal market.*
· *The Asia/Pacific region mainly exports agricultural products.*

As you listen

3 **8.2** Write down what the figures represent.

4 Write T (true), F (false) or NM (not mentioned) next to each of your predictions.

Listen again

5 Write in the missing figures.

After you listen

6 Was there any surprising information in the lecture?

Writing

1 With a partner, write down four or five key generalisations that you can draw from the diagram.

2 The three texts on page 93 describe the diagram. Read them all quickly. Which one do you prefer?

3 Now read them again, evaluate them according to the criteria in the table following the texts, and make notes in the table.

4 What advice would you give to each writer about how to improve the text? Choose one of the texts: redraft it to make it better.

a

This diagram shows the world trade flows of billions of U.S. dollars in 2001. The world trade flows have two side, that is internal trade and external trade.

It is clearly that Western Europe has the highest internal trade and the highest external trade is between Asia/Pacific and North America.

In Western Europe, the internal trade is 1,677 billion dollars, followed by Asia/Pacific which is 722 billion dollars; the North America is 391 billion and the Rest of the World is 285 billion dollars. In external trade, the largest scale of trade is between Western Europe and Rest of the World, from 333 billion of Western European's export to 312 billion export of Rest of the World. Second one is between Asia/Pacific and North America. Asia/Pacific export is 376 billion and North America's is 207 billion. The smallest scale is between Asia/Pacific and Rest of the World. That is 96 billion from Asia/Pacific and 174 billion from Rest of the World.

To sum up, it can be said that the Rest of the World's internal trade is the smallest one, it relies on external trade especially with Western Europe much more than other areas of the world. And Western Europe has the highest internal and external trade amount so that it become the most developed area in the world.

b

WTO, World Trade Organisation, is a very important organisation in the world. It helps trade's development. So it's a very good system of trade.

The WTO consists of North America, Western Europe, Asia Pacific and Rest of the World.

In order they are: Western Europe, Asia Pacific, North America and Rest of the World.

Let's see the trade of Asia, they sell 252 billion to Western Europe, 96 billion to Rest of the World and 391 billion to North America. About Western Europe, they sell 195 to Asia, 333 billion to Rest of the World, and 265 to North America. And Rest of the World sell 312 billion to Western Europe, 174 to Asia Pacific, 287 to North America. And North America sell 207 billion to Asia, 168 billion to Western Europe and 205 Rest of the World.

WTO really a good system in the world.

c

This diagram shows the world trade flows and figures among Western Europe, North America, Asia/Pacific and Rest of the World in 2001. The source is from WTO and the unit is a billion US dollar.

Firstly, Western Europe had the greatest amount of internal trade at 1,677. It was over twice compared Asia/Pacific (722) and over 4 times compared to North America (391). However, the interesting fact in the trade flows and figures of Western Europe is that the amounts of export to other places were bigger than those of import except to Asia/Pacific. Only in Asia/Pacific region, the importing figure of trade was higher than exporting in Western Europe (respectively 195 and 252).

Not surprisingly, North America imported more than exporting from other places, in contrast Asia/Pacific exported more than importing to other 3 regions.

Overall, there was the biggest amount of trade in Western Europe and was followed by Asia/Pacific and North America.

Criteria	Text a	Text b	Text c
Task completion Does the text include all key info, and only relevant info? Is the info accurate? Is the info clear?	*No - should be about past, not present*	— only relevant info accurate	— No — Yes No
Organisation & linking Is the info organised in a logical order? Are main points and supporting points clear? Are ideas clearly linked?	followed by — Yes that — better the largest — yes more than	Yes — No — Yes	— Yes — Yes — No
Vocabulary & grammar Are the most appropriate words used? Is the grammar accurate? Is there a good range of grammar and vocabulary?	— Yes — Yes No	— Yes — Yes — Yes	*Reasonable range, some good vocab, but quite a lot of errors in grammar*

5 Now write a 200-word description of the following graphic.

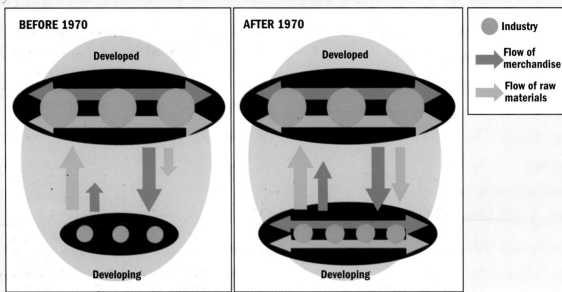

Listening

Before you listen

1 What do you know about Christopher Columbus? Try to complete the notes about his life.

> **Christopher Columbus**
>
> Born: _August 25 1451 Italy_ Died: _15 May 1506_
>
> Country of birth: _Genva Italy_ Adopted country: _Spain_
>
> Occupation: _sellar / Explorer / sailor_
>
> Main achievement: _Discovered a new world
> find china & Japan._
>
> _May octor_

As you listen

2 [🔊] **8.3** Now listen to the introduction to a lecture about Christopher Columbus to check and complete the notes.

3 There are headings in the box below that can be used to organise notes on the main part of the lecture. Listen to the main part of the lecture and put the headings in the right order.

practical	negative	intellectual	medical	positive	cultural

Listen again

4 Write the headings in the box on a piece of paper, then listen to the main part of the lecture again and make notes under the headings.

Expressing unreality

In the lecture about Christopher Columbus, the lecturer said:

> 'Although Columbus wasn't actually the first European to land in the Americas, it was his arrival that started the European colonisation of the Americas, and this was to totally change the course of world history.'

5 In what ways did Columbus' arrival in the New World 'totally change the course of world history'? Using your notes from the lecture, discuss with a partner.

Here are two sentences that describe the results of Columbus' arrival in the New World.

a *Columbus (was) one of the first Europeans to arrive in the New World, so Spain was the first coloniser of the Americas.*

past

b *Europeans colonised the Americas, so the main languages in the Americas are European.*

6 Now imagine that Columbus *didn't* arrive in the New World, and that Europeans *didn't* colonise the Americas ...

c *If Columbus hadn't been one of the first Europeans to arrive in the New World, Spain might not have been the first coloniser of the Americas.*

Present consequence

d *If Europeans hadn't colonised the Americas, the main languages of the Americas wouldn't be European.*

Present consequence

These two sentences describe situations that did not or cannot happen in the past, the present or the future: they are *unreal*. Each sentence has a condition clause, beginning with *If*, and a result clause.

7 Draw a circle around the finite verbs in sentences a–d. The first one in a is done for you. What are the differences between the verbs in a and c, and in b and d? How are the result clauses of c and d different?

8 Now think of some more results of Columbus' arrival in the New World and write at least two sentences using structures like those in c and d.

Speaking

1 Spend five minutes making notes for the following talk. The talk should last 2–3 minutes.
- Describe an important person in your country's history.
- What did he or she do?
- When?
- What impacts did this have?

2 Work with a partner. Take turns to give your talk. The listener should:
   a make sure that they have understood. They need to remember the information, so clarification questions may be required after each person has spoken.
   b make a note of any grammar mistakes that they hear, and tell their partner about them after they have spoken.

3 After each of you has spoken, find a new partner and repeat the activity. Do this with five different partners. Each time you speak you should aim to speak more:
- clearly
- fluently, and
- accurately.

4 After everyone has given their talk, sit with a partner and together make a list of all the people that the other students spoke about.

For example

	Spoke about	Achievement
Pierre	Louis Pasteur	Invented pasteurisation process

Listening

8.4 Coffee is the world's second most traded product, after petroleum. You are going to hear a radio programme comparing coffee grown in the shade and coffee grown in the sun.

Before you listen

1 Look at the table below. Do you know what all of the words mean?

As you listen

2 Make very brief notes to complete the table.

	Shade	Sun
Kilograms per hectare per year	*traditional* 550 Kg *thousand 120KK*	@ 1600 Kg
Lifetime of coffee plants	*8* 34 yrs *30 years*	*12 to 15 yrs fruited*
Flavour	*choice*	
Producer		
Weeding		
Chemical fertilisers	X	
Pesticides	X	
Irrigation	X	

Remove dead grass 2

After you listen

3 Complete the following summary of the main point of the programme. Listen again if you are not sure.

Teresa Saldana wants us to ..., because ...

Growers 10%

Exporters 10%

Shippers and Roasters 55%

Retailers 25%

4 Do you personally believe the situation depicted in this graphic is fair?

'Fair traders' argue that we can reduce these impacts by:
  a paying directly to the farmers (thus cutting out the 'middlemen'), and
  b paying more for coffee, so that farmers do not have to use intensive, environmentally damaging farming techniques.

5 Does this seem like a reasonable idea to you? What drawbacks might there be to this kind of plan?

6 Now think of another commodity from your own country—perhaps an agricultural product (such as rice or corn) or a mineral (such as coal or iron) or a manufactured product (such as steel or furniture).

7 Make a table of the positive and negative impacts that the production of this commodity has in your country.

8 In your opinion, do the positive impacts outweigh the negatives? Can the negative impacts be reduced in any way?

9 Explain your table to a partner.

Writing

Preparing to write

When you write an essay about an issue, you often have to present both sides of the argument, even though you only agree with one side. This shows that you have thought about both sides of the topic, and it therefore makes your argument stronger.

1   In the radio programme about coffee, you heard the views of people who support fair trade. Now try to imagine the views of a free trade supporter.

For example

By growing coffee on all kinds of ground, growers can make more money.

2   Here is the structure of an essay about the impacts of Christopher Columbus' discovery of the New World. Complete the following statements about this essay:
   a   The writer thinks that Columbus' impacts are mainly *positive/negative*.
   b   The writer's real opinion comes *before/after* the opposing opinion.
   c   The writer's real opinion is supported by *more/fewer* opinions than the opposing opinion.
   d   The writer uses expressions that make the opposing opinion *closer/more distant* from herself.
   e   The writer uses expressions that make her real opinions sound *more certain/less certain*.

Christopher Columbus' discovery of the New World was without doubt one of the major turning points of world history. While his arrival in America had many negative impacts on the land and its native people, the positive impacts of his discovery far outweigh the negative.

Some people claim that …

It is also argued that …

However, Columbus' voyages had a great many positive effects on the world as a whole. Firstly, it is obvious that…

In addition, we can see that …

Finally, …

Although there were a large number of unfortunate outcomes of Columbus' discovery of America, the effects on us all have been overwhelmingly positive. We must remember that great advances are almost never made without some pain.

Now write

3   Look at the writing question below. To help you get your ideas together and plan your essay, complete the notes following the question.

> Some people believe that *free* trade in coffee is good for everyone. Others think that *fair* trade is more important.
>
> What is your view?

Essay plan

My view: for free/fair trade

Arguments for free trade:

Arguments for fair trade:

4   When you are ready, write the essay, following your plan. Remember to state your view clearly in the introduction.

No man is an island

Tuning in

1 What kind of life do you imagine these people have? Make notes to build up a profile for each person, including details like age, family, education, occupation, interests, values, lifestyle and any other aspects of their life that you can think of.

2 Compare your profiles with another group.
a To what extent do you agree or disagree?
b Who had the most detail?
c Who had the most believable description?

Photo	Age	Family	Education	Occupation	Interests	Values	Lifestyle	Other
a	Late 20	Single maj	University	Bussin m. lawua.	No gnte.		Bussy Life	gym No time
b	40	big family		Sell St Vendor	mother		Poor Life	
c	20	young famil	un	Fisherman	Physical Job	South Africa	1	Busy
d	20 early	No married.	welled-	Model	meda media people		Income buy good	travel choune
e	80	4 cretive	wd	Former		Some shoot Bohea		wath Footb

3 🔊 **9.1** Listen to another group doing the same task. **Note:** The order of the pictures above is the same as the order you will hear in the discussion.

Reading

Before you read

The text you are going to read is from a book by Elliot Aronson called *The Social Animal*. It is about social psychology. Try to answer the following questions before you read the text.

1 What do psychologists study?

2 What do social psychologists study?

3 How do you think social psychology might be useful?

4 Some say 'man is a social animal'. What does this mean?

As you read

5 Answer questions 2 and 4 above. The other two questions are not answered in the text.

What is Social Psychology?

1 As far as we know, Aristotle was the first person to formulate basic principles of social influence and persuasion. He was probably not the first person to observe that man is a social animal, nor the first to marvel at the truth of that statement while simultaneously puzzling over its triteness and insubstantiality. Although it is certainly true that man is a social animal, so are a host of other animals, from ants and bees to monkeys and apes. What does it mean to say that man is a 'social animal'? Let's look at some concrete examples:

a A college student named Sam and four of his acquaintances are watching a presidential candidate make a speech on television. Sam is favorably impressed; he likes him better than the opposing candidate because of his sincerity. After the speech, one of the other students asserts that he was turned off by the candidate—that he considered him to be a complete phony—and that he prefers the opposing candidate. All of the others are quick to agree with him. Sam looks puzzled and a trifle distressed. Finally, he mumbles to his acquaintances, 'I guess he didn't come across as sincere as one might hope for him to be.'

b A second grade teacher stands before her class and asks, 'What is the sum of six, nine, four, and eleven?' A girl in the third row puzzles over the question for several seconds, hesitates, raises her hand tentatively, and, when called on, haltingly answers, 'Thirty?' The teacher nods, smiles at her, says, 'Nice work, Peggy,' and pastes a gold star on her forehead. She then asks the class, 'What is the sum of seven, four, eight, three, and ten?' Without wasting a moment, Peggy leaps to her feet and shouts, 'Thirty-two!'

c A four-year-old boy is given a toy drum for his birthday. After pounding on it for a few minutes, he casts it aside and studiously ignores it for the next several weeks. One day, a friend comes to visit, picks up the drum, and is about to play with it. Suddenly the young 'owner' tears the drum from his friend's grasp and proceeds to play with it as if it had always been his favorite toy.

d Mary has just turned nine. For her birthday, she received a Suzie Homemaker baking and cooking set—complete with 'her own little oven.' Her parents chose this present because she seems very interested in culinary things, and forever helping mommy set the table, prepare the meals, and clean the house. 'Isn't it wonderful,' says Mary's father, 'how at age nine she is already interested in being a housewife? Little girls must have housewifery built into their genes.'

2 What is social psychology? There are almost as many definitions of social psychology as there are social psychologists. Instead of listing some of these definitions, it might be more informative to let the subject matter define the field. The examples presented above are all illustrations of socio-psychological situations. As diverse as these situations may be, they do contain one common factor: social influence.

Read again

6 Which example is about:
  a possessiveness?
  b conformity?
  c gender roles?
  d self-esteem?

Try to match them before using your dictionary to check these words.

7 Have you ever experienced situations similar to the examples?

8 How is social influence relevant to each example?

After you read

9 Do you think humans are more of a 'social animal' than other animal species? Why, or why not?

10 Make lists under the following headings.

11 Think of an example for each point.

12 What can, or should, be done to maximise the positives and minimise the negatives?

Positive aspects of social influence	Negative aspects of social influence
	e.g. sometimes people/kids imitate the bad behaviour of others

Vocabulary

Word attack

1 Find the words *diverse* and *illustrations* in the final paragraph of the reading text on page 99. What do they mean in this context?

Synonyms

> ... Sam and four of his acquaintances ...

2 What is the difference between:
  a an acquaintance and a friend?
  b a colleague, workmate, and co-worker?

3 Are there words in your first language that make the same distinctions?

4 Put the names of <u>family</u>, <u>friends</u>, <u>acquaintances</u>, <u>colleagues</u>, and <u>other people</u> you know onto the sociogram below. The inner circles represent people with whom you have a close relationship; the outer circles represent people with whom you have a less close relationship.

5 Spend a few minutes explaining your sociogram to a partner.

Words that go together

6 Make a list of six pairs of words from the text. Each word must have some kind of relationship with its partner.

For example

formulate + principles
relationship: collocation (meaning = to make principles)

sincere + phony
relationship: meaning (both about honesty, or lack of honesty)

sincere ➝ sincerity
relationship: word family

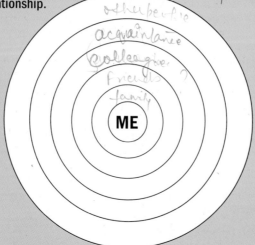

Speaking

1   Make a list of all the groups to which you belong.

For example

family, school, class, clubs, workplace

Some groups of people like to be different from others in society. Sometimes these groups form a subculture, with their own distinctive way of dressing, speaking and behaving.

2   How would you classify the groups in these pictures?

3   What subcultures exist in your culture?

4   How are they different from mainstream society?

5   How do you personally view these groups?

6   How are they viewed by other members of society in general? Why?

Describing people

1   Match the questions and answers below.

What's she like?	She's about my height, long brown hair, glasses.
What does she look like?	Well, she can be a bit grumpy sometimes, but she's generally quite cheerful.
Who does she look like?	Apparently she takes after her father.

2   Which question is about:
   a appearance?
   b resemblance/similarity?
   c personality?

3   Look at these example sentences and then choose the best word(s) to complete the rules in the box.

They look quite scruffy and dirty.

They look like they're soldiers or something.

> When we describe appearance, we use *look* + noun/clause/adjective to describe features that we can see. We use *look* + *like* + noun/clause/adjective to describe our opinion based on what we can see.

Listening: Family life cycle

Before you listen

The table below illustrates the family life cycle (FLC), a concept developed by sociologists to explain the various phases of family life.

1 There are obviously gaps in the table, which you will complete as you listen, but first see how many you can predict with a partner.

As you listen

2 🔊 **9.2** Complete the table. Make very brief notes, which you can check with a partner after you listen.

After you listen

3 This table shows typical phases in English-speaking cultures. In what ways would the FLC differ in your culture?

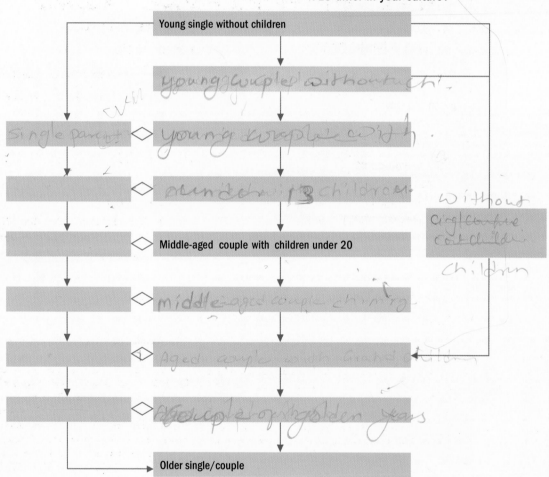

Young single without children

young couple without ch'

single parent ◇ young couple with

◇ couple with children

Middle-aged couple with children under 20

◇ middle-aged couple ...

◇ Aged couple with Grand...

◇ couple golden years

Older single/couple

without couple with children children

Reading

Before you read

The text you are going to read begins like this.

> Many of us like to think we gain independence from our parents as we grow, yet the family we are born into is extremely influential in shaping our values and the future lifestyle we choose. For instance, …

1 Write two or three more sentences to complete the paragraph.

2 Compare ideas with a partner, and check each other's grammar.

3   What cultural or family values do you see reflected in this photograph?

The text below is from a marketing textbook. It examines the way our families influence our behaviour as consumers. In other words, it discusses the way families influence what we buy.

4   How do you think:
   · your family influences what you buy?
   · your stage in the family life cycle (FLC) influences what you buy?

Make a list of examples.

For example

   Ask parents for advice about what to buy
   More money to spend if no children
   When young, spend more on ...

As you read

5   Skim read the text to see if your examples are mentioned.
   a   Tick your examples if they are mentioned.
   b   Make a note of any other examples that are mentioned.

External influences on consumer behaviour

Family

Many of us like to think we gain independence from our parents as we grow, yet the family we are born into is extremely influential in shaping our values and the future lifestyle we choose. For instance, it is not uncommon for young people to seek their parents' advice when purchasing major items like a car or home. While choosing a partner may bring another dimension with different values, the family of origin, i.e. our parents, will still have a considerable influence on us.

Of significance also is a person's *family situation*. This determines what will be purchased through need as against what a person would like to purchase through want. Consumer needs are often determined by the position of a person within the *family life cycle* (FLC). This refers to the age of those in the family and its composition. The table illustrates a modern FLC, which shows the path people take and the family situations available through life. Traditionally, the FLC comprised the stages of people's lives, which typically saw them moving from single to married status, having children and then growing old as a couple, with one partner usually surviving the other. Families within society have altered: couples quite often choose not to have children;

other people raise children alone because they have never married or because of divorce or separation. (The branches out to the right and left in the table show the life cycle of such people.) These new family types have separate needs and wants. A couple without children has more money to spend on a home, leisure activities, and travel. A person living or raising children alone may desire a smaller property with less gardening to be done. Determining at which point in the FLC a person is gives very clear indications of his or her spending patterns and therefore of potential market opportunities.

What is purchased will be influenced by a person's age and where he or she is in the family life cycle. The number of people in the family will also determine their spending. Parents with children under five spend on nappies, toys, baby food, babysitters and perhaps a mortgage. These are strong priorities for the budget. However, a couple whose children have left home might find it easy to fund an overseas trip every year or to invest in a new home or car. McDonald's identified an important target market in families and provided play facilities, a Ronald McDonald image, and an eating-out option that might be viewed as more affordable to families.

After you read

6 Go back to the profiles on the first page of this unit (page 98).

    a What stage of the FLC do you think these people are at?

    b What are their wants?

    c What are their needs?

    d What kinds of things do you think they spend their money on or invest in?

Vocabulary

Which sense?

The word *determine* is used a number of times in this text, with different meanings.

For example

> Paragraph 2: Determining at which point in the FLC a person is gives very clear indications of his/her spending patterns and therefore of potential market opportunities.

> Paragraph 3: The number of people in the family will also determine their spending.

7 Use your dictionary to identify what *determine* means in each of these cases.

8 Which meaning is more common in this text?

What is the difference?

9 The words *influence* and *determine* are similar, but not the same.

    a Which word is (much) stronger?

    b Which word belongs in which sentence below?

> The colour of your eyes is _____ by the colour of your ancestors' eyes.

> Your personality is probably _____ by your family.

Grammar: Information flow

10 Here is the beginning of paragraph 2. Do not look back at the text. You have a choice for sentences 2, 3 and 4. Which version (2a or 2b, 3a or 3b, etc.) seems the best way to continue the text each time?

> **1** Of significance also is a person's *family situation*.
>
> **2a** What will be purchased through need as against what a person would like to purchase through want is determined by family situation.
>
> **2b** Family situation determines what will be purchased through need as against what a person would like to purchase through want.
>
> **3a** Consumer needs are often determined by the position of a person within the *family life cycle* (FLC).
>
> **3b** The position of a person within the *family life cycle* often determines consumer needs.
>
> **4a** Family life cycle refers to the age of those in the family and its composition.
>
> **4b** The age of those in the family and its composition is referred to as the family life cycle.

11 Compare your choices with a partner, then compare with the original. **Note:** the original uses pronouns in a few places where this exercise has used full nouns.

12 Do pronouns show:

    a old, known information?

    b new information?

13 In written English, do pronouns usually come:

    a near the beginning of a sentence?

    b near the end of a sentence?

14 Choose the correct words to make the following summary true.

> In written English, old, known information usually comes near the *beginning/end* of the sentence and new information comes near the *beginning/end*. This helps information flow smoothly for the reader.

Sexist and non-sexist language

1   Look at these examples, taken from this unit.

> 'No man is an island.'

> '... man is a social animal.'

> 'Of significance is also a person's family situation. This determines what will be purchased through need as against what a person would like to purchase through want.'

> 'What is purchased will be influenced by a person's age and where he or she is in the family life cycle.'

> '... every parent of a teenager knows that their peers really do have a determining impact on their personality and behaviour.'

In English, we often face the problem of sexist language—language that excludes one of the sexes (usually women) from what is being described. Writers and speakers have several options when they are faced with this problem.

2   In the example sentences, which option did the speaker or writer choose?

   a   Use *they* or *their* even though the noun being referred to is singular.

   b   Use *a person* and *a person's* to mean 'either a man or a woman'.

   c   Use *he* or *she*, *he/she*, *(s)he*.

   d   Use the sexist language anyway (this is normal in more traditional language).

3   Do you face this problem in your language? Why? How do you solve the problem in your language or in other languages you know?

Writing: Personal influences

Several external pressures influence the behaviour of consumers. The obvious one is culture, which dictates the norms and values of a society in which a person lives. Other external influences can be the person's family, lifestyle, social class, and reference groups he/she associates with.

1   The paragraph above is from earlier in the same book on consumer behaviour. Use the same paragraph frame, but rewrite it so that it is true about your own personal influences in some area of your life—as a student, an employee, a sportsperson, etc.

For example

A number of people have influenced me as a teacher. The obvious ones are my own teachers in the past, who ...

2   Write at least 100 words on this topic. Do not write your name on your text.

3   Pass the texts around the class, and see if your classmates can guess whose is whose.

Speaking: Hopes, plans and intentions

1 **Find someone in your class who:**

_1_ ... thinks they'll get married in the next five years.

_2_ ... is planning to do their university studies overseas.

_3_ ... knows what sort of job they hope to get in the future.

_4_ ... would like to visit the same countries as you.

_5_ ... is thinking of emigrating.

_6_ ... intends to study an unusual subject at university.

_7_ ... will probably be living in the same place as now, in ten years.

_8_ ... is intending to learn another language.

_9_ ... plans to sit IELTS very soon.

Grammar: aspect and the future

1 **What is the difference between the following pairs of sentences:**
  a in grammar?
  b in meaning?
  (**Clue**: it's not really about time.)

I'm planning to sit IELTS soon.

I plan to sit IELTS soon.

I'm intending to learn another language.

I intend to learn another language.

One difference between Present Simple (*I plan to ...*) and Present Continuous (*I'm planning to ...*) is that continuous aspect focuses on the activity more than the goal.

Activity   Goal

_I'm __planning__ to sit IELTS soon._

Therefore, when we use continuous aspect with verbs like *plan, hope, intend,* and *think*, it feels as though we are still thinking about it, we are not sure yet, or the plan is not definite.

2 **Complete the sentences below with true statements about your own plans and hopes, and then explain them to a partner. Use the time phrases in the box to help you.**

I intend to... _____

I'm hoping to... _____

I'm thinking of... _____

I plan to... _____

next week/month/year
in the next few days/weeks/months
in the next couple of weeks/months
in a couple of days/weeks/months
by the end of the month/year
sooner or later

Writing

1 In some countries, it is acceptable for couples to live together before they get married. How acceptable is this in your country or culture? Is the situation changing?

This graph shows the marriage expectations of men and women in Great Britain in 2001. For each group, the different bars represent these opinions:

· Have not really thought about the future
· Will probably get married at some point
· Planning to marry
· Will probably just keep living together without marrying
· Other

2 Try to match the opinions to the bars on the graph.

Marriage expectations in Great Britain, 2001

Percent axis: 0, 10, 20, 30, 40, 50

Males   Females

3 Choose the best words to complete this sentence.

The *number/amount* of men *planned/planning* to get married *is/are* slightly higher than the *number of women/women*.

Now write

4 The graph here gives information on Britain. It does not have a title or labels on its X and Y axes. What information do you think it is showing? Can you label the axes?

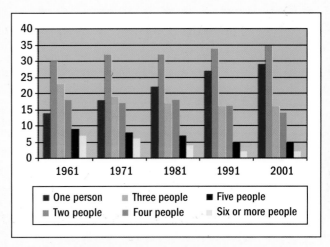

- One person
- Two people
- Three people
- Four people
- Five people
- Six or more people

5 Write a 150-word report describing the information in the graph. You have twenty minutes only.

Listening: Interview

Before you listen

You are going to hear parts of an interview in which a controversial book by Judith Harris, *The Nurture Assumption,* is discussed. The book is about the 'nature or nurture' debate: are we who we are because of our ancestors and genes (nature), or because of the way that our parents raised and taught us (nurture)? The first two paragraphs of her book are on the right.

Heredity and environment. They are the yin and yang, the Adam and Eve, the Mom and Pop of pop psychology. Even in high school I knew enough about the subject to inform my parents, when they yelled at me, that if they didn't like the way I was turning out they had no one to blame but themselves: they had provided both my heredity and my environment.

'Heredity and environment', that's what we called them back then. Nowadays they are more often referred to as 'nature and nurture.' Powerful as they were under the names they were born with, they are yet more powerful under their alliterative aliases. Nature and nurture rule. Everyone knows it, no one questions it: nature and nurture are the movers and shapers. They made us what we are today and will determine what our children will be tomorrow.

1 Do you believe that we are more influenced by our genes or by the environment in which we live? Place yourself on the following line according to your view.

Nature/Heredity/Genes ←————————————————→ Nurture/Environment

As you listen

2 9.3 Decide whether the following statements are true (T) or false (F). Harris believes that:

a Earlier views about the role of parents are based on bad research.

b Genes are not significant in determining personality and behaviour.

c The environment is not significant.

d Parents don't really matter.

e Friends are more significant than parents.

f The most important job of parents is to teach their children.

After you listen

3 Here is a reaction to Harris' argument. Is it supportive or critical?

4 Have you changed your own views after listening to the interview?

Dr Stanley Greenspan, Child Psychiatrist

It's going to tell parents it doesn't make a difference what you do. It doesn't make a difference if you are loving, if you are warm, if you are intimate. So the worst part of this is that parents—I think most parents are too smart for that—but that any parent who believes the message, they could devalue what's so important about what they do give to their children—the love, the warmth, the security, the building blocks of healthy self-esteem, healthy thinking, and healthy patterns of communication.

Speaking

1 What were your favourite toys as a child?

2 Many people argue that toys have a significant influence on children, and that the influence can be very negative. For example, they claim that toy guns can make boys violent, or that dolls give girls unrealistic expectations regarding their physical appearance. Do you agree?

3 Should parents take care with the types of toy they give their children?

Writing

'Parents should choose their children's toys carefully.'

Write a 350-word essay on this topic.

4 Here are some sources of evidence that could be used to support an opinion on this issue. Classify them as:
- Science
- Local news
- International news
- Logic
- Personal experience

a When I was young I had toy guns, ...

b I remember a case in my local newspaper where ...

c Every year there is a story from the USA in which ...

d Research has shown that ...

e It seems clear to me that someone who plays with guns as a child must be more likely to be violent as an adult.

5 What types of supporting argument do you think are best in the IELTS exam?

Reading

Before you read

One way to find answers to the nature–nurture question is to study twins. They have similar or identical DNA, and sometimes they are separated at birth (for example, because they are adopted by different families), so the effects of environment and heredity can be separated. And more recently, scientists have been able to clone animals—produce exact copies, or identical twins—so that they can do controlled experiments in order to answer these questions.

1 Do you think that if you were cloned, your identical twin would grow up to be exactly the same as you?

2 How do you personally feel about the idea of being cloned? For example, does the idea disgust, excite, or not interest you?

As you read

3   First, skim read the text to identify the writer's position on question 1.

4   Then read again more carefully, and make notes on supporting arguments. Organise your notes to show the structure of the argument.

NATURE vs NURTURE

It must be emphasised that while cloning produces an exact nuclear genetic duplicate of the donor's DNA, this does not guarantee that the cloned individual will be physically or behaviorally identical to the donor.

For example, identical twins share identical nuclear genomes just as clones do. In addition, identical twins share identical mitochondrial DNA as well. Yet it is clear that identical twins are neither physically nor behaviorally identical to one another. If they do not have identical diets and nutrition, then they will not be the same height or weight. Or they may suffer dissimilar injuries, or wear their hair different lengths. Identical twins will often not share the exact same values or beliefs. They often do not like the same sports. They usually choose different occupations. They do not always choose similar friends or mates.

If genetically identical twins, (or clones) were raised in different environments then their physical and behavioral characteristics would differ accordingly. Imagine identical twins who are separated at birth. One is raised by a middle-class French family living in Marseilles. The other twin is raised by a Kickapoo Indian family living on the Kickapoo Indian Reservation in Oklahoma, USA. How identical will these genetically identical people end up looking and acting? Will they think alike? Will they feel the same way about the same kinds of things? Will they have the same beliefs? Will they dream alike? Will they have the same needs and desires? Will they like the same kinds of people, foods, drinks, clothes? Obviously the answer is no. One will dress, speak and be French. The other will dress, speak, and be a Kickapoo Indian.

Their differences will be readily apparent. But will they have any significant similarities? If so, can these similarities be the result of their having identical genomes?

In short, the environment in which genetically identical individuals grow and develop shapes their physical and behavioral appearances in many significant ways. The genome codes for potential. The genome is not deterministic of many significant physical and behavioral characteristics, because the environment acts upon this genetic potential to determine the final characteristics of the plant or animal.

This is the essence of the 'nature–nurture' debate: What is the ratio of genetic to environmental influences in understanding the source and expression of various biological and behavioral characteristics?

After you read

5   Compare your notes with a partner.
  a   Have you identified the same supporting arguments?
  b   Has either of you made too many or too few notes?

Speaking

6   Are there any circumstances under which genetic engineering is OK? For example, is it acceptable to try to:
  ·   change the personality of your children?
  ·   change the appearance of your children?
  ·   produce identical twins for scientific experiments?
  ·   avoid a hereditary disease?

7   Discuss your views in a small group.

10 Creatures great and small

Tuning in

APTERYX MANTELLI

DoDo

Rhinoceros
(Africa)

Gorilla

1   One of these animals is not like the others: which one is extinct?

2   What is the difference between an extinct animal and an endangered animal?

3   Do you know the names of the other animals? What problem do they all share? Try to think of more animals in the same situation. Why are they in this situation?

Listening

Before you listen

You are going to hear a lecture about the blue whale. The information in the talk can be grouped under these headings.

·   Physical dimensions
·   Location
·   Communication
·   Numbers

1   For each heading, write down at least two questions that you have. Share your questions with a partner.

As you listen

2 **10.1** Listen to the lecture and try to answer the questions that you and your partner have written. Which ones were you unable to answer?

Writing

Before you write

1   Use the statistics from the lecture to make a graph or table about the numbers of blue whales. Before you do this, think about the advantages and disadvantages of displaying the data in each of the following formats.

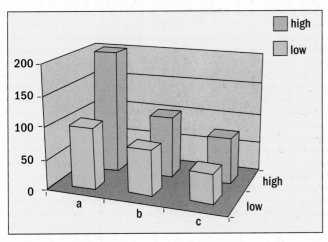

Listen again

3   This time, note down the statistics about the blue whale population that you hear. Make sure you get the right numbers, because you will need to use the information in the next section.

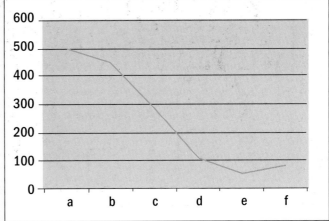

Year	High	Low
xxxx	200	100
yyyy	150	75
zzzz	100	50

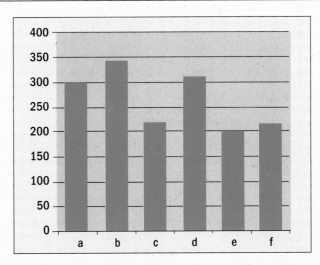

Describing statistical trends

2 Look at these examples.

The number of endangered animal species in the world has risen to 2151 in the last six years.

The number of endangered animal species in the world has risen by 195 in the last six years.

3 Which sentence describes the level that the number has reached? Which one describes the amount of the change?

4 One of these sentences is not correct in meaning. Which one? (**Clue:** What exactly is increasing?)

✗ a *Some whales, such as the minke whale, have increased significantly in recent years.*

b *The number of some whales, such as the minke whale, has increased significantly in recent years.*

c *Some whale populations, such as the minke whale, have increased significantly in recent years.*

d *Some whales, such as the minke whale, show a significant increase in numbers in recent years.*

5 The information in one of these sentences about the blue whale population is not correct. Which one?

a In the 1930s, the population was between 30 and 40 000.

b In the 1930s, the population fell to between 30 and 40 000.

c By the 1930s, the population had fallen to between 30 and 40 000.

In this context, the preposition **by** means:

a during this time.

b during or before this time.

Now write

6 Write a report describing the graph or table that you have made.

Pronunciation

A It is estimated that there were over 200 000 blue whales at the beginning of the twentieth century.

B There are many different estimates of whale populations.

1 In which sentence is *estimate* a verb, and in which is it a noun?

2 The sound of one of the vowels changes. Which one? You can use your dictionary to check.

3 Do you know any other words that have the same spelling for the verb and the noun forms, but different pronunciation?

Speaking

> When we are hungry, the elephant is food, when we're full, the elephant is beautiful.
>
> Old Man, Zambesi Valley

Elephant hunting is banned in most countries. Although the elephant population in Zimbabwe at the end of the twentieth century was not endangered, many people still opposed elephant hunting in Zimbabwe.

1   Skim the following passages and decide whether each one makes points *for* hunting or *against* hunting.

a

Almost 10 000 elephants roam Zimbabwe's communal lands, often wandering out from neighbouring national parks. In these communal areas, an elephant or two can quickly munch their way through a family's crops, trampling those that they do not consume, and destroying the family's only source of subsistence in the process. Elephants also threaten people's lives—a local newspaper has reported that over 100 people have been killed by elephants or buffaloes in Kariba since 1980.

b

The environmental groups who oppose elephant hunting have serious problems with killing elephants and other wild animals for use as an economic resource. Other environmental groups claim that the elephant population in Zimbabwe is not doing well enough for hunting to take place.

c

In some districts ... elephant harvesting is the only source of income. With a trophy fee of up to US $12,000 or more, together with a daily hunting fee of $1,000, one elephant can realise $33,000 over the course of an average 21-day hunt. In addition, revenues are raised through the hunting of other trophy species. Normally the safari operator retains the daily fee, whilst local communities receive the full trophy fees, plus negotiated fees for the rental of the hunting concession. As a rural family of eight would expect to subsist on about $150 per year in Zimbabwe, this is no small amount.

d

It is largely agreed that the demand for ivory caused a decline of the African elephant in the 1970s and 1980s.

Government considers ban on elephant hunting

Under pressure from the international environmental movement, the Minister for the Environment announced today that ...

The government has called a conference to discuss this plan. The following groups have been invited.

Elephant hunters	Park rangers
Ivory traders	Travel agents
Conservationists	Local villagers

2   Divide into groups. Each group takes one of the roles. How do you feel about the hunting of elephants? Prepare for the conference.

3   Now divide into new 'conference' groups. Each conference group should have one representative from the original groups (i.e. one elephant hunter, one park ranger, etc).

4   Take it in turns to make your points and answer questions from the others. When everyone has spoken, take a vote: will your conference group advise the government to ban elephant hunting or not?

Reading

Before you read

1 Which answer would you give to the following question? Spend a few minutes thinking about your answer.

Why save endangered species?

a *We should save endangered animals because ... (give reasons)*

b *We shouldn't bother trying to save them, there's nothing much we can do about it.*

c *It doesn't really matter, it's a natural process anyway: look at the dinosaurs!*

d *Who cares? People are more important than animals or plants.*

2 Now discuss your answer with a partner. Do you agree? (See the *Useful language* box.)

When we disagree with someone, we do not usually just say 'I disagree' because it can be quite rude unless we know the other person very well. We are more likely to show disagreement by acknowledging the other argument, then giving counter-arguments, or asking questions.

> *Useful language*
>
> *Yes, but ... Maybe, but ...*
> *I suppose that could be true, but ...*
> *Don't you think that ...*

3 Then do a quick survey of the class, to see how many people gave each answer.

As you read

4 Skim read the text very quickly (just two minutes). Which answer(s) from Exercise 1 does it give to the question in the title?

Why Save Endangered Species?

Since life began on this planet, countless creatures have come and gone—rendered extinct by naturally changing physical and biological conditions.

If extinction is part of the natural order, and if many other species remain, some people ask: 'Why save endangered species? What makes these animals and plants so special that money and effort should be spent to conserve them?'

The American Government answered these questions in the Endangered Species Act of 1973, stating that endangered species of fish, wildlife, and plants 'are of aesthetic, ecological, educational, historical, recreational, and scientific value to the Nation and its people'. In this statement, the government was summarising a number of convincing arguments made by scientists, conservationists, and others who are greatly concerned by the disappearance of unique creatures.

Unfortunately, we cannot attribute the accelerating decline of our wild animals and plants to 'natural' processes. Biologists know that today's dangers to wildlife most often result from habitat degradation, environmental pollution, the introduction of exotic (non-native) organisms, and exploitation—all generally as a direct result of human activities.

Although conservation efforts have begun in recent years, mankind is still exterminating entire species at an ever-increasing rate. Since 1620, more than 500 species, subspecies, and varieties of our nation's plants and animals have become extinct—lost forever. By contrast, during the 3000 years of the Pleistocene Ice Age, all of North America lost only about three species every 100 years. The situation today is even worse in other parts of the world.

A No creature exists in a vacuum. All living things are part of a complex, delicately balanced network called the biosphere. The earth's biosphere is composed of ecosystems, which include plants and animals and their physical environment. The removal of a single species within an ecosystem can set off a chain reaction affecting many other species. It has been estimated, for example, that a disappearing plant can take with it up to thirty other species, including insects, higher animals, and even other plants.

B Each living thing contains a unique reservoir of genetic material that has evolved over eons of time. This material cannot be retrieved or duplicated if lost. So far, scientists have partially investigated only a small fraction of the world's species and have begun to unravel a few of their chemical secrets to determine, among other things, possible benefits to mankind. No matter how small or obscure a species, it could one day be of direct aid to all of us. It was 'only' a fungus that gave us penicillin, and certain plants have yielded substances used in drugs to treat heart disease, cancer, and a variety of other illnesses.

At least a quarter of all prescriptions written annually in the United States contain chemicals discovered in plants and animals. If these organisms had been destroyed before their chemistries were known, their secrets would have died with them.

C Many seemingly insignificant forms of life are beginning to show important benefits in areas such as agriculture. Some farmers are beginning to use insects and other animals that compete with or prey on certain crop pests, as well as using plants containing natural-toxin compounds that repel harmful insects. These are called 'biological controls,' and in many cases they are a safe, effective, and less expensive alternative to synthetic chemicals.

D Many individual species are uniquely important as indicators of environmental quality. The rapid decline in bald eagles and peregrine falcons was a dramatic warning of the dangers of DDT—a strong,

once widely used pesticide that accumulates in body tissues. (Its effect on these birds was to hamper fertility and egg-hatching success.) In another example, certain plants, such as the eastern white pine, are good indicators of excess ozone, sulphur dioxide, and other air pollutants. Species like these can alert us to the effects of some contaminants before more damage is done.

E Aside from the more utilitarian reasons for preserving endangered species, many people believe that every creature, after adapting for thousands or even millions of years to fit a constantly changing environment, has an intrinsic value. Exterminating other forms of life is not only shortsighted, but wrong—especially since the species could never be replaced. Mankind would also lose; being accustomed to diversity in nature, the quality of human life would be diminished.

Read again

5 Match the headings below with sections A–E. You will not need two of the headings.
- Environmental Monitors
- The Benefits of Natural Diversity
- Contributions to Industry
- Intrinsic Value
- Contributions to Medicine
- Feeding the Hungry
- Contributions to Agriculture

6 Which paragraph lists the causes of extinction mentioned in the text? List the causes.

7 Read the following sentences. According to the article, is the information true (T), false (F), or not mentioned (NM)?
- **a** Extinction is a natural process.
- **b** Humans have caused the rate of extinction to increase.
- **c** When a plant becomes extinct, it has more consequences than when an animal becomes extinct.

- **d** Scientists have managed to save some animals.
- **e** Plants and animals can alert humans to pollution.
- **f** Farmers use biological controls because they can be cheaper than chemicals.

After you read

The US government stated that endangered species have the following values:
- aesthetic (= beauty)
- ecological
- educational
- historical
- recreational
- scientific

8 Which of these are *not* explained in detail in the main body of the text? Can you think of examples for each one?

Vocabulary

9 Paragraph 3 talks about *convincing arguments made by scientists*. Do you find the arguments in this text convincing?

10 The text also talks about animals *evolving*—which relates to the theory of *evolution*. Can you explain the basic theory of evolution to your partner? It is a controversial theory. Do you find the theory convincing?

Cause and effect

A *We cannot attribute the accelerating decline of our wild animals and plants to 'natural' processes.*

1 In the sentence above, draw a circle around the part that describes the cause, and underline the part that describes the effect.

Attribute means 'to say that one thing is the cause of another thing'. So we could actually rewrite the sentence above like this:

> We cannot say that _____ is/are the cause of _____.

B *Biologists know that today's dangers to wildlife most often result from habitat degradation, environmental pollution, the introduction of exotic (non–native) organisms, and exploitation ...*

2 Again, in sentence B, circle the cause and underline the effect.

3 In this particular sentence, there is actually a third link in the causal chain.

C *... all generally as a direct result of human activities.*

4 Are 'human activities' a cause, or effect? Put these three parts of the causal chain into the following table.

· habitat degradation, etc.

· human activities

· accelerating decline

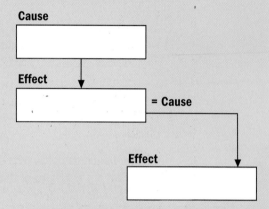

Speaking

1 Make a list of three key problems in your country or in the world. What, in your opinion, are the causes of the problems? Note down at least two for each problem.

2 Work with a partner. Explain the problems and causes to each other. As you listen, make notes. If you do not understand something, ask your partner for clarification.

3 From your notes, write a brief summary of what your partner told you.

For example

> *Maxim believes that the main problem facing the world is ... He attributes this problem to ... / He believes that this is caused by ...*

4 Exchange summaries with your partner, to evaluate whether they are an accurate summary of what each person said.

5 What solutions are there to your problems?

Listening: The economics of conservation

Before you listen

1 Do you think the following table indicates a serious situation?

2 What do you think *documented* means here?

Table 1. Number of Species and Documented Extinctions, 1600–1995.

	Number of Species	Extinctions Since 1600
Vertebrates	47,000	321
· Mammals	4,500	110
· Birds	9,500	103
· Reptiles	6,300	21
· Amphibians	4,200	5
· · Fish	24,000	82
Molluscs	100,000	235
Crustaceans	4,000	9
Insects	>1,000,000	98
Plants	250,000	396
Total	~1,600,000	1,033

As you listen

3 🔊 **10.2** You will hear the introduction to a lecture. Choose the correct answer.

The speaker thinks the problem is:
  a serious
  b exaggerated
  c underestimated.

She thinks that economics:
  a is the cause of the problem
  b is the solution to the problem
  c has nothing to do with the problem.

4 In the second section you will hear a description of the benefits that wild species and their environments bring us. Complete the notes, by matching words in box A with words in box B.

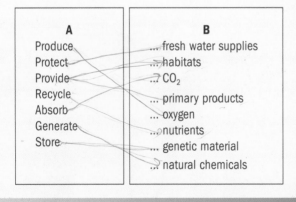

A	B
Produce	... fresh water supplies
Protect	... habitats
Provide	... CO_2
Recycle	... primary products
Absorb	... oxygen
Generate	... nutrients
Store	... genetic material
	... natural chemicals

5 In the final section, you will hear an explanation of the main causes of species extinction, and a discussion of economic solutions. Complete the notes below.

Problem	Economic solution?	How? (make brief notes)
1 Excessive *Harvest*	Yes/No	ownship – to local people – look after
2 Introduction of exotic *species*	Yes/No	economic Proble Board security
3 Habitat *loss*	Yes/No	Hard soft make disaster land es forest Individual Charring poverty, national

After you listen

6 Look back at the reading text on page 114. Do the author of that text and the speaker in this lecture agree on the problem?

7 They list different benefits of natural environments. How are the lists different?

8 Do you think they would agree on the solution to the problem?

Reading

Before you read

The following humorous essay from *New Scientist* magazine aims to give readers a bit of fun. It argues that humans would be better off if we had wings.

1 With a partner, brainstorm the pros and cons of wings for humans.

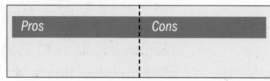

Pros	Cons

2 What do you think? Would we be better or worse off with wings?

As you read

3 What, in your opinion, are the three most interesting benefits mentioned in the text?

4 Read the text slowly and carefully; it is designed to be read for pleasure, and to make you think.

There may be quite a few words or expressions that you do not know: the first time you read, try to guess what they mean. Simply identifying whether the meaning is positive or negative will be helpful.

On the desire of wings

HUMANS have lost the evolutionary race. We are born without wings. It's a crucial omission and we are making the environment pay for it.

We like to think we're the bee's knees of the natural world but we're nothing more than bumbling flatfoots. That's why kookaburras laugh and midges torment us. We are grounded for life and, in our frustration, we're wrecking the planet.

Wings might seem just fun and frippery, but they would also save the environment. If we could fly, we would not be trampling ecosystems underfoot. Natural habitats that now get bulldozed would flourish because we wouldn't need roads. There would be no demand for cars, so there wouldn't be emissions problems.

The common housefly travels 300 times its body length in one second. If in a few generations we could match that, we would reach 2000 kilometres per hour, which would make ozone-destroying aircraft and land-grabbing airports unnecessary.

Society would benefit enormously if we could fly. Our philosophy about the private ownership of land would have to change because fences would become useless. Nets wouldn't stop people flying into your garden—as anyone knows who has tried in vain to keep birds out of fruit crops. And domestic rooftops would become public resting places.

The justice system would not need to guard expensive prisons because felons would simply have their wings clipped. Sports stadia would consist of only the pitch, with spectators hovering over the action. Stairs, escalators and lifts would be as superfluous as bridges and tunnels. Buildings would have smaller ground plans and, instead, rise upwards, with entrance porches on every level.

If we had wings, not only would we not need to plunder so much of the Earth's resources, but we'd also be better guardians of the environment. Woodland would not be cut down because trees would be vital resting places as we flitted through the troposphere. We'd be more aware of the changes to Earth as we surveyed it daily from on high. And we'd soon appreciate any changes to air quality at all heights.

There would be some drawbacks. Clothing would have to be unflatteringly tight and aerodynamic—but our perception of human beauty would soon change so that we'd delight at a glimpse of plush, plump plumage. Demand for the best addresses would push the prices of mountain eyries sky-high. Electricity pylons and overhead cables would have to go. There would, inevitably, be the occasional crash landing in rush hour as soaring commuters got spun by the wing-tip vortices of others.

But it would be worth these minor hassles. The dinosaurs clearly recognised the merits of wings, and went so far as to evolve into birds. That left us to inherit the Earth—an inheritance we seem determined to fritter away.

Humans clearly have an intuitive inkling of the need to fly. It comes up again and again, in nursery tales and sophisticated mythology from all over the world.

If we had evolved wings the world would have been blessed. For the sake of the planet, biologists should stop growing ears on the backs of mice and start putting feathers between our shoulder blades, before it's too late.

Time's running out. Must fly.

After you read

5 With a partner, discuss the benefits that you noted down in Exercise 3. Did you both identify the same points?

Focus on organisation

6 The introduction suggests that the authors will mention only environmental benefits, but in fact they also mention another type of benefit. Which type?

7 The authors use different types of paragraph structure in this text. Some of the paragraphs have General ➤ Particular organisation, with very clear topic sentences, followed by examples. Which paragraphs?

Speaking

8 With a partner, think of another evolutionary improvement to humans: a third eye, two heads, a wheel instead of legs, etc.

9 Make a list of advantages that this modification would bring. Would there be any drawbacks?

10 Explain your ideas to classmates. Who has the best idea?

Writing

11 Now write your own essay, in a similar style to the one you have just read. It should be:
· humorous
· well-organised and clearly signposted
· accurate in grammar and vocabulary (use your dictionary if you are not sure about anything).

Listening

Before you listen

1 In the essay about humans having wings on page 118, the last sentence was *Must fly*. Do you know what this expression means? In what situation would a speaker say it? Why did the writer use it in this essay?

As you listen

2 🔲 **10.3** In the box below are the topics that students often talk about when they run into each other unexpectedly. As you listen to two students chatting, number the topics that they talk about in the order they talk about them. The first one has been done for you.

sport	holidays	weather
study **1**	relationships	paid work
music	hobbies	money
living arrangements		meeting again

Listen again

3 As well as *I've got to fly*, these speakers use a number of conversational expressions. Listen to the conversation again and try to note some of them down.

4 Check with a partner that you both understand these expressions. Which ones would you *not* use in the IELTS speaking test?

Tuning in

No Smoking

PG **PARENTAL GUIDANCE RECOMMENDED FOR PERSONS UNDER 15 YEARS**

1 What does each picture show?
2 What is the situation in your country?

For example

You don't have to wear a seat-belt in the passenger seat in Japan.

Listening

Before you listen

1 What is your opinion on each of the issues below?

As you listen

2 **11.1** Write Y (yes) or N (no) to indicate the speaker's opinion on each issue. Note: Not all of the issues are mentioned.

Do you think it is necessary for a government to:	Male	Female
a require everyone in cars to wear a seatbelt?	Y	Y
b set minimum pay rates?	Y +	Y
c establish a compulsory retirement age?	N N	N
d ban smoking in public places?	N x	N0
e control immigration?	Y	Y
f impose high taxes on alcohol?	N	N0
g pay mothers when they stop work to have babies?	✓	✓
h set maximum speed limits for drivers?	✓	✓
i prohibit advertising to children?	NG x	✓ NG

Modifying opinions

1 Put the word or phrase at the end of the line into the correct place in the sentence. The first one has been done for you as an example.

certainly

1 Yeah I/do   certainly

2 Minimum pay rates are necessary.   definitely

3 Yeah, there should—there should be minimum standards.   certainly

4 I don't agree with that that's necessary.   I don't think

5 Well then they could always be asked to retire.   I guess

6 They could be dealt with in the same way as other people in a similar job.   probably

7 I think in some public places, it's appropriate to ban smoking.   probably

8 I think you need to control immigration.   definitely

9 But yeah, there seems to be a need for some controls.   certainly

10 It's just a matter of imposing higher taxes.   I suppose

11 But there has to be a maximum speed limit.   of course

2 Listen to the speakers again and check your answers.

3 Write a + symbol or – symbol next to each word, to show whether it makes the opinion stronger or less strong.

For example

certainly +

Speaking

The structure of the extract below is similar to the final phase of the speaking test.

1 Write **D** in the box where the speaker is describing the situation, and **O** where she is giving her opinion about the situation.

A: Yeah how about the autobahn in Germany, though? Is there a speed limit there?

B: Umm, the thing is, there is no speed limit there, but people generally stick to a limit ... but it's like they're very organised when they drive, you know how they have the fast lane, the medium lane and the slow lane.   i ☐

A: And they're on straighter roads as well I guess.

B: They're very straight. And when you go in the fast lane, you only go to overtake someone, then you move out of it. So it's always clear. It's not like someone sits in the fast lane doing 50 K.   ii ☐

A: So maybe we don't need speed limits either?

B: Well, they're in big powerful cars, on good, straight roads. I don't think it would work here, because ...   iii ☐

2 Look at a–i on page 120. Work with a partner. Take turns to talk about each of the points.

· Describe the situation in your country.

· Give your opinion on if or how the situation could be improved.

Listening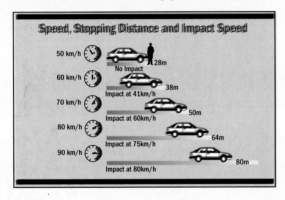

You will hear a lecture on the relationship between speed and the risk of an accident in which someone is injured.

Before you listen

1   What is the procedure for getting a driving licence in your country?

2   Do you think this procedure should be changed in any way—for example, in order to make it easier or more difficult to get a licence?

3   The following opinions are quite common. Do you agree with them?
    a   Traffic police only give speeding tickets to raise money for the government.
    b   Speeding is safe if you are a good driver.

4   What does the following graphic illustrate?

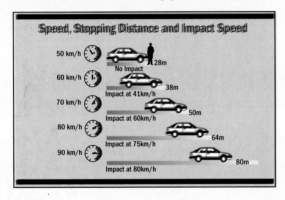

As you listen

5   **11.2 Listen to section 1.**
    a   Check that you understood the graphic correctly.
    b   Complete the table below, which shows how risk increases with speed.

Speed	Relative Risk
60	1.00 (base)
65	2
70	4·16
75	10·6
80	31.81
85	56·55

6   In section 2, you will hear three reasons why risk increases with speed. Complete the notes with one or two words in each space.

    1   Small diffs in speed = big diffs time to impact & ability to avoid ___an accident___

        Less time to:

        Recognise the ___danger___

        Decide on action (swerving or ___Breaking___)

        Complete evasive ___action___

    2   Small diffs in speed before braking = big diffs in ___Serious enjury___

    3   Small diffs in impact speed = big diffs in probability of ___too high___

After you listen

7   Do you believe this research?

8   Do you think you will drive more slowly after hearing this information?

9   What do you think can or should be done to increase road safety?

Writing

1   Write a 150–200 word summary of the table on speed and accident risk, including the reasons why the risk increases.

2   When you have completed the summary, assess it for the following points.

·   Conciseness and accuracy: does it contain all—and no more than—the key information?

·   Organisation and linking: is it logically organised and clearly linked?

·   Grammar and vocabulary: is the grammar and vocabulary accurate and appropriate?

Reading

Before you read

1 As you can tell from the headline, this article reports that smoking and drug use by teenagers in the USA has dropped. What possible reasons can you think of for this drop? Make a note of the reasons in the diagram below.

As you read

2 The article mentions four possible reasons for the drop. Are they the same as yours? If not, add them to the diagram.

3 According to the text, have the causes of the decrease in smoking been proven?

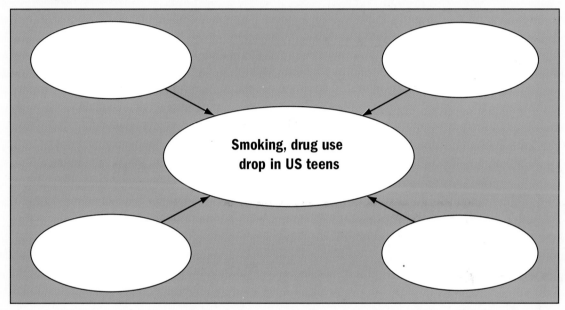

4 Draw a graph of the survey findings.

Smoking, drug use drop in US teens

by Maggie Fox

18 December 2002

REUTERS—Smoking, drinking and drug use are dropping among United States teens, an annual survey shows.

This meant prevention messages were working, the survey's authors and health officials said.

Smoking dropped 4 to 5 percentage points among 8th, 10th and 12th graders, the survey found.

Health officials said they were heartened and said they will continue to do what they have been doing. 'Prevention is an absolute priority. Prevention does work,' said Charles Curie, head of the Substance Abuse and Mental Health Services Administration.

Among 8th graders, aged 13 to 14, 10.7 per cent said they had smoked tobacco in the past thirty days, a big fall from the peak of 21 per cent in 1996 and down from 12.2 per cent last year.

Lloyd Johnston, a University of Michigan researcher who led the study, said several factors could have affected smoking.

'These include increasing prices, less tobacco advertising that reaches young people, more anti-smoking ads and a lot more negative publicity about the tobacco industry.'

In 1975, when the survey started, 73.6 per cent of 12th graders said they had smoked at some time in their lives. That dropped to 63 per cent in 1991 and 57.2 per cent last year.

Anti-smoking campaigners welcomed the finding.

'After experiencing alarming increases in youth smoking rates during the first half of the 1990s, we have turned the tide and today we can celebrate the fact that smoking among high school seniors is at its lowest level in at least twenty-seven years,' said William Corr, of the Campaign for Tobacco-Free Kids.

Using *mean*

This meant prevention messages were working, the survey's authors and health officials said.

5 It is possible to put the word *that* into this sentence. Where?

6 The first verb in this sentence (*mean*) is in the past tense. Why?

7 Try replacing *mean* with these verbs.

show	suggest	prove
demonstrate	imply	indicate

Which one(s):
a make the meaning stronger?
b make the meaning weaker?
c is/are similar in strength to *mean*?

After you read

8 This article is about the USA. How is the situation similar or different in your country?

9 Do you agree that smoking, drug use and drinking (alcohol) are problems:
a for teenagers?
b for adults?

10 If these are problems, which is the most serious? Why?

Speaking

1 If you want to solve or prevent a social or public health problem, what, in your view, is the most effective way of doing so?
- an advertising campaign
- new laws
- special taxes
- an education programme

2 Is there any other way to deal with these problems?

3 What, in general, is better: persuasion or compulsion?

4 Which approach, persuasion or compulsion, is evident in each of the news excerpts below?

LA schools ban soft drinks

LOS ANGELES—Soft drink sales will be banned to the 735 000 students in Los Angeles County schools amid worries about increasingly overweight children being fed junk food.

McDonald's taking waistline worries to heart

CHICAGO—McDonald's has made a weighty decision: to cook its French fries in a new oil that reduces fats linked to heart disease.

Coca-Cola starts youth physical fitness programme

ATLANTA—Soft drink giant Coca-Cola Co., accused in recent years of helping to fuel rising childhood obesity in the United States, unveiled today a campaign designed to make adolescents more physically fit.

Obesity hitting younger children in NZ, experts say

As obesity reaches epidemic levels across the developed world, New Zealand health experts are worried that the problem is affecting increasingly younger children. In response, some health campaigners advocate banning food ads during children's television hours and banning soft drinks from schools.

Listening

11.3 You will hear three people giving their views on the subject of obesity and advertising.

Before you listen

1   What views do you think each person will express on the relationship between obesity and advertising?
  i   Dr Richard Wilson, head of the National Institute for Dietary Research
  ii a representative of the Association of Food Producers and Processors
  iii a university student

2   Each person speaks in a different situation. Which person do you think will be speaking as part of:
  a   a research survey?
  b   a radio interview?
  c   a press release?

As you listen

3   Now listen to check your predictions.

Listen again

4   This time, make notes on how each person supports their basic position on the subject.

Speaking

1   In groups, design a campaign to deal with a social or public health problem such as speeding, smoking, gambling or underage drinking. In your group, decide on:
  ·   the problem you want to address
  ·   who your target audience is (teenagers, adults, male, female, etc.)
  ·   the medium you are going to use and what combination (education programme in schools, TV advertising, posters, magazine advertising, etc.)
  ·   the message you want to get across
  ·   exactly how you are going to communicate your message.

2   Present your idea to the class.

3   As a class, decide who:
  a   has identified the most significant or interesting problem.
  b   has designed the most effective campaign.

Reading

Before you read

1   What is a *brand*? Why is advertising important for brands?

2   Work by yourself: write down the first five brand names that you think of.

3   Compare your list with those of other students. How similar are they?

4   Do you think that your list reflects your personal preferences or lifestyle in any way?

As you read

5 The following article reports one major fact, and two opinions responding to that fact. As you read, write notes from the text in the table below.

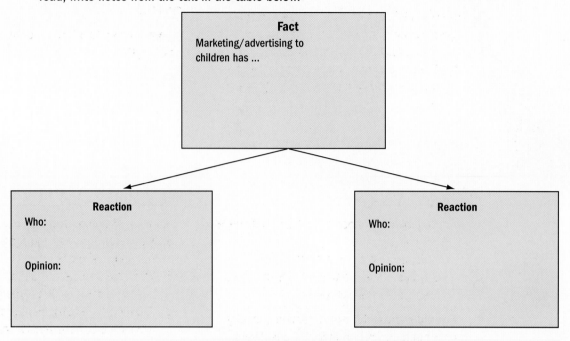

Fact
Marketing/advertising to children has ...

Reaction
Who:

Opinion:

Reaction
Who:

Opinion:

Experts split on branding for kids

The explosion in the advertising of food and drink to children in the past decade has divided expert opinion over whether it is an essential part of growing up or harmful to health, say two new reports.

Items such as Spiderman cereal, Barbie dolls who work at McDonald's and battery-operated sweets that spin in the mouth are contributing to a global epidemic of obesity, eating disorders and emotional problems, claims research in medical journal the Lancet.

But the Social Affairs Unit, an independent right-wing think-tank, argues in a pamphlet published yesterday that learning to handle advertisements is part of education.

'Young people should not be protected by increased regulation from advertising of products such as snacks, fizzy drinks, computer games and alcohol,' it says. 'Those who seek to impose further regulation do not have the research evidence on their side ... and may do harm.'

Spending on marketing to children, which has been regarded as increasingly acceptable in the past decade, rose to US$12 billion (NZ$25.5 billion) in the United States in 1999 as companies realised children could influence what their parents bought.

Doctors at a meeting organised by the Stop Commercial Exploitation of Children Coalition in New York last week warned that marketers were trying to own children's minds.

The brand names of food and drinks appeared on toy cars, and fast-food chains issued 'educational' card games.

A new kind of 'interactive candy' incorporated a lollipop into a battery-operated handle and carried names such as 'sound pops' and 'hot licks' which were operated 'when your tongue turns it on'.

The sexualisation of these products and the constant exposure to 'over-sexualised and underfed' images in the media were contributing to body image and other emotional problems, the meeting was told.

In its editorial, the Lancet recommends more radical solutions, including taxing soft drinks and fast foods, subsidising nutritious foods, labelling the content of fast food and prohibiting marketing and advertising to children.

But in his pamphlet for the Social Affairs Unit, *Growing Up with Advertising*, Adrian Furnham, professor of psychology at University College London, says many factors influence young people, most importantly their parents and peers.

'Around fifty years ago a myth was born about the power of advertising ... It is a conspiracy theory totally unsupported by the data ... Manufacturers spend vast sums to increase their total market share by small percentages.'

After you read

6   Which side of the argument do you personally favour?

7   Do you think that the article shows any bias towards one side of the argument or another?

   a   If so, which side does it favour?

   b   Or do you think that the article treats the two points of view in a balanced, neutral way?

According to Adrian Furnham, 'around fifty years ago a myth was born about the power of advertising'.

8   Do you agree that the power of advertising is a myth?

Reading

Before you read

1   Are the following statements true (T) or false (F), in your opinion?

   ·   Girls are smarter than boys.

   ·   Boys are better at some things than girls.

   ·   Men get all the best jobs.

2   If you disagree with the statements, modify or completely change them to reflect your own opinion.

As you read

The following text is about Britain.

3   According to the text, are these statements true (T), false (F), or not mentioned (NM)?

   a   Girls do better than boys at school.

   b   There are more women than men at university.

   c   Women do better than men in all subjects.

   d   Men earn more than women.

   e   Women get more financial advantage from university than men.

   f   Women and men with the same qualifications earn the same amount.

   g   The difference between men's and women's income is decreasing.

4   Which of the following sentences (A–D) best summarises David Bell's argument?

   A   Girls need to increase their advantage over boys at school, so that they can decrease their disadvantage at work.

   B   Girls do much better than boys at school, but men do better at work.

   C   School is unfair to boys, while work is unfair to women.

   D   Something must be done to improve the performance of boys at school.

Girls must do even better—schools chief

GIRLS, who already outperform boys in most exams, need to get even further ahead to make up for the discrimination they will suffer when they go out to work, the Chief Inspector of Schools believes.

Girls are far ahead of boys in national curriculum tests, a higher proportion of girls than boys go to university, and women win the best degrees in all but four subjects. But David Bell says they need to do even better 'if they are to gain the benefits that are properly theirs'.

A study by the Organisation for Economic Co-operation and Development last month showed that the gap in earnings with men was only half as great for women with degrees as it was for non-graduates competing with similarly qualified men. 'This means that girls get proportionately more value simply in terms of employment from university-level qualifications than boys. That is a significant finding for me,' Mr Bell said.

'Education beyond upper secondary level brings a particularly high earnings premium for women, although it has to be said that women earn less than men of similar educational attainment.

'The achievement of girls continues therefore to be a matter of pressing concern if girls are to overcome some of the disadvantages that are still inherent in our economy.'

Vocabulary

According to the text, girls outperform boys at school in Britain. Here, *perform* means *do*, and the prefix *out-* means *better than*. So *outperform* means *do better than*.

outdo	outgrow	outlive
outnumber	outplay	outrun
outsell	outsmart	outvote
outweigh		

5 The prefix *out* often has the meaning of *more*, *better*, or *longer*. What do you think the following words mean?

6 Check your guesses in a dictionary, then write an example sentence for each word.

Written and spoken language

The following sentences are packed with lots of information.

For example

A the Lancet recommends more radical solutions, including taxing soft drinks and fast foods, subsidising nutritious foods, labelling the content of fast food and prohibiting marketing and advertising to children.

B … said several factors could have affected smoking.

'These include increasing prices, less tobacco advertising that reaches young people, more anti-smoking ads and a lot more negative publicity about the tobacco industry.'

C Girls are far ahead of boys in national curriculum tests, a higher proportion of girls than boys go to university, and women win the best degrees in all but four subjects.

Each of these sentences lists a number of points. For example, sentence **a** lists four 'radical solutions':

· taxing soft drinks and fast foods

· subsidising nutritious foods

· labelling content of fast food

· prohibiting marketing and advertising to children

1 How many factors does sentence b list?

2 How many better results for girls does sentence c list?

These examples are typical of formal, written language. We tend to put more information in less space than we would use when we are speaking.

3 Re-write each of the sentences so that the information is less dense, and so that the grammar is more like spoken English.

For example

A The Lancet recommends four quite radical solutions. First, it recommends that the government taxes soft drinks and fast foods. A second solution is to …

Speaking

In the article about girls and education, David Bell argues that women suffer from discrimination in employment.

1   What groups do you know of that believe they are discriminated against?

2   Do you think that positive discrimination, where a company chooses a candidate for a position partly because they are a woman or come from a racial minority, is a good idea? What positive or negative consequences might it have?

3   Who would you choose in each of the situations below?
  a   Make notes for and against each candidate.
  b   Get together with two other students to discuss your views and make a decision.

You need to hire a mechanical engineer for your large ship-building company

> Mary Thomas is 23. She is the top mechanical engineering graduate from her class at university, and has already published two engineering research articles. This would be her first job.
>
> Peter Brown is 25. After leaving school, he worked for two years as a mechanic in a factory before beginning a mechanical engineering degree at university. He recently graduated with average grades; he did not have a lot of time for study as he has had a successful university sports career.

You are on the committee that decides which students can enter medical school. There is only one place left.

> John Watson is 18. His father is a plastic surgeon and his mother manages a private hospital. He has high grades in science from school and he speaks fluent Chinese, as his family lived in Hong Kong for three years when he was a child. His hobby is computing.
>
> Mark Smith is 37. He was a male nurse before quitting work to look after his two children after his divorce. His children are now at high school and old enough to look after themselves. He would like to train as a doctor and eventually become a paediatrician.

Writing

Some people believe that groups such as women, older people, ethnic minorities and the disabled do not receive full access to education and employment opportunities. They argue that it is therefore the government's responsibility to ensure equal opportunities for disadvantaged groups.

> What can or should the government do to ensure equal opportunities for everyone in society?
>
> What is your view?

There is no single, correct answer to an essay question. A good essay is one which expresses a clear, well-argued, personal response to the topic. There are many ways that you can do this.

1 Which approach would you take *in this case*? In other words, what is your personal view on this issue?

2 Expand the outline below (A, B or C) which reflects your personal view with supporting points.

3 Write the essay.

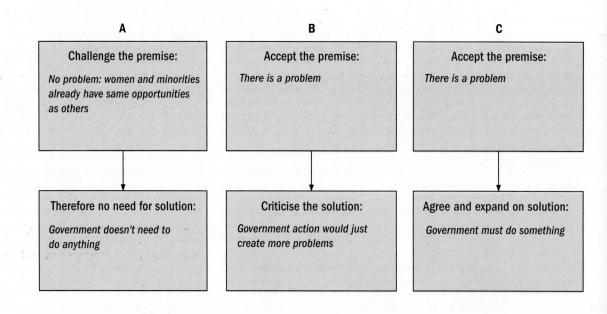

A

Challenge the premise:

No problem: women and minorities already have same opportunities as others

↓

Therefore no need for solution:

Government doesn't need to do anything

B

Accept the premise:

There is a problem

↓

Criticise the solution:

Government action would just create more problems

C

Accept the premise:

There is a problem

↓

Agree and expand on solution:

Government must do something

Vocabulary

The box below contains key vocabulary from this unit.

limit	prevent	law
ban	required	rules
prohibited	discriminate	impose
restrict	principle	

1   **Use the words in the box to complete the gaps below.**
- They want the government to change the _____.
- This is a very important _____—one which I believe in very strongly.
- One of his key responsibilities is to discipline students who break school _____.
- I try to stick strictly to the speed _____.
- The government is considering legislation to _____ immigration.
- Following the death of a boxer last month, there have been many calls to _____ the sport.
- Advertising by tobacco companies will also be_____.
- The French response was to _____ restrictions on salmon fishing.
- The public still need to do a lot more to help _____ crime.
- It is illegal for employers to _____ against people on the grounds of sex or marital status.
- Overseas students are _____ to produce proof of proficiency in English.

Speaking

'Do to others as you would have them do to you.'

This statement outlines a principle, also reflected in some religious doctrines, that many people find reasonable, and try to live by.

1   **What principles guide you in your life?**

2   **Where did these principles come from?**
- parents
- friends
- a religion
- a personal philosophy

3   **Do you ever find it difficult to keep to these principles?**

4   **Do you think principles like this should be taught at school?**

Tuning in

1 What is happening here?

2 What deeper meaning does this situation represent?

3 What is the connection between the picture and the advertised product?

Advertisers like to make a connection between certain values and their product. Below are some values which advertisers like to appeal to.

4 Tick the ones that are represented in the advertisement above.

5 Discuss your choices with your partner.

- ☐ Masculinity
- ☐ Femininity
- ☐ Environmental awareness
- ☐ Hygiene
- ☐ Fashion
- ☐ Family
- ☐ Physical comfort
- ☐ Independence
- ☐ Ambition
- ☐ Community
- ☐ Materialism
- ☐ Tradition

- ☐ Physical attractiveness
- ☐ Power
- ☐ Competitiveness
- ☐ Control
- ☐ Health
- ☐ Security
- ☐ Progress
- ☐ High technology
- ☐ Hard work
- ☐ Friendship
- ☐ Social status
- ☐ Nostalgia

6 Does this advertisement appeal to you, personally? Would it be effective in your culture?

Reading

Before you read

1 The advertisement on the previous page depicts a crossroads, where someone has to make an important choice. Do you personally find it easy to make big decisions?

As you read

2 **12.1** Listen to the poem as you read.
The poem is about:
a a travel decision
b a life decision
c both.

Read again

3 What do you think: True or False?
a It was an autumn morning.
b The decision was easy.
c He took the second path.
d He took the less common route.
e He thinks he will go back to the other one on another day.
f He regrets his decision.

THE ROAD NOT TAKEN

by Robert Frost

Two roads diverged in a yellow wood,
And sorry I could not travel both
And be one traveler, long I stood
And looked down one as far as I could
To where it bent in the undergrowth;
Then took the other, as just as fair,
And having perhaps the better claim,
Because it was grassy and wanted wear;
Though as for that the passing there
Had worn them really about the same,

And both that morning equally lay
In leaves no step had trodden black.
Oh, I kept the first for another day!
Yet knowing how way leads on to way,
I doubted if I should ever come back.

I shall be telling this with a sigh
Somewhere ages and ages hence:
Two roads diverged in a wood, and I
I took the one less traveled by,
And that has made all the difference.

Speaking

1 Draw a map of paths of your life up to this point, and possible future paths. Each fork should represent a major choice and decision. Label the forks.

2 Explain your map to your partner.

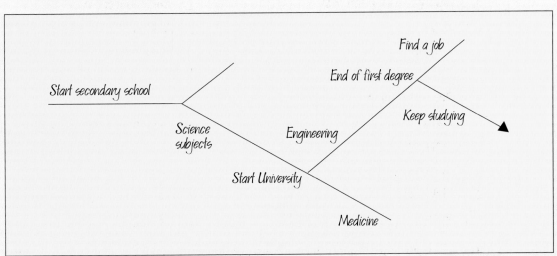

What if ...?

1 How could your life have been different? Choose a point in the past where you made an important decision. Write four sentences describing the possible consequences if you had made a different decision.

Condition		Result
If + Past Perfect	A	would/could/might + Perfect infinitive (have done, etc.)
	B	would/could/might + Present infinitive (be, live, be living, etc.)

For example

If I'd stayed at school for another year, I would've ...

If I'd studied Spanish, I'd be ...

Check your grammar

This type of sentence has two possible structures.

If + Past Perfect, *would* + Perfect infinitive (*have done*, etc.)

would + Present infinitive (*be, have, live*, etc.)

In both cases, the condition is in the past, which means that it cannot be changed.

2 The difference is that one result is about the past, and one is not. Which one is about the past, A or B?

3 Check that the grammar of the sentences that you wrote is correct.

4 Finally, explain your sentences to a partner.

Reading

Before you read

1 Is the glass half-full or half-empty?

2 What would an optimist answer?

3 What would a pessimist answer?

4 Are you an optimist or a pessimist?

The text on page 135 is from an article giving advice to managers. As the headline suggests, the article claims that optimists 'are more successful in work, health and life in general than pessimists.'

5 Why do you think this may be true?

As you read

6 Which paragraph or paragraphs contain the following information? The first one has been done for you as an example.

a General claim: optimists do better than pessimists. *Paragraph 2*

b How to identify optimists and pessimists.

c General behaviour of optimists.

d How pessimism can be controlled.

e How optimism profiling is done.

f How optimists react physically to stress.

g Work that optimists are good at.

h Contrasting rates of illness.

i Research evidence that optimists produce more.

j Why pessimists can be useful to a company.

k General behaviour of pessimists.

l Work that pessimists are good at.

m How optimism ratings are calculated.

Optimists are better performers than pessimists

1 Is the glass half-full or half-empty? Depends whether you're an optimist or a pessimist.

2 But those two words are more than casual labels: research has established that optimists have a consistent and upbeat way of dealing with adversity and that they are more successful in work, health and life in general than pessimists.

3 Optimists bounce back from trying times, generally with good grace, and see failure as a stepping-stone to success. Any problem tends to be minimised and dealt with later while the rest of life goes on as usual.

4 Their upbeat approach, resilience and perseverance makes them ideal for jobs in high-pressure areas where setbacks are part of the territory: sales, brokering, public relations, presenting, creative jobs and high burn-out posts. They are often a company's visionaries.

5 Pessimists, however, risk unravelling and sinking into depression when one thread of their life breaks. They are less likely to cope well with setbacks; they give up early or seek excuses.

6 Both types can be identified through optimism profiling, based on the pioneering work of American psychologist Martin Seligman, of the University of Pennsylvania.

7 Various studies, quoted in Seligman's book, *Learned Optimism*, found that pessimists have twice as many infectious diseases as optimists.

8 In hundreds of studies, people with high optimism scores out-performed and out-produced those with low scores, equating in sales terms to 20 to 40 per cent greater productivity.

9 More recent research shows optimistic and resilient people's belief that they have control over seemingly uncontrollable events enables specific molecules to be released by the brain that increase stress resilience, reduce anxiety and make for a less vivid emotional memory of stressful events. What you think and how you explain good and bad events to yourself—explanatory style—is the key to resilience, and is one of the things optimism testing captures.

10 The optimism profiling test sets up 12 situations—half good and half negative—and asks you to vividly imagine them, and record a likely major cause for each. The first situation—'You meet a friend who compliments you on your appearance'—is easy enough to imagine. You might scribble 'wearing something unusual/interesting'.

11 But pinpointing likely causes for other scenarios may be tougher: 'You give an important talk in front of a group and the audience reacts negatively' and 'You meet a friend who acts hostilely towards you.'

12 The test requires you then to rate the cause for each scenario on one-to-seven scales, which measure:

a Personalisation—Is this cause something about other people or circumstances, or something about you?

b Permanence—Is this a one-off cause or always a part of life?

c Pervasiveness—Does this cause affect just this thing, or all areas of your life?

13 The results deliver measurement of two specifics—reaction to adversity and reaction to success. Your reactions to both success and adversity are rated on a scale of one (low optimism) to five (high optimism). Then everything is crunched into an 'overall optimism rating', with each band representing 20 per cent of the population.

14 Heavy pessimism can be moderated. Among the techniques is 'thought-stopping', a way of blocking unhelpful rumination—you make an appointment with yourself to worry about it, and the unconscious mind feels relieved of it. And in practice, people generally never get around to the appointment—the need to worry has gone. Another major technique is learning how to dispute one's own critical internal explanations.

15 However, mild pessimism does have its place. According to Seligman, the mildly downbeat do well in low-pressure settings on jobs requiring a keen sense of realism: design and safety engineering, contract negotiation, law, statistics, technical writing, quality control, industrial relations management, and technical and cost estimating.

16 Says Seligman: 'The company also needs its pessimists; they must make sure grim reality intrudes upon the optimists. The treasurers, the business administrators, the safety engineers—all these need an accurate sense of how much the company can afford, and of danger.'

Word attack

7 Paragraph 2 says that *research has established that optimists have a consistent and upbeat way of dealing with adversity.*

   a In this context, *established* probably means _____.

   b Does *upbeat* probably mean *positive* or *negative*?

   c We usually *deal with a* _____ so this is what *adversity* probably means.

8 Paragraph 15 says that *According to Seligman, the mildly downbeat do well in low-pressure settings.*

There are two clues to the meaning of *downbeat*.

   a It is probably the opposite of _____.

   b The previous sentence in paragraph 15.

What do you think it means?

9 Paragraph 4 says *their upbeat approach, resilience and perseverance makes them ideal for jobs in ...*

   a What is the main point of this paragraph?

   b Do you need to understand the words *resilience* and *perseverance* to understand the main point?

After you read: Designing a questionnaire

This is how optimism profiling, explained in the article, works.

10 Follow the steps yourself.

---

1 Imagine this situation vividly.

You meet a friend who compliments you on your appearance.

2 Write down a likely cause for the compliment: _____

3 Rate this cause on the following scales (i.e., why did it happen?):

Because of other people/the circumstances   Because of me

  1   2   3   4   5   6   7

One-off cause   Always part of life

  1   2   3   4   5   6   7

Only happens in this case   Affects all parts of my life

  1   2   3   4   5   6   7

---

11 Now follow the same procedure with the following two scenarios.

  · You give an important talk in front of a group and the audience reacts negatively.

  · You meet a friend who acts hostilely towards you.

12 When you have done the procedure for all three scenarios, compare your answers with a partner. Which of you appears to be more optimistic?

Reading

Before you read

1   How long do you think humans will continue to live on this planet?

As you read

2   Label the clock with the following events from the text.

- Planet Earth is formed
- Life on earth begins
- Life on earth ends
- Current time
- Seas disappear
- Earth disappears

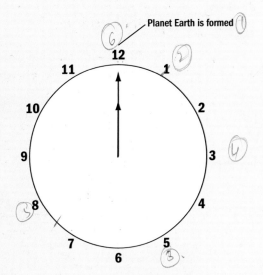

Planet Earth is formed

Beginning of the end has already begun

LONDON—The end of the world is not merely nigh*— it has already begun, claim two scientists.

Earth has already started the process of turning into a burned out cinder which will eventually be swallowed by the sun, according to US experts Donald Brownlee and Peter Ward.

They calculate that Earth's 'day in the sun' has reached 4.30 am, corresponding to its age of 4.5 billion years.

By 5 am, the billion-year reign of animals and plants will come to an end, say the Washington University astrobiologists.

At 8 am, the oceans will vaporise, and at noon—after 12 billion years—the expanding sun will engulf the planet and melt away any evidence that it ever existed.

'The disappearance of our planet is still 7.5 billion years away, but people really should consider the fate of our world and have a realistic understanding of where we are going,' said Brownlee.

'We live in a fabulous place at a fabulous time. It's a healthy thing for people to realise what a treasure this is in space and time, and fully appreciate and protect their environment as much as possible.'

Brownlee and Ward outline the Earth's doomsday timetable in a new book, *The Life and Death of Planet Earth.*

They use current knowledge of the planets, stars, and biology to provide a glimpse of the second half of life on Earth and what is likely to follow.

The scientists argue that higher life will be removed in much the same way that it came into being— ecosystem by ecosystem.

Eventually scorching heat will drive land creatures into the sea. But in the end even the oceans will become too hot for complex life forms.

'The last life may look much like the first life—a single-celled bacterium, survivor and descendant of all that came before,' the authors write.

The chances of humans surviving by moving to another planet or moon are not good, they claim.

*nigh = near

3   Do the following statements reflect the claims in the passage? Write (Y) Yes, (N) No or (NG) Not Given.

a   The sun is getting bigger. *Yes*

b   Life on earth will disappear suddenly. *No*

c   Life began in the ocean. *NG*

d   Thinking about the future is good for the present. *Yes*

e   Life in the sea will last longer than life on land. *Yes*

f   Moving to another planet is unlikely to be successful. *10 Yes*

After you read

4   Do you agree or disagree with the following statements?

- Thinking about the end helps us appreciate the present.

- We are not likely to survive on other planets.

- Human science and technology can solve this problem.

Speaking

1 The table below lists a set of global issues. For each issue, note down optimistic and pessimistic scenarios for the future.

Pessimistic scenario		Optimistic scenario
	Medicine	
	Global warming	
	Information technology	
	Genetic engineering	
	Education	
	World economy	

2 For each issue, are you personally more optimistic, or pessimistic?

3 With a partner, take one issue and survey the class. Is your class on the whole more optimistic or pessimistic on this issue?

Listening

4 12.2 Listen to other groups doing the same task.

5 Do they mention the same possibilities?

6 Do you agree or disagree with their personal views?

Writing

1 Write a report describing the following graphic.

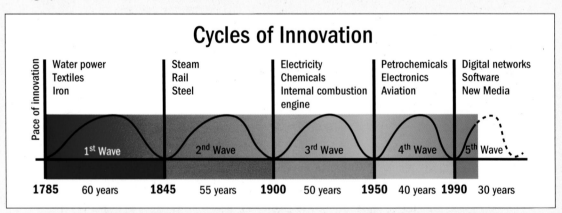

Speaking

2 Do you think it is possible for change to continue at this rate, or have we reached a natural limit?

3 What do you think will be the next big technological advance?

> It pays to be an optimist. But a little realism helps, as well.

4 Write a 250-word essay on this topic.

Listening: The future of work

Before you listen

1 *Time* magazine recently predicted that the following jobs would disappear during the 21st century:

- Stockbrokers, Auto dealers, Mail carriers, Insurance & Real estate agents
- Teachers
- Printers
- CEOs (chief executive officers)
- Prison Guards
- Truck Drivers
- Housekeepers
- Fathers

2 Why do you think each of these jobs might be under threat? Do you agree with the list?

Dr Michio Kaku, a physicist who thinks about the future, made contrasting predictions in his 1997 book, *Visions: How Science Will Revolutionize the 21st Century*. In the book he discusses jobs which will be 'in' (i.e., important in the future) and jobs which will be 'out' (i.e., may disappear). You will hear an excerpt from a review of his book.

As you listen

3 🔲 **12.3** Here is a list of jobs mentioned by Kaku. Write *in* or *out* next to each job, according to what the speakers say. The first one has been done as an example.

- Broadcasters   *in*
- Actors
- Journalists
- Printers
- Travel agents
- Car dealers

- Software developers
- Doctors
- Cleaners
- Teachers·
- Hotel staff

Listen again

4 Make a note of the reason why each job will be in or out. **Note:** there are many examples, but only a few general reasons.

For example

Broadcaster: creative, requires common sense

After you listen

5 Where do the *Time* article and Kaku disagree?

6 Do you personally agree more with the *Time* article, or more with Michio Kaku?

7 What do you think is the future outlook for the area that you currently work in, or hope to work in?

Reading

Now you have reached the end of this course, you are probably about to sit the IELTS exam. This text has some advice on sitting exams, and particularly on dealing with nervousness or anxiety.

Before you read

1 Some people enjoy exams. Do you?

2 What do you do to prepare for tests?

3 Do you get nervous or anxious?

4 What do you do, if anything, to control your anxiety?

As you read

5 There are 8 sections in the text. Next to the numbers 1–8

- write **B** if the strategy is most useful **before** the exam
- write **D** if it is useful **during** the exam
- write **B/D** if it is useful both before and during the exam.

1 _____		**5** _____
2 _____		**6** _____
3 _____		**7** _____
4 _____		**8** _____

Test Anxiety Reduction

Dr Carla Trujillo
UC Berkeley College of Engineering

1 Optimal Level of Performance

We have an optimal level of performance whenever we're doing anything that requires us to demonstrate something about ourselves, whether it be knowledge, a performance, or a sport. If we are too anxious, we exceed our optimal level and perform at a poorer rate due to the inability to concentrate, reason, or remember. On the other hand, if we are not excited enough, let's say due to exhaustion, we perform below our optimal level and perform poorly for similar reasons and with similar results. Therefore, the goal of performance anxiety reduction is to keep your performance level at the optimal or middle area, where you remain alert, attentive, but not over- or under-stimulated.

2 Have a Back-up Plan

We must always have back-up plans. Construct back-up plans for all that you do to insure that you will still obtain your desired goal no matter what the consequences are of the test you are taking. Ask yourself what will happen if you fail this test? What will happen if you fail the class? Will you simply have to repeat the class? Will this mean that you will no longer be able to be the engineer or scientist that you were intent on becoming? Of course not. If you create a back-up plan, or a 'worst case scenario,' you know that you have constructed a mechanism that will insure achieving your goal no matter the outcome of a particular test.

3 Assess Your Study Skills

When studying for a class, assess your knowledge of the material. Do you understand what is being taught in class? Are you studying properly? Do you review your notes after lectures? Do you study with others or at least try to do problem sets together? Do you speak to the professor if you're having any difficulties? Are you assertive about asking questions during class? Do you get extra tutoring help if necessary? Do you tape record lectures where you may be having problems?

You may need to slow yourself down while studying. Try getting a notebook with blank paper and dedicate one to each class. When you are reading your textbook, or any readings for the class, outline what you are reading in a careful and concise way. Make this outline good enough to enable you to review the outline for exam preparation in the future. Sometimes we are anxious when we are studying which doesn't enable us to learn the material properly, so slowing yourself down while you read enables you to absorb the material better.

4 Positive Visualisation

On the night before your exam (right before you go to sleep works well), find a quiet place to relax. Close your eyes. Pull your eyes to the top part of your head, roll up and back, then take two slow, deep breaths. Do this a couple more times. This is to get you more relaxed. Now, visualise yourself in the classroom taking the test. See yourself receiving the test, then calmly, confidently taking the exam. You are organised and alert. You are enjoying taking the test because you want to demonstrate just how much you know about the material. Create this movie in your head. You are in command and in control. Repeat the positive visualisation again in the morning, right before you get out of bed. When test time comes you will have already seen yourself confidently taking the test. Refer to this personal movie anytime during the test. This positive visualisation will help you realise what you are capable of achieving.

5 Breathing

If there is anything to take with you in learning test anxiety reduction, take the breathing exercise. You can do breathing exercises at anytime, before, during, and after the test. Breathing helps you stay emotionally grounded and rids the body of excess tension. It is also an effective way of reducing stress of any kind and only takes a moment to do.

If you can, close your eyes. Inhale through your nose deeply and slowly. Exhale slowly through your mouth. Do this two to three times or whenever you feel excess anxiety building up. This is an easy and effective exercise to do throughout the test.

6 When the Test is Handed Out

When the test is handed out, do a quick breathing exercise if necessary. Quickly assess the test. What are the major point items on the test? What do you see expected of you on the test? Try to very quickly calculate how much time you should spend per question so that you attempt to complete the test. Go for the major point items over smaller points. Work quickly and efficiently. Use your personal positive visualisation 'movie' to keep up your confidence and the breathing exercises to keep your energy at the optimal performance level.

7 Recover Your Academic Self-Esteem

Go back in your memory through time and try to remember all your accomplishments since you were a child. This will refresh your memory regarding how smart you were and continue to be.

8 Bringing Yourself To Consciousness During an Exam

If, during an exam, you find yourself starting to blank out or panic, try to stop and ask yourself these questions:
   What am I doing?
   Why am I doing it?
   What am I going to do about it?
   If you can come to some sense of consciousness during a moment while you are panicking or blanking out, you can possibly bring yourself to a calmer place because by recognising what you are doing, you give yourself a sense of control. Regaining control of your thoughts and emotions during an exam is crucial to doing well.

Read again

6   Read the text again more carefully and slowly. Your task is simply to think about and, where appropriate, do what the text suggests.

After you read

7   Do you think you will use any of the suggestions in the IELTS exam?

Speaking: Looking back, looking forward

Spend a few minutes thinking about the following questions. Then discuss them with a partner.

As a result of doing this course:
   a Has your English improved?
   b Have your chances of doing well in IELTS improved?
   c Which is more important for you, **a** or **b**?
   d How will you use your IELTS result?
   e How do you expect or hope to use English in the future?

Academic Word List

abandon	benefit	consist	displace	facilitate
abstract	bias	constant	display	factor
academy	bond	constitute	dispose	feature
access	brief	constrain	distinct	federal
accommodate	bulk	construct	distort	fee
accompany	capable	consult	distribute	file
accumulate	capacity	consume	diverse	final
accurate	category	contact	document	finance
achieve	cease	contemporary	domain	finite
acknowledge	challenge	context	domestic	flexible
acquire	channel	contract	dominate	fluctuate
adapt	chapter	contradict	draft	focus
adequate	chart	contrary	drama	format
adjacent	chemical	contrast	duration	formula
adjust	circumstance	contribute	dynamic	forthcoming
administrate	cite	controversy	economy	foundation
adult	civil	convene	edit	found
advocate	clarify	converse	element	framework
affect	classic	convert	eliminate	function
aggregate	clause	convince	emerge	fund
aid	code	cooperate	emphasis	fundamental
albeit	coherent	coordinate	empirical	furthermore
allocate	coincide	core	enable	gender
alter	collapse	corporate	encounter	generate
alternative	colleague	correspond	energy	generation
ambiguous	commence	couple	enforce	globe
amend	comment	create	enhance	goal
analogy	commission	credit	enormous	grade
analyse	commit	criteria	ensure	grant
annual	commodity	crucial	entity	guarantee
anticipate	communicate	culture	environment	guideline
apparent	community	currency	equate	hence
append	compatible	cycle	equip	hierarchy
appreciate	compensate	data	equivalent	highlight
approach	compile	debate	erode	hypothesis
appropriate	complement	decade	error	identical
approximate	complex	decline	establish	identify
arbitrary	component	deduce	estate	ideology
area	compound	define	estimate	ignorance
aspect	comprehensive	definite	ethic	illustrate
assemble	comprise	demonstrate	ethnic	image
assess	compute	denote	evaluate	immigrate
assign	conceive	deny	eventual	impact
assist	concentrate	depress	evident	implement
assume	concept	derive	evolve	implicate
assure	conclude	design	exceed	implicit
attach	concurrent	despite	exclude	imply
attain	conduct	detect	exhibit	impose
attitude	confer	deviate	expand	incentive
attribute	confine	device	expert	incidence
author	confirm	devote	explicit	incline
authority	conflict	differentiate	exploit	income
automate	conform	dimension	export	incorporate
available	consent	diminish	expose	index
aware	consequent	discrete	external	indicate
behalf	considerable	discriminate	extract	individual

induce	maximize	phase	rely	sufficient
inevitable	mechanism	phenomenon	remove	sum
infer	media	philosophy	require	summary
infrastructure	mediate	physical	research	supplement
inherent	medical	plus	reside	survey
inhibit	medium	policy	resolve	survive
initial	mental	portion	resource	suspend
initiate	method	pose	respond	sustain
injure	migrate	positive	restore	symbol
innovate	military	potential	restrain	tape
input	minimal	practitioner	restrict	target
insert	minimise	precede	retain	task
insight	minimum	precise	reveal	team
inspect	ministry	predict	revenue	technical
instance	minor	predominant	reverse	technique
institute	mode	preliminary	revise	technology
instruct	modify	presume	revolution	temporary
integral	monitor	previous	rigid	tense
integrate	motive	primary	role	terminate
integrity	mutual	prime	route	text
intelligence	negate	principal	scenario	theme
intense	network	principle	schedule	theory
interact	neutral	prior	scheme	thereby
intermediate	nevertheless	priority	scope	thesis
internal	nonetheless	proceed	section	topic
interpret	norm	process	sector	trace
interval	normal	professional	secure	tradition
intervene	notion	prohibit	seek	transfer
intrinsic	notwithstanding	project	select	transform
invest	nuclear	promote	sequence	transit
investigate	objective	proportion	series	transmit
invoke	obtain	prospect	sex	transport
involve	obvious	protocol	shift	trend
isolate	occupy	psychology	significant	trigger
issue	occur	publication	similar	ultimate
item	odd	publish	simulate	underground
job	offset	purchase	site	underlie
journal	ongoing	pursue	so-called	undertake
justify	option	qualitative	sole	uniform
label	orient	quote	somewhat	unify
labour	outcome	radical	source	unique
layer	output	random	specific	utilise
lecture	overall	range	specify	valid
legal	overlap	ratio	sphere	vary
legislate	overseas	rational	stable	vehicle
levy	panel	react	statistic	version
liberal	paradigm	recover	status	via
licence	paragraph	refine	straightforward	violate
likewise	parallel	regime	strategy	virtual
link	parameter	region	stress	visible
locate	participate	register	structure	vision
logic	partner	regulate	style	visual
maintain	passive	reinforce	submit	volume
major	perceive	reject	subordinate	voluntary
manipulate	percent	relax	subsequent	welfare
manual	period	release	subsidy	whereas
margin	persist	relevant	substitute	whereby
mature	perspective	reluctance	successor	widespread

Unit 1, Listening 1.1

OK … so I used to live quite close to my primary school, just about a hundred metres down the hill, in fact. I can still remember the school quite clearly, although I haven't been back there for more than thirty years now.

When you walked in the gate, there was a big concrete playground in front of you. It had these seats around the outside that we sat on to eat our lunch. There was an office block on the left—the principal's office and secretary, and—I'll never forget—a nurse's clinic and small dental clinic on the right.

The classroom I was in during my first year at school was directly across the playground from the gate, and my second year classroom was just to the left of that, I think.

There were a couple of fields behind the classrooms and down the hill to the right. I remember on the weekends we used to slide down that hill on cardboard boxes …

Unit 1, Listening 1.2

1 There was an office block on the left.
2 There were a couple of fields.

Unit 1, Listening 1.3

Over the last twenty-five years, researchers in education have made two important points: the first is that learning is more important than teaching; and therefore, what students do is much more important than what teachers do. Think about that for a moment—what students do is much more important than what teachers do.

And the second point, which follows from the first, is that students take different approaches to learning; or in other words, students learn in different ways. It's possible to divide these different approaches into two main types: the *deep* approach to learning and, by contrast, the *surface* approach to learning.

Let's look first at the deep approach. Students who take a deep approach aim to understand and use the subject. They also value the subject: they think it's important and, usually, enjoyable. What are the characteristics of these learners? Well, first of all, they actively try to understand the material they are learning and the subject in general; and second, they are motivated by interest; they also take a general view of the subject and relate different ideas to each other; for example, they relate new ideas to what they've already learned, and they relate ideas to their everyday life and experience. Finally, they tend to read and study more than the course actually requires them to. So, that's the deep approach.

Students who take a surface approach on the other hand, have the main aim of passing an exam or getting a qualification. They are not so interested in the subject itself or in really understanding it. Of course, teachers generally think that most students take this approach. How can this approach be characterised? Well, for a start, these students try to learn in order to repeat what they have learned: they memorise information needed for tests; they make use of rote learning—that is, they repeat information again and again until they can remember it by heart. Second, they take a narrow view and concentrate on detail, rather than on the 'big picture. And they tend to do only what the course requires them to do and no more; finally, they are motivated by fear of failure—they are afraid to fail the exam.

Educators believe that the most effective *students* are those who take a deep approach, while the best *teachers* are the ones that encourage students to take a deep approach: to be motivated, interested and really try and understand what they are learning.

Unit 1, Listening 1.4

Part 1

S: So do you think computers in education are useful?
N: Yeah, quite a lot, actually. I certainly wouldn't agree with 'to improve education, forget computers'. I'd say I'm more in favour of them than against them.
S: In what way do you think they're useful?
N: Well I think computers can be very motivating for many students: they're actually more interested in what they're studying because it's coming to them through a computer.
S: But there are students who don't like computers, and I think it can have the opposite effect on them … although I suppose everyone is exposed to computers now and there'll be less and less of these people as time goes by. And also, a lot of adults use computers at work … maybe they don't want to study the same way that they work.

N: Yeah, I guess so. Umm, I suppose those kinds of technical issues and problems can actually reduce the time that you spend learning in the end.
S: I also think it's a mistake to think that you can replace the classroom with a computer, because part of that's, y'know, a valuable learning resource is mixing with all the other students and learning from them. Interacting with a computer is certainly not like interacting with another person.
N: Yeah, but I think there are some students who really like not having to interact with other people … interacting with a computer is safe for them. I guess it really all depends on your individual learning style, doesn't it? There's also an issue about access to computers … umm students who have less knowledge of computers, or students who don't actually have access to computers in everyday lives, maybe they get disadvantaged in, umm, education that makes use of computers.
S: Well, I suppose if computers do come to dominate education, then some people will have a limited education because not all schools can provide the same kind of facilities, can they?
N: No, you're right.

Part 2

A: What's your opinion on computers in education, Martin?
M: Well I certainly think they have a place, but it's quite limited.
A: Yeah, right, they're like a useful … tool, but it all—really depends on the skill of the user.
M: Mmm … basically, students need to interact with humans to learn effectively … y'know, they find it hard to find answers on the computer … or rather, they can't find the reasons for the answers on the computer … and they can't get help easily when they get stuck.
A: Right … I'd say the most important thing is that computers should be a *part* of a well-designed education system, not the central—not the main factor.
M: And I think it's easy to forget other technology that can be useful in the classroom, apart from computers … video, I think, can be very motivating, because sight is such a strong sense … it really helps students understand and remember.
A: Sure … Outside technology, the quality of the teacher is especially important … I remember some fantastic teachers from school…they made learning fun, and when it's fun, it's memorable too.
M: The personality of the teacher is the key for me: I found that I got the best results with teachers who had a strong personality … y'know, a confident teaching style.
A: Mmm … Having small class sizes is also a real advantage if possible…I mean, you can have lots of computers in a classroom, but if there's too many students for each teacher, then I think the quality of the education will be lower.
M: Yeah, I agree. I also think in general that we need to offer teachers higher pay … to attract higher-quality teachers. I know that a lot of teachers leave—end up leaving the job because they don't feel they are respected in a financial sense.
A: I think that also applies in terms of the social status of teachers … it's not a profession that's respected socially any more … We need to give teachers support— more support in several different ways: umm, more money, more training … in the end, that's what will lead to improved education.
M: Mmm … basically, we need to find a balance between *human* resources and *technological* resources.

Unit 2, Listening 2.1

When I was a kid, we used to go to the Mediterranean coast every summer. We'd usually stay a couple of weeks and we'd go down to the beach every day to swim.

Unit 2, Listening 2.2

Topic 1

A monsoon climate is one where the wind changes direction with the season, and this brings a major change in the weather. We usually think of the monsoon as the rainy season, but actually it refers to the climate pattern over the whole year. The best-known example is in the Indian Ocean area. Here, the wind blows from the south-west, across the Indian Ocean, from about April to October, usually bringing heavy rain. Then, from October to April, it blows in the opposite direction, from the north-east, and it's much drier. Other areas of Asia also experience monsoons: parts of China, Japan and Korea, for instance, and Indonesia and Thailand in South-East Asia. One welcome effect of the monsoon rains is that they cool temperatures after the hot spring months. They also damp down dust storms and their most vital role is to provide water for agriculture. But they can also have unwelcome effects: heavy monsoons bring floods, sometimes the winds bring dangerous tropical storms, and sometimes the rains don't come at all, which is devastating for an area which is so dependent on the monsoon rains.

Topic 2

Water pollution comes from both direct and indirect sources. Water is polluted *directly* when we throw or pour something straight into the water that shouldn't be there: household rubbish, waste from factories, etc. *Indirect* sources include pollutants in the soil, like agricultural fertilisers and pesticides, which enter the groundwater or wash off the land into rivers, and air pollution from things like cars and factories, which enter the water supply from rainwater. What can we do about it? Well, better science will help: new technologies in factories and cars mean that we will put less pollution into the air, which means less pollution to get into our water. But personal choices are also important: every time we decide to drive rather than walk, or whenever we buy products with lots of packaging, we're helping to put more pollution into the air or the ground, and we know that it will eventually find its way into our water.

Topic 3

Well, there are quite a lot of pluses compared to other ways of generating electricity: for example, no fuel is burnt, so there's minimal pollution; and the water is provided free, by nature; and it's renewable: when it rains, it fills up the reservoir, the lake that holds the water, so the fuel is almost always there. In fact, if it looks so good, why don't we use it all the time? Well, basically because there are a lot of drawbacks: you need *lots* of water, and *lots* of land to build the dam and the reservoir; and it takes an awful lot of money and time and construction. Also, most of the good spots for hydro stations have already been taken, so it's really difficult to build new ones.

Unit 2 Listening 2.3

Well, there are quite a lot of pluses compared to other ways of generating electricity: first of all, for example, no fuel is burnt, so there's minimal pollution; secondly, the water is provided free, by nature; and a third advantage is that it's renewable: when it rains, it fills up the reservoir, the lake that holds the water, so the fuel is almost always there. In fact, if it looks so good, why don't we use it all the time? Well, basically, because there are a lot of drawbacks. One important drawback is that you need *lots* of water, and *lots* of land to build the dam and the reservoir. Which leads to the second problem, it takes an awful lot of money and time and construction. But perhaps the biggest issue is that most of the good spots for hydro stations have already been taken, so it's really difficult to build new ones.

Unit 2, Listening 2.4

E: Umm, it's used for drinking …
D: Yeah, that's the most obvious one … it can be drunk in lots of different ways.
E: You mean by animals?
D: No, I mean as other kinds of drinks—coffee, tea and so on.
E: So it's made into other drinks?
D: Yeah.
E: OK.
D: Water is used for washing … washing the car
E: Washing, yeah
D: Ourselves and our clothes …
E: Dishes …
D: Dishes, yeah … cars and things … water is used to … wash your house
E: Bodies, cars, houses, windows … cleaning your teeth
D: It's used in the production of a lot of things, like paper … there's a lot of water involved in making paper.
E: Mmm, OK … umm, what else? Cooking …
D: Cooking of course, yeah, boiling and so on.
E: Yeah … swimming
D: And boating, fishing … social uses
E: Right, sports activities … it's used for skiing and skating on, when it's frozen.
D: What about cars, keeping the engine cool … in the radiators of cars and trucks?
E: And for heating too.
D: And heating, yeah, so for cooling and heating.
E: Making electricity …
D: Yeah, producing electricity, hydroelectric power

E: Dams and things
D: For transport … boats, ships … submarines …
E: Yeah, right … for watering crops, irrigation, that's a really important use.
D: Yeah, so for producing food … that's about all I can think of.

Unit 2, Listening 2.5

Water is used to … wash your house
Water is used for washing … washing the car.

Unit 2, Listening 2.6

OK, so what you can see here are the trends in water use in different categories in the US, over 40 years from 1950 to 1990. The units are billions of gallons per day.

So, the most striking feature is the massive increase—about 500% in fact—for electricity production. It went up from about 40 billion gallons in 1950 to about 195 billion gallons in 1990. And that doesn't even include hydroelectricity: this graph just shows the water that's used for cooling in nuclear and fossil fuel stations—you know … coal, gas and oil stations.

Rural use, mainly drinking water for farm animals—that's it in front here—is the smallest category—only about 8 billion gallons in 1990, but it doubled over this period. That's mainly because livestock farming has become a lot more intensive—farmers are able to put a lot more animals on their land. Public supply … is another one that's kept going up. That's partly population pressure, of course—there were about 250 million Americans in 1990, compared to 150 million in 1950, but the public supply went up a lot more—it nearly tripled, and in fact more water is now used for public supply than is used in industry.

The trends with irrigation and industry in fact are a little more promising. You can see that irrigation—the light blue—peaked at about 130 billion gallons in 1980 and then started falling, and industrial use—the yellow—peaked in 1980 also. That's basically because technology got better: you know, machines have been computerised so that they only water plants when it's really necessary, and so they give just the right amount. There's less waste.

Unit 2, Listening 2.7

B: So why do you personally drink bottled water?
F: Oh, mainly for the taste … and the convenience—it's always good having a drink with you.
B: Well, I'd agree with you that it does taste better than tap water.
F: There's the health aspect too: I know it doesn't really come from a place like the picture on the label, but it's still a pure and natural product.
B: Oh come on! It sounds like you're a victim of their marketing tricks.
F: No, no I'm not. I don't have one preferred brand, I don't mind which one I buy. What about you, don't you ever buy bottled water?
B: Oh, yeah, I do sometimes … I'm like you, I just get whichever brand is cheapest. But actually I'd rather buy a water filter and use that—just as good as the bottled stuff, and cheaper in the long run.
F: I suppose so, but bottled water's not exactly expensive relative to other sorts of drinks, is it?
B: Yeah … I guess what I really object to is something as plain and unaltered as water becoming a luxury: y'know, some kinds of water are better than others, more expensive than others. It's all just packaging.
F: Sure, but you could say that about a million kinds of products—that's what marketing's all about! Anyway, it *is* different for water: in lots of countries, there really are different grades of water, and sometimes you really can't drink the water from the tap—not safely, anyway. You're just lucky you come from a country where you can actually drink water straight out of the tap. I think you're right about the packaging, though: it seems really wasteful.
B: Mmm, I always think it's a lot of quite sophisticated designing and production to just use once then throw away … So do you think it's just a trend, like a fashion? Are we all going to get sick of water soon and move on to something else?
F: No, I don't think so … people are more and more aware of staying healthy, and it's all part of that … I'd say bottled water is here to stay.

Unit 3, Listening 3.1

Interview 1

A: Hello there, how can I help you?
S: Hi, umm, I was wondering if you could just give me some advice. Umm, yeah, I've just finished secondary school, and umm, well, I know what field I'm inter-

ested in, but I—I don't really know how to get there, y'know, what to do …
A: Mm-hmm, OK. Which—which field are you interested in?
S: Advertising.
A: All right. Why advertising, why does that interest you?
S: Uhh, well, I suppose I'm creative and … quite artistic and so I'd really like to use my abilities in that field … and umm, yeah, I've always thought that advertising's very relevant to everyday life, it's … something that we see everywhere.
A: Mmm … and why are you interested in those particular areas, the creative and artistic areas?
S: Well, I've studied art, and also economics, at secondary school, and umm … I've always been interested in ads … I analyse good ads, and …yeah.
A: OK, well the first thing to do for you really is, umm, we should make a list of all the advertising courses available. Now, umm, I can show you a very good website which helps you do this, that shows all the courses that are available in this country.
S: OK … and umm, do you advise a university or polytech?
A: That depends really. Umm, in terms of polytech, you can go there straight after secondary school, they offer very, ahh … practical courses, which is good … you would then probably start at a lower level, within a company, and … and work your way up. In terms of university, you'd have to first do a degree that wasn't connected with advertising, and then specialise … so for example, maybe do a degree in film and television studies, and then do a post-graduate diploma in advertising.
S: Right.
A: This course is obviously longer than going to a polytech, but then you would probably start working in a company, in an advertising company, at a higher level.
S: And umm, how would I go about choosing a course?
A: Well, you have to look at first of all the more general features, that is, the reputation of the school or university that you're thinking about, and umm, lifestyle factors like how convenient is it for you, for where you live and so on … but it's also important to look at very specific things, such as the exact content of the particular course you're looking at, the price, of course, the reputation of the teachers who are who—are in that department … the opinion of the industry, of the employers in the advertising industry … concerning that particular course.
S: Right. Well, it's been very helpful, thank you very much.
A: You're welcome.

Interview 2

A: Hi, what can I do for you today?
S: Hi … umm I've just finished secondary school … well, actually I—I just don't know what career to choose, I don't know what to study. The thing is, I want to study something useful, y'know something that leads to a job.
A: Mmm, yeah … in general, you can divide tertiary courses into two groups, there are the non-vocational courses … now these teach you very useful academic skills and thinking skills, but there is no specific job that they're leading to afterwards … and then of course there are the other courses that are … are vocational or professional, and they do lead to jobs, so things like … a law degree quite clearly leads to being a lawyer.
S: OK.
A: Generally, I tell people that they should start with their—with their own interests, because if you enjoy what you're studying, then … probably you'll get a job that you like afterwards. Umm, we actually have some very useful software … that helps you to assess … your interests and the kind of occupations that you will find interesting … so at some stage I'll show you that, and maybe we can get you started there.
S: OK.
A: What subjects did you enjoy doing at school?
S: Well, I, umm, I didn't like maths or the sciences very much … but, yeah, I really like languages, and I like history and geography as well.
A: OK … why do you think you liked these subjects?
S: Umm, I think because they're connected to cultures … and they're about real people and … and their lives.
A: Well, those interests, they sound to me like they point in the direction of an Arts degree, really.
S: Mmm, yeah, but I don't want to be a teacher.
A: Well, it's not the only choice, if you're, if you have an Arts degree … there are many possibilities, and one thing I can do is help you to … to research the other kinds of career paths that graduates in languages and social sciences can follow. There really are no limits for any degree at all. Umm, for example, just recently,

I talked to a language graduate who then went on to become a financial analyst in her first job … so that's a good example.
S: Right.
A: So may be we can have a look at that software now …

Unit 3, Listening 3.2

Section 1

A majority of Americans in general are in this category, and an even higher percentage of managers: one study found that 60 per cent of the managers they surveyed were clearly this type.
Employees of this type are the ones who, first of all, work long, hard hours under constant time pressure. In other words, they routinely work under the conditions that lead to overload and burnout. Secondly, they often take work home at night or on weekends, and they're unable to relax when work ends—they can't leave the office at the office. They also seem to be constantly competing with themselves, always trying to do better and setting incredibly high standards that are extremely difficult to maintain. Lastly, this kind of person tends to become frustrated by their work situation, they often express irritation with the work efforts of others —no-one else ever works hard enough; and they often seem to be misunderstood by their superiors.

Unit 3, Listening 3.3

Section 2

The sad truth is that Type As are much more prone to the worst outcome of stress—heart attacks. One study found that compared with Type Bs, Type As are twice as likely to suffer from heart disease. It's ironic that in most companies and organisations, Type As are the ones that are typically on the 'fast track' to the top, to the management positions. And in general, they tend to be more successful than Type Bs. However, it's interesting that at the *very* top, in the executive positions of big corporations, Type As do not tend to be as successful as Type Bs, because the Type Bs are more patient and take a broader view of things. The key is to change from Type A to Type B behaviour, at least in some aspects; but, of course, most Type As are unable to make this kind of a change or to manage their Type A characteristics. And, in fact, they are generally unwilling to even try to do so.

Unit 3, Listening 3.4

Section 1

Over the last couple of generations, there has been little change or variation in the way that people work. People have started a job after they leave school and continued in the same job, or at least the same company, until they retire. It has, in fact, been a job for life. And people have worked more or less the same hours: 9 to 5, Monday to Friday or Monday to Saturday. Now, on the other hand, there are more changes in career—people change from one job to another—and people are not just working 9 to 5. There are, in fact, many alternatives to the traditional way of working … and companies that are trying to attract good staff really should consider some of these alternative work arrangements. There are good reasons for considering these alternatives … for example, the company could attract staff who can't, or won't, work traditional hours. For example, mothers who are returning from maternity leave after having children, or those who are caring for elderly relatives … or even those who are wanting to spend more time on leisure, or with their family.

Unit 3, Listening 3.5

Section 2

The first alternative to consider is the job-share. This is where one job is shared by two people. It differs from part-time work because the job can't be done part-time; in fact, it is a full-time job, and is shared by two people. So these two people must communicate with each other.
The part-time job, the second alternative, is of course when people work less than full-time, and where there is less need to communicate with colleagues.
The third alternative is flexi-time. This is where the worker, the employee, works flexible hours which he or she has agreed with the employer. For example, the worker may choose, and the employer may agree, that the worker can work a 5-day week in 4 days, so that they have a 3-day weekend; or the worker may be able to start and finish at any time during the day as long as he or she works for 8 hours.
The fourth alternative is tele-commuting. This is where the worker works from

home for part or all of the week using telecommunications, and the worker is in constant communication with the office by phone, by fax or by computer. The worker may need to attend work once a week or so for a face-to-face meeting with colleagues.

The fifth alternative, working from home, is very similar, but there's less need to stay in constant contact with the office, so the worker has less need to visit the office, may in fact live quite a long way from the office.

Unit 3, Listening 3.6

B: OK, so what we're looking at here is the idea that 'The unemployed don't want to work because everyone who really wants a job can find one.' What do you think about that?

A: Yeah, yeah, I think that's probably quite close to the truth … umm, I hear about employers all the time who desperately need workers, and they can't find people. And yet there's all these people who say they can't find jobs. I mean, what's the problem here?

N: No, I have a problem with 'don't want to work', umm, because I don't believe that unemployed people don't have jobs because they don't *want* to work, it's because they really can't get jobs in the right area, y'know, in the area where they live.

A: In the area that suits them …

B: Yeah, so there's the location factor, as well as the education factor.

A: Mmm.

N: The qualifications they've got matching the qualifications needed for the jobs that are actually available.

A: Yeah I can see what you mean … I mean, saying that they don't want to work, I guess they do possibly want to work but, y'know, why couldn't they just perhaps do a slightly different job, even if it doesn't suit them, you often just have to change your career direction, don't you?

B: So what could we say … '*Some* unemployed don't want to work'?

N: Yeah, that would be closer … I'd go with that.

A: Yeah, mm …Yeah, we don't know how many, what percentage of them don't want to work, but I think you could say that *some* don't … and of course some do. Yeah.

B: Would it be 'most', 'the majority' …? Or just 'some'?

N: I wouldn't go more than 'some'. I'd say that most people genuinely, if they could work, they would be working.

A: Mmm, yeah, I'd go along with that, actually.

N: What about the second part of the sentence?

B: '…because everyone who really wants a job can find one.'

A: Well, we need to change that to 'because *most* people', I guess. Well, no, 'because *some* people who really want a job can find one'.

B: '*Some* unemployed don't want to work because *some* people who really want a job can find one'… that doesn't make sense, does it?

A: 'Some unemployed don't want to work, but the majority …

N: '… who really want a job…

B: '… can't find one.' '… but most unemployed people … really want a job but can't find one.'

N: So: 'although some unemployed don't want to work, many unemployed really want a job, but just can't find one.'

A: Yeah, that sounds good.

B: I'm happy with that.

Unit 3, Listening 3.7

a Have you recently been able to concentrate on whatever you're doing?

b Have you recently lost much sleep over worry?

c Have you recently felt that you were playing a useful part in things?

d Have you recently felt capable about making decisions about things?

e Have you recently felt constantly under strain?

f Have you recently felt you couldn't overcome your difficulties?

g Have you recently been able to enjoy your normal, day-to-day activities?

h Have you recently been able to face up to problems?

i Have you recently been feeling unhappy or depressed?

j Have you recently been losing confidence in yourself?

k Have you recently been thinking of yourself as a worthless person?

l Have you recently been feeling reasonably happy, all things considered?

Unit 4, Listening 4.1

N: So, Sarah, what do you think this is?

S: Well, that to me looks like a microchip embedded in a tooth.

N: Hmm. What do you think they use it for?

S: Umm … could be a microcomputer…

N: Yeah? For tracking people?

S: Could be. Identification chip.

N: Identification chip! Sounds good.

S: So maybe it sends a signal to a computer when you go through a scanner or something.

N: Ahh. So they can tell where you've been, where you're from … I dunno … Could be that … Maybe it's for listening … a secret James Bond gadget for listening and spying on people.

S: Mmm.

N: OK. What about this other one? What do you think this is?

S: Looks like a moon buggy. Don't you think?

N: It does. Do you think it's on Mars?

S: Doesn't look like it's on Mars … it could be a desert somewhere I suppose.

N: Yeah.

S: Looks like a radio-controlled device.

N: Yes, yes … sounds right.

S: It's definitely doing research … looks like it's got instruments on there to do research …Yeah, this looks like a camera …

N: Solar panels …

S: Soil extractor …

N: Yeah, all those sorts of things.

T: OK, well, actually guys, you didn't do too badly. The first one is Fido—it's a NASA robot for exploring the surface of Mars, looking for water in particular. And the second, well that's an audio tooth implant. It enables messages to be sent to you in secret. A dentist implants a tiny device in your tooth and a colleague can send you messages. The messages vibrate through your jawbone and this actually allows you to hear them.

Unit 4, Listening 4.2

So let's now talk about the year 2020. Take out your calculator. You can calculate mathematically that chips will cost one penny in the year 2020. What does that mean? Let's talk about some of the gadgets and then what the effect will have on society. First, the Internet. Some people say that well there are going to be homeless on the web—people with no homepage, the homeless on the web. Well, I don't think so. In the future you'll talk to your watch. Your watch will access the entire database of the planet Earth—you'll talk to it in English, Japanese, or whatever, and it'll talk back to you in English, or Japanese. When you want access to a cell-phone or a laptop, you will talk to your tie clasp, which will have the power of a cell-phone and a laptop combined. Your earrings will access the geo—the global positioning satellite—orbiting 18,000 miles overhead, and your earrings will tell you your location to within 20 feet. Think of it, think of all the parents who will buy this for their children—one needs to know exactly where their kids are on Saturday night. A tremendous market for these earrings. Your glasses will have the Internet in them. If there's an emergency meeting at the home office, your home office calls and says mandatory meeting at home office, you're at the beach for god's sake. No problem, you hear your glasses ring, you pick up your glasses and say 'hullo', your boss says 'mandatory meeting' and you say, 'no problem, download the meeting in my glasses and I will participate via teleconferencing.' You will never have to leave the beach. These glasses will also recognise people's faces—a limited set of faces. How many times have you been at a cocktail party and bumped into somebody and you say to yourself 'is this Jim, John, Jake, who is this person?' Your glasses will tell you 'it's Jim, stupid. Remember? You met him last week. You want me to download his entire biography for you in your lens?'. OK? Think about it. How many times have you been at a cocktail party and not known who to suck up to? You'll know when these glasses become public—and you'll see them in today's programme. OK? Your clothes will have chips in them. They'll only cost a penny. What happens today if you're on a lone country road and you have a heart attack? The answer is you die. In the future your clothes will monitor your heartbeat, send a signal to the ambulance, locate your coordinates within twenty feet, and download your entire medical history to the ambulance while you're unconscious. And when you go to the bathroom, your toilet will be smart. This already exists. Matsushita has made the smart toilet, which will revolutionise preventive medicine. You go to the toilet, relieve yourself, and your toilet says 'you eat too much. Too much animal fat. Too much sugar. Too much salt.' Isn't the future wonderful?

Unit 4 Listening 4.3

Section 1

I: Is there life on other planets? It's a question many of us ask from time to time, and which some people are trying to answer. Recently Project Encounter sent a message to space, looking for intelligent life. With me in the studio to discuss this development and the search for intelligent life in space I have Dr Nick Mandretti, an astronomer at the national observatory. Welcome Dr Mandretti.

M: Thank you. Nice to be here.

I: Now before we look at this project ... even if there are E.T.s out there, it can't be easy to communicate with them. What difficulties do we face?

M: You're quite right. We face some formidable difficulties. The first, in fact, is language. How do we know extra-terrestrials will understand us? It's difficult to communicate with someone from another country. Just think what it must be like to talk to someone from another *planet*. And if they send *us* a message, how will we recognise it?

Then there's size. Space is big. If we are sending a message to the universe, which part do we send it to? If we want to listen, which part do we listen to?

And finally there's time. Because space is big, it takes a long time for any message to get anywhere. We may all have been dead for millions of years before any message we send now is received.

Section 2

I: Despite these difficulties, some people are trying. What can you tell us about them?

M: Well, I suppose there are two main groups, taking very different approaches. On the one hand there's the SETI League—SETI stands for Search for Extra Terrestrial Intelligence—and on the other there's Project Encounter.

I: So how are they different?

M: Well, for a start, the SETI League is a bunch of scientists, engineers, radio enthusiasts and astronomers—some amateurs, some university academics. The group was set up in 1993 with the aim of looking for alien intelligence. What's different is that there are thousands of members of this group all around the world who use satellite dishes on the roofs of their houses to search the sky for messages from space. They then use special software on their personal computers to analyse the radio signals they pick up from space and see if anything is a meaningful message.

I: And have they heard anything yet?

M: Well, the SETI League amateurs haven't ... yet, but astronomers at Ohio State University may have, once. On 15 August 1977 the university 'Big Ear' radio telescope picked up a narrow-band signal. It was from the direction of Sagittarius and it lasted for 37 seconds. It's now known as the 'Wow!' signal, because of what one astonished astronomer scribbled in the margin of the computer printout. Unfortunately they looked in the same area of space again, but it was never repeated and still nobody knows what it was.

I: Wouldn't it be easier to search using one of these big university radio telescopes?

M: Actually, no. Even the biggest telescope can only point at one one-millionth of the sky. So even if there is a signal, there's a 99.9999 per cent chance that the telescope will be pointing in the wrong direction. The home satellite dishes are much smaller—only 3–5 metres across, but there are so many in the league— more than 5000, that they can cover the whole of space.

I: OK, so what about Project Encounter?

M: Well Project Encounter was set up in the late 90s and basically it's a private business. It does include some academics—astrophysicists and astronomers— but any member of the public can pay to send a message to space. So if you ever wanted to talk—or try to talk—to aliens, this is the way to do it. They will record your message, translate it into digital form, and send it out to space. They also include some scientific messages which aim to tell extra terrestrials about life on earth: where we live, how we live, what we look like, etc. They aim these messages at just a few stars where they think there is a good chance of finding planets which will support life.

I: Well from what you were saying earlier, the chances of this approach actually being successful are pretty slim. But it's a nice idea—maybe I'll pay my money and give it a go! Thanks a lot for joining us. It's been fascinating.

M: You're welcome.

Unit 4, Listening 4.4

A: So you've been to Bhutan, is that right?

B: Yeah, that's right; I went there about three years ago.

A: Right. How long did you spend there?

B: We were there for ten days in total. Are you interested in going there or something?

A: Yeah, I am actually. It seems so mysterious, so difficult to get to. Y'know, the sort of place hardly anyone else has been to. What did you think of your trip there, overall?

B: Oh, brilliant, not like anywhere else I've been to. I really wish we could've stayed longer.

A: Yeah? They've got a kind of restricted tourism policy, haven't they? To stop too many people going there and staying too long?

B: They have, yeah. I don't know what the actual number limit is, but they definitely make sure there's not too many tourists in the country at one time. It certainly seems like a good idea when you're there.

A: Right. But once you're there, you can plan your own trip, I suppose?

B: No, no way. You have to actually plan your itinerary and have it officially approved before they give you the visa and all that.

A: Oh really?

B: And all the time you're there, you have to have an official government guide to show you around—and make sure you don't go anywhere or do anything you're not meant to. They eat with you and everything.

A: I didn't realise it was quite so controlled ... sounds a bit sinister, really.

B: Yeah, it is a bit annoying ... but somehow it sounds worse than it is in practice, at least in our case. Our guide was a pretty cool guy, actually, and they have a fair bit of discretion to change your official plan. I mean, a couple of times, we heard about something we wanted to see that wasn't on our itinerary, and he just said, 'Yeah, OK, we can do that'. What they're trying to do is protect the culture, keep it a bit isolated from Western culture ... and the other cultures around Bhutan.

A: OK. So how different is it from Nepal? Must be quite similar in some ways.

B: Um ... yeah, in some ways ... I mean, the scenery is obviously quite similar – although Nepal's much more densely populated, I think. There's some big cultural differences, though, and they've got the tourism policy thing, so the culture is less affected by western culture than Nepal's.

A: But do you reckon you get to see the real culture? Don't you end up with a kind of officially approved version with all the negative bits taken out?

B: Um, yeah, I guess so, a bit ... y'know, when they're in public everyone there has to wear like the national costume, and apparently, if they get caught not wearing it three times, they get thrown in jail! So that sort of thing is a bit forced, a bit false, but ... I mean, you make your choice between over-protecting your culture a bit or seeing it changed completely by outsiders ... and they've made the opposite choice to Nepal. I've been to Nepal too, and I'd have to say that I actually prefer what Bhutan has done, I think it's had a positive effect ... but I guess that's seeing it just as a tourist.

A: Yeah, right. What do you reckon the Bhutanese think about it all? Are they happy to go along with all the rules?

B: It's a bit hard to say. I mean, the guide obviously says that everyone's OK with it, and it's not like you see the locals complaining about it ... but then they get to control what you actually see and hear, so a tourist doesn't get the chance to hear the other side of the story, I s'pose ... but if you look at the standard of living in Nepal, and the health and education and stuff like that, compared to Bhutan, the Bhutanese are way better off than the Nepalese ... so you've got to say that whatever they're doing, it's working for them.

A: So you think I should make the effort to go there?

B: Oh yeah, definitely. I mean, it is a hassle to get it all organised, and it's more expensive than going to Nepal, but it's really worth it in the end.

Unit 5, Listening 5.1

The ancient game of *Go* was invented in China about 4000 years ago, and it has spread to become the most popular board game in Asia. It is also gaining in popularity throughout the rest of the world. It has been played in Japan since 740 AD, in Europe since the late 19th century, and in Britain since 1930.

The English word *Go* is borrowed from the Japanese—*Go*—but it is known by other names in other countries. For example, in Korea it is known as *baduk*—

which is spelled *b-a-d-u-k,* and in Chinese it is known as *wei chi,* spelled *w-e-i c-h-i* …

The game is played on a board with 19 by 19 intersecting lines, which of course form squares. But unlike chess or checkers, where you place the pieces on the squares, in *Go* you place stones on the intersections—the points where the lines cross each other. One player has black stones and the other has white stones, and they take turns to place the stones on the board. The aim of the game is to capture territory by placing your stones around your opponent's stones. Once you have completely surrounded the stone, you capture the stone, and remove it from the board. The winner is the player that has captured the most territory at the end of the game.

The game is interesting because it is intellectually very challenging. The rules are very, very simple, but the strategies to win the game are very complex. In chess, computer programmers have been able to program computers to beat world champions, but so far attempts to program computers for *Go* have been unsuccessful.

The most important *Go*-playing countries are Japan, Korea and China, which all have professional players, and where it is estimated that there are more than 50 million players in total. Major tournaments in these countries attract sponsorship from large companies and they are very big sporting events. More recently, young people have turned away from *Go,* as they have from other traditional elements of Asian culture. In spite of this, there are still about 10 million *Go* players in Japan, for example, of whom about five hundred are professional.

Unit 5, Listening 5.2

Section 1

… And if you want to know why computer games seem to play such an important part in your kids' lives, a consumer survey released today might give you some answers. The results show that people enjoy playing computer and video games for a variety of reasons. Not surprisingly, the reason most often mentioned, by 88% of respondents, was that they're fun. The fact that they're challenging came next, mentioned by 71%; that they can be played with friends and family was next on 42%—although my son has never asked me to play a computer game with him! Anyway, 36% of respondents said computer games offer a lot of entertainment for the price, and 19% thought they offer a way for players to keep up with the latest technology.

Section 2

The survey also reveals what kind of games are most popular. Those who play console games—those are the ones you plug into your TV—console game players have no clear favourite: driving and racing games are the most popular, with 39% playing them regularly, but action games and sports games are both just 1% behind, and role-play and adventure games are a little further back on 31%. People who play games on their computers tend to play puzzles and board or card games most often, with 35% mentioning them; 28% say they like playing action games, and finally sports games and simulations are both played by 23% of the respondents.

And who exactly plays these games? Well, for both console games and computer games, players are predominantly male—62% of them for computer games and 72% for console games. Ages show a slightly different pattern: console game players are mostly under 30, while computer game players are more evenly spread in terms of age.

When it comes to buying the games, it's clear that the young players have to ask others to pay for them: 96% of those who buy console games and 90% of computer game buyers are over 18. And although it's mainly men who play the games, men and women buy them in roughly equal numbers.

Unit 5, Listening 5.3

A

1

Do you like adventure? Want to visit places most people will never go to? Then come along and join up. At only $20 for a year's membership, we're about the best value club on campus. You only need some strong boots, a backpack and a sleeping bag to take part in our weekend activities …

2

For students who like to relax by exercising their minds, this is the club you're looking for. Learn how to play one of the oldest and most challenging games in the world, and take part in regular competitions and plenty of social events …

3

Our main aims are to provide support, information and fun for students who are new to this country. We also want to introduce our cultures to other students on campus, so even if you don't come from our part of the world, we would love to welcome you to our meetings and activities …

4

Are you interested in more than just snapshots? Would you like to get better equipment but don't know how to choose? Do you want to learn the techniques that the professionals use? We can help you do all of this and more. With technical and artistic courses, regular trips to great locations and discounts on equipment and supplies, you'll improve your techniques—and have heaps of fun.

B

C: Hi, how are you?

S: Great thanks. I think I'd like to join up.

C: Excellent. OK, I just need to enter your details into our database …

S: Right.

C: Now, what's your first name?

S: Stephen.

C: Is that with a 'v' or a 'ph'?

S: It's s-t-e-p-h-e-n.

C: And your family name?

S: McKenzie … that's capital M, small c, capital K e-n-z-i-e.

C: OK … um, I need a postal address, a phone number and an e-mail address, if you've got one.

S: Sure … my postal address is 63B Featherston Avenue, Eastern Bay, postcode 6419, my phone number is …

C: Hold on, not too fast … Featherston is f-e-a-t-h-e-r-s-t-o-n-e?

S: No 'e' on the end.

C: Featherston Road, was it?

S: No, Avenue.

C: Right … now, phone number?

S: 7492 6472

C: And finally, your e-mail?

S: It's Stephen-dot-'m' at freemail-dot-com

C: OK, great. Now, that's $25 for a year's membership …

Unit 6, Listening 6.1

1

And it has been officially announced that today, October 12 1999, is the day of six billion: the United Nations has calculated that Earth's six billionth inhabitant will be born today. However, experts are nowhere near as sure about what the world's population will increase to in the next 50 years. The optimists predict that the rate of global population growth will actually fall, and that as a result, the population will only rise by about 1 billion. The pessimists, on the other hand, tell us that the population is likely to increase at the same rate as it is increasing now—and that there will be over 10 billion of us by the year 2050.

2

T: So do you see what this graph is telling us, Andrew?

S: I think so … umm, the total population has increased …

T: Well, not exactly … these bars, they show the number of people who are living in cities, and the other ones, what do they show?

S: Umm, the number of people living in the countryside?

T: Right, good. So what does the graph show us about those numbers?

S: Oh, I see … the number of people who are living in cities has been increasing but the number of people living in the countryside has been falling. But what country is it about? Is it about this country?

T: No, no, it's not about one country in particular … it shows a global trend, so the situation in individual countries may be quite different from this graph.

3

People who study population usually identify four main stages in the development of a population. In the first stage, when the birth rate is very high, but death rates tend to fluctuate a little, you get a fluctuating population, the population doesn't change a great deal but it goes both up and down. In the next stage, birth rates stay very high, but the death rate drops dramatically because of advances in medicine and in social services, etc., which help people to live longer. So in the second stage, you tend to get a fairly rapidly increasing population, because the birth rate remains high but the death rate is falling. In stage 3 of this population transition, you get a falling birth rate, as people tend to use contraceptives more, as people start to work longer and therefore delay having a baby until later … so the birth rate is falling, the death rate stays fairly low and stable, so the rate of increase, while the population continues to increase, the rate of increase falls. And then in the final stage of the population transition, population tends to stabilise, because both birth rates and death rates fall.

4

I: Today on the programme, we're talking to Professor Diana Thomas, who has recently completed a major study of the origins of Americans. Welcome, professor.

G: Thank you, it's a pleasure to be here.

I: Firstly, why is this topic of such interest to your fellow Americans?

G: Well, I'm sure you've heard the States described as a 'melting pot', and that's quite a suitable description. If you look at where our people have come from over the last two hundred or so years, which encompasses the so-called 'great waves' of immigration, if you look at the origins of immigrants over that period, you'll see that although the majority of them, around 65%, came from Europe, very significant numbers came from all parts of the world: from other parts of the Americas, from Asia, Africa and Oceania. So, you see, the fact that there are so many different cultures making up American society makes the American people very interested in their origins.

I: Yes, I understand why that would be the case. What sort of people is your book aimed at and how do you think it will be received?

5

A: Have you done that homework assignment?

B: Umm, which one do you mean?

A: The one where we have to say what those graphs mean and what they imply.

B: No, not yet. Shall we look at them together?

A: Yeah, OK … Let's see … they're comparing population at different times, aren't they?

B: Right. I think I've seen this kind of thing before. It's kind of a profile … look, it shows how many people there are in each age group for men and women.

A: So in this one, the biggest number is in the kind of middle-aged group, but in this one, it's in the older group, around 60.

B: Yeah, that's the ageing population thing that's a problem for some countries.

A: Mmm, right … I think it must be only for developed countries, though, cos developing countries still have really high birth rates, so their profiles would have more in the young age groups.

B: Yeah.

Unit 6, Listening 6.2

OK, so during the 20th century, Egypt experienced very, very rapid population growth … the population, after the war … after the Second World War, doubled every 20 years or so, to reach a peak of … well, not a peak, but to reach a total of over 60 million in the year 2000.

OK, now the problem with this rapid population growth is that there is actually not very much land that people can live on in Egypt. Egypt is a very big country, but a lot of the country is covered by desert, by the Sahara desert … and 95% of the population live in a very narrow area, close to the banks of the Nile River. This area is very fertile, you can grow a lot of food there … but it is still a small area, relative to the size of the population. So the population of Egypt tends to be very crowded together, along the sides of the Nile.

Now, another problem, apart from the crowding is that, because there is such a large population for a relatively small area of land, is that Egyptians cannot produce enough food, cannot grow enough food, for their own population, so they actually have to import a lot of their food, and this is quite difficult … for a developing country to afford to import that food.

A further problem is that the population is very young … overall, there is a relatively high proportion of the population which is young, and this means that there is a lot of demand on the education system, and it's expensive to educate everybody, and because it's expensive, it's not possible to … provide a complete education for everybody, so literacy levels, and general education levels are relatively low in many parts of the country. This of course leads to economic problems, because these people are not able to get skilled jobs … they tend to work in low-paid labouring jobs, and this is not good for the overall economy.

Unit 6, Listening 6.3

New Zealand has a population that is growing slowly … of course, this is a good thing in terms of having a stable, quite a stable society where there is enough education and medical care and jobs, in general … but there are some issues … problems to do with population, that New Zealand is facing.

OK, so, as in many developed countries now, the problem is, or what could

become a problem is the profile of the population. In New Zealand the profile of the population, the number of people in the country in each age group, shows that there is an increasing number of people who are over 50 … people who are retiring from their jobs, they're beginning to need more health care and so on. And people are tending to have less—to have smaller families, and to wait till they're older to start their families. So all this means that the age profile of New Zealanders has changed … and this is, as I said, similar to what is happening in many other developed countries.

Now, on the other hand, another force that is … acting upon the population of New Zealand, another important force, is immigration. Immigration to New Zealand has gone through several different stages, with waves of people from certain parts of the world coming at different times. The most recent waves have been Polynesian immigrants—from the islands of the South Pacific —and immigration from Asian countries. This continual flow of immigrants is a good thing for New Zealand, because a larger population helps a country to compete economically with larger countries … it also keeps a flow of educated and experienced people coming into the population and into the workforce … and the society becomes more multi-cultural. Of course, immigration also has challenges, presents some problems for a country, like how to integrate them—integrate the immigrants into the society.

Unit 6, Listening 6.4

A: So do you think advertising has a significant effect on people's behaviour?

B: Umm, I think … people, especially young people nowadays, are quite sophisticated about advertising, they know when they're being manipulated, but they sometimes … they choose to accept that … so y'know, they pick up fashions off advertising and they buy those products, if that's what their friends are doing too.

A: Yeah, I agree with that to some extent, but I kind of think, umm, that even when we know we're being manipulated, the advertisers are manipulating us in other ways we don't know about … it's like they're always a step ahead of us.

B: Oh, I don't know … I don't think it's that subtle … I think most people are smart enough to ignore advertising most of the time.

A: Well, what about fashion magazines? …Y'know, the ads they have tell us what kind of body we should have, how we should think about other people … and it's quite difficult to separate the advertising from the articles, the edited bits. Even though people understand it's just advertising, they still try to have that kind of body, those clothes and so on.

B: Some people, sure … but I don't think that most people are really deeply affected. Anyway, it's more like the advertising reflects what people already think and want, it doesn't cause it or change it … it's the result, not the cause.

A: Yeah, maybe … but look at how advertising has changed in the last few years … umm, a lot of it now is not so focused on a product, but on the brand and how it's, like, part of your lifestyle … sometimes they don't even show the product, they just use emotion to make you think, yeah, I need that brand in my life to make me feel good.

B: Yeah, that's true … I don't think that's necessarily bad, though. Those ads are often quite creative, it's like they're another kind of art … and if they make you feel good about your life or your community, what's the problem? They're not asking you to actually buy anything!

A: No, I suppose not. I just think it's kind of dishonest … we shouldn't need brands and products to make us feel good. Advertising just seems like such a waste of money and effort to me … it's like companies spending time and money to get us to spend more money … a big money cycle.

B: Not always though. What about charity ads asking people to give money for starving children and all that … and y'know, ads to stop smoking or to make people drive more slowly? The people who make those ads aren't getting any profit out of them, are they.

A: Yeah, but what if they just spent the money they use to make the ads to actually do something … like buy more food for the starving children! Wouldn't that be more useful?

Unit 7, Unit 7.1

1

F: Well I heard this story, I think it was in California, there was supposed to be a problem with the alligators … no, maybe it was in Florida … Anyway, there was apparently this problem with the alligators, they were getting into the sewerage system and causing trouble. They were getting in there when they were small, then growing bigger and damaging the pipes and so on.

M: Right, and they were also like, coming up out of people's toilets and getting into their swimming pools and things.

F: Yeah, yeah ... I guess they were just attracted to cities and people ... y'know, easy living.

M: Do you think it's just an urban myth?

F: Umm, no, I think it probably happens there ... I mean, they have alligators in that part of America, and the same kind of thing happens with bears in other parts of the US, so ...

2

M: When I was younger, about twelve I think, I went to a big swimming pool complex with water slides and all that ... I was there with my older brother, he would have been fourteen or so. Anyway, in the water slides, the tunnels, apparently these guys had been stopping halfway down and like, putting razor blades into the slide ...

F: Oh, that's sick.

M: Yeah, and they were sticking up so that the next person down the slide would get really badly cut.

F: Did it ever really happen?

M: I'm not sure ... but the worst thing was that my brother made me go down the slides before him to make sure they were safe!

3

F: This happened to a friend of mine ... or maybe a friend of a friend...

M: Oh, right, one of those stories.

F: Yeah ... well, this woman went into a hamburger restaurant and bought a chicken burger ... and she was sitting there eating it, then she got this crunchy bit and she thought it must be a piece of crisp vegetable or something ... anyway, she took another bite, and it was crunchy again and it also tasted pretty bad ... so she opened the burger and took out the chicken fillet, and there was this dead grasshopper in it ... well, half a grasshopper!

M: Yeah, I've heard the same one, but it was a dead mouse ... and it happened to a friend of *mine*!

F: Oh really?

4

This is a story I heard in Egypt when I used to live there. Women in Egypt, or particularly women in poor parts of the city and the country, wear a lot of gold—usually gold bracelets on their arms, because they are basically a way of saving for the future—they feel it's safer than having money in the bank. So they have all of these gold bracelets all the way up their arms. Anyway, this guy I know—he'd been working in Cairo for years—said that this guy he knew had been driving through one of the poor parts of Cairo in a taxi, when the taxi stopped to let this woman all dressed in black—like they normally are—get in. Taxis stop to pick up extra passengers all the time. And this woman looked kind of nervous, anxious. And the guy looks across and sees that there's blood on her dress, and sees this arm sticking out with all these gold bracelets on it. She'd cut it off someone! ... But I heard a few people tell that story and I'm not sure if it's true or not.

Unit 7, Listening 7.2

and she was sitting there eating it, then she got this crunchy bit and she thought it must be a piece of crisp vegetable or something... anyway, she took another bite, and it was crunchy again and it also tasted pretty bad ... so she opened the burger and took out the chicken fillet ...

they feel it's safer than having money in the bank. So they have all of these gold bracelets all the way up their arms. Anyway, this guy I know—he'd been working in Cairo for years—said that this guy he knew had been driving through one of the poor parts of Cairo in a taxi, when the taxi stopped to let this woman all dressed in black ...

Unit 7, Listening 7.3

Making an animated movie these days is obviously a very complex, high-tech process—at Pixar it involves hundreds of staff—but it can basically be broken down into four main stages: development, pre-production, production and—finally—post-production. Each of these main stages involves a number of sub-stages, and these are what I've been asked to run through quickly with you now. OK—so, the first main stage—development, is where the team actually creates the story. The very first step is when someone at the company comes up with a story idea, and they 'pitch' the idea to other members of the development team. It's basically a sales pitch—they're trying to sell the idea to other members of the team.

The next step is to write the text treatment, which is really just a short document that summarises the main idea of the story. So it's not a full script, just a summary of the story.

Artists then take the treatment and use it draw the storyboards. You've probably seen these before—they're like a hand-drawn comic book version of the movie. They give the director an idea of how to put the movie on screen.

The final step in the development stage is for the voices to be recorded. At first this is just done by staff in the company—so, you know, one of the artists and maybe the writer might do a voice, but later professional actors are brought in to do the recording.

Work then moves into the pre-production phase. Essentially what happens now is the team works on the technical problems with making the film.

The first step here is for the art department to create the look and the feel of the movie. They figure out the detailed look of the characters, do the lighting, the colour, design the sets, stuff like that.

Next the models are made of the characters. Sometimes they are sculpted by hand, sometimes they are modelled in 3-D directly onto computer. Models are also made of the sets at this point.

The next stage is to 'dress' the sets—in other words, add detail like chairs, curtains, toys—basically try to make a believable world.

OK, so, now phase three—the actual production, is ready to begin.

First up, the shots are laid out—the crew translates the story into 3-dimensional scenes and shoots them from a variety of camera angles so the director and the editors have choices about what they can put into the final version.

Then the animators actually go to work. In the old days this meant drawing the characters' movements, but these days they use special animation software to make the characters move through each scene and fit in with the layout, set and the voices—which you'll remember have already been recorded.

At this point production has finished and the post-production can start. This is where the final movie is polished up.

First the lighting team completes the 'look'. This is kind of like stage lighting, except they use digital light to emphasise the mood and emotion of every scene. Then the masses of computer data—all the different information on sets, colours, character movement and so on—are 'translated' into frames of film. Pixar uses a huge computer system, but even though every frame only represents 1/24 of a second of screen time, it can take about six hours of computer processing ... which means a whole film takes literally millions of hours of computing time.

Finally, the editorial team adds the final touches—the music, sound effect, special effects and it's all put on film or into a form for digital projection, ready to be shown.

Unit 7, Listening 7.4

1

A: Hi. How are you?

B: I'm good.

A: Very good. So listen, we're going out tonight, that's the plan, right?

B: Yeah, that's the plan.

A: OK. So have you thought about what sort of thing you'd like to do?

B: Well, I rather fancy seeing a movie actually, and maybe have dinner.

A: Yes, food sounds good. I was actually thinking about seeing a play.

B: Oh really?

A: Yeah, I haven't seen anything live for a long time.

B: That's a good idea. What would you like to see?

A: Well, it's funny. The other day on Sunday I was listening to the radio. Amanda Jones came on. She's directing a play called 'The Birthday Party'.

B: I've heard it's really good.

A: And I thought it could be a good bet. It's also on at the University Theatre, so it's a reasonable price.

B: Oh right. So how much is that?

A: Umm, well, it's $18 if you're under 25.

B: That's not us then, is it?

A: No ... it doesn't really matter though.

B: We could have something to eat first.

A: Yeah, yeah, that'd be good. We could go to Ken's Yakitori quite early, like, round 6.30 ...

B: OK, well, that's great. So what time would you like to meet? Shall we meet in town or should I pick you up?

A: We'll meet at Ken's.

2

A: Hello.

B: Hi Bridget, it's Mark here.

A: Hi Mark, how's it going?

B: Oh, OK. Just had a really hard week at work, glad it's over!

A: Definitely! So what are you up to this evening?

B: I was just about to ask you the same thing. D'you wanna catch a movie?

A: Oh yeah … what did you have in mind?

B: I wouldn't mind seeing the latest episode of *Star Wars* … whaddaya think?

A: Umm … I didn't really like the last episode, so I'm not that keen actually. How about something a bit sort of upbeat? A comedy?

B: All right … uhh, there's a new one with Mel Gibson and Julia Roberts, isn't there? A romantic comedy.

A: Yeah, right. That sounds like the sort of thing we need on a Friday evening. Where's it on at?

B: Hold on, I'll just have a look … umm … here we are, it's on at Central Cinemas at 6.30, 7.45 and 9.15. Which one shall we go for?

A: Well why don't we go for the early one and then have something to eat afterwards? Just a burger or something.

B: Yeah, OK … we'd better get going then, it's 5 o'clock already. How about we meet there at about 6.00?

A: Out in front of the building?

B: Let's say inside, in front of the ticket desk.

A: OK, great. See you soon, then.

B: Yeah, see ya.

3

A: Hey, you guys, wanna go to the game on Friday night?

B: Can you still get tickets? I thought they'd all sold out?

A: I know this guy who's got three tickets he can't use, and he'll sell them to us for the price he paid originally.

B: Good deal! I'm in.

C: I don't wanna go to a football match!

B: Come on, you've never been to a live game before, have you? It'll be a really good match.

C: I don't even know who's playing.

B: It's Central United against Western Districts, it's the final.

C: And how much are the tickets?

B: $20 each.

C: $20! I can see two movies for that.

B: This is much better than a movie. Come on, I promise you'll enjoy it.

C: … All right. But you'll have to explain everything to me … So how do we get to the ground?

A: The bus is probably easiest, do you think?

B: Yeah, and cheapest. We can catch it from the stop outside the university library. If we get the bus at about 5.30, that'll give us plenty of time before kick-off.

A: OK, so we'll meet at the bus stop at 5.30. I'll bring the tickets with me.

B: Excellent. It'll be great.

C: See you at the bus stop, then …

Unit 8, Listening 8.1

D: What do you think this one is? It looks a bit like rice, doesn't it?

M: Yeah, yeah, because of the water there.

K: I think it could be rice, yeah.

M: It looks like a rice paddy, yeah?

K: How about this one?

D: Could be corn … maize?

M: I wonder if it's … I don't know … it looks a bit like sugar cane.

K: Mmm.

D: Yeah.

K: Mmm.

M: It's quite dry.

K: It *is* sugar cane.

M: Yeah maybe corn doesn't have the same thing at the top.

K: Corn's usually pretty green, too.

M: Mm, yeah.

K: That looks quite dry.

D: Yeah. What about this one?

M: Probably wheat, isn't it? It looks like a field of wheat.

D: Yeah.

K: What about the nice bright red one?

D: Gotta be chillis, doesn't it?

K: Chilli peppers?

M: Yeah, I reckon. Heaps and heaps of chilli peppers.

D: Not sun-dried tomatoes.

K: No coz they're too long and thin.

D: Mm. What are those berries? The last one. Some kind of berries?

K: Umm … could be.

D: What do gooseberries look like?

K: Gooseberries are green, aren't they?

M: No, but look, it's going black. I think they're coffee beans.

D: Mm, yeah, definitely they're coffee beans.

K: So where do they all come from, do you reckon?

M: Well rice is from Asian countries, isn't it? Is it from China? First?

D: Either China or Japan.

K: Yeah well, wild rice was originally right throughout Asia, but as far as they can tell, the first people to start growing it domestically were from Thailand. A long, long time ago.

M: Yeah?

K: From at least 4000 BC. How about the wheat?

M: It's been in lots of countries, for ages. But apparently originally it was the Middle East.

D: Wow, I wouldn't have picked that. What about the chillis?

K: Chillis—South America.

D: Yeah?

M: Yeah, apparently Columbus found them there, and he took them to Europe.

K: Oh, OK.

M: And apparently the name pepper is a mistake. He thought they were related to pepper, like salt and pepper, but they're not. Yeah, yeah. They reckon they might've been from Bolivia, but they're not sure.

K: What about coffee? Where do you think coffee comes from. I think it sounds like South America, too, but …

D: A hot place. Africa.

M: I had no idea it was from Africa originally.

D: It was actually from Ethiopia.

M: Oh, right.

D: Then they took it over to the Arabian peninsula.

M: They were quite good businessmen, weren't they?

D: About 1500 years ago. And the price has kept on going up!

M: I suppose that's why things spread, isn't it. You know … because people … like it, and want to export it.

D: Mm, I guess so.

M: And take it somewhere else.

D: Yeah, bartering … and trading.

M: Swap it for other resources.

K: What about sugar cane? Where do you think that's from?

D: That's a toughie, because it's all over the world, isn't it?

K: Yeah.

D: There's heaps of it in Australia.

M: Yeah, and I had it in Brazil, ah, so it's in South America. I don't know where it comes from originally. Some place hot.

K: Well originally it's supposed to have come from Papua New Guinea.

D: Mm.

K: In the South Pacific, 8000 years ago.

M: Ah, so a totally different part of the world from South America.

K: Then it was taken to other parts of the world.

D: I guess that's how all these things spread, with people taking them with them …

Unit 8, Listening 8.2

OK, so what you can see in the diagram is the value of trade flows within and between different regions of the world in the year 2001. The data is from the WTO—the World Trade Organisation—and the units are billions of dollars US. The figures *inside* the boxes are trade between countries inside the region—so for example, in 2001 there was $1677 billion worth of trade between different countries inside Western Europe. And these figures next to the arrows obviously represent the trade *between* countries—or, sorry, regions rather than countries. So Western Europe exported $255 billion worth of goods and services to North America, and imported $188 billion in return.

Perhaps I'd better clarify what some of these region labels refer to. Western Europe refers basically to the European Union countries. North America is obviously Canada and the US, but it actually also includes Mexico, because these three countries are partners in NAFTA—the North Atlantic Free Trade Agreement. Asia/Pacific's pretty straightforward, I think—it includes Australasia—Australia and New Zealand—along with the South and East Asian countries. So that leaves the Rest of the World, which is a bit of a mixed bag—Africa, obviously, but also the Middle East and Eastern Europe.

OK, so what's the diagram telling us? Well first of all, that trade *within* regions accounts for a significant portion of world trade. This is pretty clear with Western Europe, isn't it, but it's also true in particular of the Asia/Pacific region—with $722 billion worth of *internal* trade. The North American figure is perhaps surprisingly low—'only' $391 billion, but these figures show only trade between countries in the region, for example, Canada and the US, or the US and Mexico. They *don't* show sales *inside* the States—which is by far the biggest market in the world. So you could say this data is a little misleading. And then, of course, we've got the Rest of the World with just $285 billion worth of internal trade.

Let's have a look at the external trade figures, then. You'll notice here that the situation is slightly better for the Rest of the World: in this particular year they had exports of $287 billion to North America, $312 billion to Western Europe, and $174 billion to the Asia/Pacific region. This is largely to do with oil supplies coming out of the Middle East. Clearly trade between Western Europe and the Rest of the World is one of the more significant flows in the world: you can see here that Western Europeans had exports of $333 billion back to the Rest of the World. There are a number of reasons for this—energy, as I just mentioned, but also geographical proximity to Eastern Europe, and historical colonial relationships with Africa—the French, Belgians and British, for example.

And you'll notice that trade between North America—particularly the US—and the Asia/Pacific region is pretty significant. There's a fairly heavy imbalance in favour of Asia/Pacific: they sold $376 billion worth of cars and electronics from Japan, for example, and other heavy industrial goods from Korea and China to North America in 2001. North America does quite a lot of trade with the Rest of the World—they imported $287 billion worth—a lot of that is trade with South America.

OK, and finally, the wealth of Western Europe, and the emerging importance of the Asia/Pacific region is pretty clear here—with 195 billion in exports from Western Europe to Asia/Pacific, and 252 billion going back the other way.

Unit 8, Listening 8.3

Section 1

First of all, some basic facts about Columbus: he was born on August 25, 1451 in Genoa, Italy, and he died on May 20, 1506 in Valladolid, Spain. Columbus went to sea at the age of fourteen; it was quite common in those days for boys to start their careers as sailors at such a young age. He became a sailor in a time when there were many exciting opportunities for European adventurers and explorers. Columbus soon left his family behind in Italy and went to live in Spain and Portugal, where explorers were looking towards the west and wondering what they might find out in the Atlantic Ocean. Of course, Columbus is famous for the voyage he made in 1492: on October 12, two worlds met on a little island in the Caribbean Sea. Columbus was actually trying to find a direct sea route to the Far East—China and Japan—but he had discovered the New World—without even realising it! Although Columbus wasn't actually the first European to land in the Americas, it was his arrival that started the European colonisation of the Americas, and this was to totally change the course of world history.

Section 2

What I'd really like to focus on now are the impacts that Columbus' arrival in the New World had, both the positive impacts and the negative impacts.

Let's start with the positive impacts. The European discovery of the Americas had a very great impact on the way that Europeans thought about the world, themselves and others. After Columbus and others had opened the way to the New World, people in Europe realised that they could now exchange ideas and information with people from all over the world. They had to accept the idea that people from the Old World were not the only humans in the world that could build civilisations and cultures. The discovery of the Americas and other parts of the world also helped to confirm for many Europeans the basic physical facts that the world is not flat, and is not at the centre of the universe. Apart from these intellectual impacts, there were a huge number of practical impacts that contributed to both the Old and the New Worlds. Some of the many kinds of food that were taken back to Europe from the Americas were corn, potatoes, peanuts

and tomatoes. The Europeans also introduced a lot of really basic things like rice, wheat, onions and sugar to the New World. Many animals also came to the New World; the most important were probably cows and horses. And it may seem hard to believe, but there were no vehicles with wheels in the Americas until Europeans introduced them.

Unfortunately, Columbus' arrival also had many negative impacts, and for many people in modern times, these negative impacts far outweigh the positive ones. Firstly, although the Europeans found a number of quite advanced cultures when they arrived, cultures with well-developed political and religious systems, they regarded all the native people they met as barbarians—they didn't actually accept that they were really humans for about 50 years. They were only useful as a source of labour in the work of finding gold and other wealth to take back to Europe. As a consequence of this way of thinking, whole cultures were destroyed along with the millions of native Americans who died. The greatest killers of the native people of the New World, however, were the diseases introduced by the Europeans. We can hardly say that the Europeans did this deliberately, but still, they certainly passed their diseases to the native Americans, with disastrous results. Within about a hundred years of Columbus' arrival, 90 to 95% of the native population in many parts of the Americas had been killed by epidemics of diseases that were previously unknown to them.

Unit 8, Listening 8.4

I: Welcome to *Planet Watch*, our weekly look at environmental matters. Now some listeners may have seen 'Shade Grown Coffee' leaflets in their local Starbucks, and may be interested to know more, and some of you may be wondering what it's all about. Well with me in the studio today I have Teresa Saldana from the Shade Grown Coffee Association. Thank you for joining us, Teresa.

TS: It's a pleasure.

I: Perhaps you could start by telling us exactly what shade grown coffee is.

TS: Well, basically it's coffee which is grown the traditional way. Coffee beans grow on bushes, and traditionally these bushes grew in the shade under other, bigger trees in hillside forests. More recently, however, some farmers and businesses have cut down the forests so that they could grow the coffee in direct, full sun.

I: And presumably they've done this because the plants grow better in the sun?

TS: Well, that's part of it. In fact, growing coffee out in the sun started in the late 60s, early 70s, because of a disease called coffee leaf rust. It was thought that the disease could be prevented by growing plants out in the sun. But actually, it turned out that the coffee leaf rust never really became a big problem in Latin America. In the meantime, though, the farmers found that they could put their plants closer together in the open sun.

I: So they got higher yields.

TS: Yes. In the shade you can get about 1000–2000 plants per hectare, and from them you get around 550 kilograms of beans per hectare a year. You get about three times as much from sun grown coffee. Three to seven thousand plants per hectare, and up to 1600 kilos per hectare each year.

I: You can see why they do it, then. It obviously makes more economic sense.

TS: It depends how you look at it. Yes, they produce more coffee, but it costs them a lot more to produce. For a start, their plants only last half as long: a coffee bush will grow for 30–34 years in the shade, but in full sun farmers have to replace them every 12–15 years, because they basically burn out. And coffee might grow better in the sun, but weeds do too, so you have to pay people to do the weeding. It's also necessary to use more fertilisers in full sun. So it's more expensive. On the other hand, with shade grown coffee, because there are more surrounding trees, there are more birds, and the birds control the insects, so you don't need to use as much pesticide. And you don't need to irrigate as much in the shade.

I: All of which must make shade grown coffee better for the environment—less fertiliser, less pesticide, less irrigation.

TS: Exactly. It's far better for the environment. Coffee should be grown in the rainforest, with all the other plants and animals around. And if that doesn't convince you, taste might! You can grow more varieties in the shade, and they are less bitter. Only a couple of types of coffee grow in the sun, and they are much more bitter.

I: Well that should be a good enough reason for anyone. So, what would you like us to do about it?

TS: We at the Shade Grown Coffee Association would like people to buy shade grown coffee only. If your local café or supermarket doesn't sell it, ask them to. We believe that by making this choice, you'll be promoting fair trade, because you'll be supporting the small-scale growers, rather than the big companies that run the sun-grown coffee plantations and you'll be helping out the environment. And of course you'll be getting a better cup of coffee as well.

Unit 9, Listening 9.1

C: Right, so what about this guy rushing up the steps, what do you think about him?

S: Looks like a businessman, don't you reckon?

N: He doesn't look that old, maybe umm … late 20s? … I suppose … he looks like he's in a hurry, he must have a pretty busy … busy job.

C: Mmmm.

S: I wonder if there's a laptop in that bag?

N: Could be … or some important documents … He's probably educated at university … got some sort of qualification.

C: Mmm … he just looks like a lawyer to me, I don't know why.

N: Yeah, definitely a lawyer or a businessman.

S: Maybe single?

N: Maybe single … umm he may have a young family, but he doesn't look like … if he has children, that they'll be very old.

S: Right…he looks like the sort of guy that goes to the gym after work.

C: Mmm … he leads a pretty busy life and maybe doesn't have time for family or any other interests. What about the woman on the right?

N: I think she looks like someone's grandmother maybe?

S: Yeah … What country do you think she's from?

N: It's hard to say … maybe somewhere in Asia … or the Middle East …

S: Anyway, she's got some sort of food that she's prepared.

N: Maybe that's one of her interests … making food for other people.

C: Yeah, or maybe just … she's a housewife … so she's cooking for her family.

S: She could be selling it, y'know, she could be some sort of market … umm, vendor, it could be her livelihood, her job.

C: Yeah …As for her interests, I don't know…

S: 26 grandchildren!

C: Yes, most probably.

S: Family-orientated, maybe.

C: And the guy with the net, he's obviously a fisherman.

N: He looks … perhaps he's from somewhere in Africa …

S: Mmm … yeah, his skin colour's quite dark.

N: If that's the case, if he's a fisherman, he's probably quite busy as well, he must have to get up pretty early in the morning … to go and put his nets out.

C: So, interests … well, this definitely looks like his job, he looks quite rugged, like y'know, he's been outdoors and … doing a very physical job.

N: He also doesn't look that old maybe about the same age as the businessman guy.

S: Umm, he might be a bit older than that.

C: Of course, being out in the sun and all that can make you look older as well.

N: Sure.

S: He might be—he might have a young family or something like that.

C: Yeah, I'd say so. The model … I presume she's a model … do you?

N: Yes … she looks like she's in an advertisement.

C: Yeah, so she's—she's pretty young … early 20s?

S: Even younger?

C: Could be … they do start quite young these days.

N: She's probably got quite a good … quite a good income if she's appearing in ads.

S: Yeah, right.

N: Interests probably involve sort of … going out and mingling with … important media people.

S: She may well have started her job quite early, so education-wise, she … she may not have completed high school, for example.

N: Yeah, that's true. She may have just gone straight out … into the modelling industry.

C: Mmm … I don't imagine she's got a family yet.

N: No, I don't think so either … she looks too young.

C: And too busy, I'd say … if she's a model, there's a high chance she might be travelling around a bit and might not have time to … get married or …

N: And the last guy?

S: He looks like a farmer … looks pretty rugged.

C: He does, doesn't he … with that hat.

N: He reminds me of an American.

S: Mmm…he looks like he's outside, in a …

N: Some sort of field.

S: Yeah, looks like he's holding some grass—no, some wheat—and that's a field of wheat behind him, so … maybe he grows crops on his farm, wheat and things.

N: He's umm … pretty old.

C: 60s, maybe?

S: Yeah … could have some grandchildren … What do farmers do in their free time?

C: Watch football, drink beer … He probably doesn't get away from the farm much, because he has to keep an eye on things … most of the time.

N: He probably has to every day, pretty much … there'd always be something to do.

C: Yeah, so it would be hard to imagine him having lots of other interests.

S: Mmm, family and farm … maybe that's it.

N: He might like to go fishing and stuff like that … he obviously lives in a rural area, so he'd be interested in outdoor things.

S: He could be a photographer.

C: He doesn't strike me as one … he doesn't look very artistic or creative.

Unit 9, Listening 9.2

OK, so what you see here is a model of the family life cycle. It basically captures the idea that the average family—whatever that may be — goes through a series of fairly typical stages. Now obviously this is going to differ from culture to culture, from country to country, and over time. A typical family now is rather different in many respects from a typical family 20 years ago, for example. But this particular model we're looking at is a reasonable representation of the stages that families tend to go through in modern Australia.

You can see that there's the same basic starting point: a young single who doesn't have any kids yet. Then there are three basic paths: the archetypal one, if you like, down the middle, where there's a couple with kids. Down the left here you have the basic path for single, solo parents. And over here on the right, the most basic path—the typical path for those without children. In fact you can see on this model there's just one cell here for the 'middle-aged couple or single without children'.

OK, so let's look down this central path. Singles get together and we've got a young couple without children, who may decide to have kids, at which point we've got a young couple with children under five—the third stage in this type of cycle. Now a couple with kids under five tends to be rather different from a family with older kids, so we make a further distinction at about 13—we have a cell here for a young couple with children under 13—in other words, before they are teenagers. The next stage we recognise is the middle-aged couple—some parents will object to being called middle aged at this point!—the middle-aged couple with children under 20. Sometimes those children hang around home for a while —so next we've got a middle-aged couple with children at home. Logically, the next one here is the couple whose children have left home—and this is where the path down the right joins up again. With the kids gone, a typical middle class couple has more time and money to spare, and here we have what has been called the 'couple in the golden years', enjoying the years around their retirement, before they get older. That's the stereotypical path for couples with children, then—the couple and their 2.2 kids.

It's pretty easy to see how the path for solo parents corresponds. Where we have a young couple with children under 5 we have a young *single* with children under 5, where there's a middle-aged couple with adult children at home, there's a middle-aged *single* with children at home, and so on, right up to the single in the golden years.

Now, let's have a look at some of the implications of this model …

Unit 9, Listening 9.3

I: You've been reading *The Nurture Assumption*, Kate. Tell us about it.

R: Well, it's a new book by Judith Harris, an American psychologist.

I: And just what is the 'nurture assumption'? It's got something to do with the nature/nurture debate?

R: Yes, that's right, Kim. The nurture assumption is the assumption that we are what we are because of environment—and particularly our parents, the way they bring us up, nurture us.

I: Which of course contrasts with the … nature assumption … that it's down to our genes?

R: Yes.

I: So what does she have to say about this … nurture assumption?

R: Well, she points out that there's good evidence for the environment, for nurture. Behavioural geneticists have found—mainly from studies of twins—that about 50% of the difference between individuals can be explained by heredity, by genes.

I: Which leaves the other half to environment.

R: Exactly. And it's long been assumed that the key part of a child's environment is family, especially parents. And as Harris documents, there's been a whole industry based on it, particularly in the States, over the last 50 years. There have been hundreds of books telling parents how to bring up their kids—you know, read to them, play them music before they're born, limit their television watching, and so on.

I: And her view is … ?

R: That they're barking up the wrong tree. That parents—and what parents do—is not that important. The research, she says, was flawed: it didn't prove anything.

I: So parents don't matter.

R: No, she doesn't say that. Parents do have an effect, but it has been exaggerated. The point is that friends matter more, it's our friends when we're kids that really influence what we become.

I: That's a pretty controversial claim. She must offer some support.

R: Yes, she does. She tells the story of a child she called Joseph. His parents came from Poland, and they settled in a rural area in Mid-West America, where they were the only people from Poland, and no other people spoke Polish. In a year or so, Joseph was speaking English like an American, and he's going to adopt the culture and language of his peers, even though he continues to speak Polish at home with his parents.

I: And how has this view been accepted by other experts?

R: Mixed: it seems some psychologists agree, others argue. But Harris still insists that those who argue for the role of parents ignore what every parent of a teenager knows—that their peers really do have a determining impact on their personality and behaviour.

I: So does she have any advice for parents?

R: Yes, well—Harris says parents can do things to affect how their children turn out—help them choose the right friends, for example.

I: And you're convinced?

R: Well, it's certainly an interesting read, and it does make sense, but personally, I'm not persuaded yet …

Unit 10, Listening 10.1

… OK, so let's look now at the—as a case study—at the Blue Whale, which has of course been very important, almost like an icon in the struggle to save whales in general.

First of all, some of the basic facts about them. Probably the most amazing thing about them is their size: the blue whale is the largest animal that has ever lived on earth, about 25 times bigger than an adult elephant, and twice as big as the largest dinosaurs were. An adult male can weigh up to 136,400 kg … to put that on a more familiar scale, that's the same as about 12 fully-laden buses! And they can grow to 33.6 m long … and in more familiar terms, that's about the same as seven stories in an office building. Now how does something that big find enough to eat? Actually, it's kind of ironic that the biggest creature in the ocean feeds almost exclusively on one of the smallest: a small crustacean about 1.5 cm long called krill. During the summer, when the blue whale does nothing but eat non-stop, they consume about 40 million krill each day, about 3600 kg in weight. But then during the rest of the year, about 8 months, they don't seem to eat anything, they live off their stored fat.

As for their location or habitat, blue whales are found in all the oceans of the world, although they usually stay in the colder zones, rather than the tropics, and prefer deeper water as opposed to areas closer to the coast. They can dive down as far as 500 m, although they don't often go deeper than about 200 m, and they can stay under for up to 20 minutes. Blue whales are quite solitary animals … they usually travel alone or in groups of two or three. They do sometimes come together in larger groups, up to 60 whales together, to take advantage of areas where there is a lot to eat. Over the course of a year, they migrate into cooler waters around the north and south poles, in the summer to feed, and then they migrate back towards the equator, into warmer waters, in the winter to breed. Like other whales, the blue whale makes a range of sounds, the low-frequency sounds that we often call their songs, as well as series of clicks. These make up quite a sophisticated language, and they're actually different for groups of whales living in different parts of the world. You probably won't even be surprised now when I tell you that the blue whale makes the loudest noise of any animal, louder than a jet engine. However, the sounds are at a frequency below the range of

human hearing, so we can only hear them via recording technology.

So how many blue whales are there now? Well, we stopped catching them commercially in 1964, but they're still categorised as one of the most endangered species of whale. The problem with saying just how endangered they are, is that it's very difficult to count them … like I said before, they tend to travel alone, and they keep moving throughout the year. Anyway, it's estimated that there were a little over 206 000 blue whales before people started killing them and about 200 000 of those were in the Southern Hemisphere. We didn't actually have the technology to be able to catch and kill blue whales until late in the 19th century, but after whalers worked out how to do it, they killed them in their thousands. By the time we were able to make any sort of count of the population, in the 1930s, the total population was down to between 30 and 40 000. When whaling stopped in 1964, the number was of course at its lowest level—but we're not even very sure about that … estimates range from 650 to 2000. Since then, the population has grown, but only slowly. In the early 1980s, researchers put the total population at about 6500, and the majority of those in the Northern hemisphere, rather than the Southern, as before. An estimate from a decade later is actually lower than the 1980s one, at between 2500 and 3000, but maybe that reveals more about the difficulty of counting blue whales than about their real numbers. As for current numbers, there have been some reports of more frequent sightings of blue whales in particular areas, but there's not really enough reliable information to say whether that means the total population has increased.

Unit 10, Listening 10.2

Section 1

OK, so what I'm going to try to do today is to argue for an economic solution to the problem of species extinction. Now some people will think this is a bit strange, because we usually think of economics as having got us in this mess in the first place. It's certainly true that today's developed economies consume more than any other societies in history. And the world's growing populations and increased lifespans —we're living longer—put a significant burden on the environment. Continuing economic growth and increasing incomes are things we all desire, but we pay a price to achieve them. Most of us make choices every day about how we trade off consumption of goods against the environmental impacts that all consumption entails. You don't make those choices because an economist told you to; you make those choices because it is your natural behaviour. That is a key point in understanding the role of economics in any environmental issue. Economics is a study of human behaviour; it is not the cause of it. Basically economics is just about how we use resources, and we can make economic choices to *protect* resources—protect the environment—as well.

Let's make no mistake—there *is* a problem. The tables you can see are very clear. And they only tell half the story. What you can see is the animals that are *already* extinct—not the ones that are in danger of extinction—already declining. We know that three-quarters of all bird species are declining; one third of North American fresh water fish are now rare; 42% of the world's 270 turtle species are now rare or threatened. Nearly half of Australia's remaining mammals are threatened. Two-thirds of the world's primates—gorillas, chimpanzees, orangutans, etc.—are threatened. Virtually all species of big cats and bears are seriously declining in numbers. Many scientists believe that we will lose over 2000 species in this century. And if we lose these species, we lose what they do for us as humans.

Section 2

Just think for a second about what animal species and the environments they live in do for us.

Plants absorb CO_2 and produce oxygen.

They protect our fresh water supplies.

They provide primary products—timber, rubber, etc.

They generate natural chemicals.

They provide habitats for animals and people.

They store genetic material that we use in industry and agriculture.

So we can't afford to take the problem lightly.

Section 3

The immediate causes of the problem are pretty well agreed. Namely:

One. Excessive harvest: put simply, we kill too many fish, whales, elephants, rhinos, and countless other animals.

Two. The introduction of exotic species: we import species from one area into another, where they can do a lot of damage. Feral cats—pet cats, introduced from Europe, that have gone wild—have done untold damage to native bird populations in Australia, New Zealand, and many other parts of the world. In Africa, introduced rats have helped wipe out many birds, including, for example, the dodo.

Third—and most important—loss of habitat. Humans move into areas where wild animals have lived and make it impossible for them to live there.

What can economics do about these?

Excessive harvest is the best-known path to extinction, because it's the one we hear about in the news. Let's consider the problem in a bit of depth.

Ask yourself 'why are animals endangered, but cows and beef cattle aren't'? Sure, I know it's a funny question, but the answer is critical to understanding the fundamental causes of this problem. If both cattle and elephants are valuable, why don't cattle owners harvest their herds to extinction? So they can continue to breed. If your livelihood depends on harvesting elephants, then why would you allow them to become extinct?

The answer is found in the economic theory of property rights. Property rights define what you can and cannot do with your property, and what others can and cannot do with it. One thing that property rights do is provide a reason for the owner of a resource to look after and profit from his or her property.

There lies the difference between cattle and elephants. Cattle owners have a right to possess, breed, sell and keep the profits from their cattle. They have a clear incentive to keep breeding cattle and to balance the numbers that they harvest with those that they keep for producing future cattle.

This is not true of elephants. Even thought the government—in most cases—owns the wild elephants, the lack of effective policing means that anyone can harvest them for their ivory. What reason is there for anyone to not harvest any particular elephant. Because there is no ability to exclude others from hunting; if you leave a young elephant to grow larger tusks, someone else will shoot it anyway. If you harvest the elephant today, you receive some income; if you don't, you receive nothing.

The answer, clearly, is to give ownership of wild elephants to the local population, and allow that population to harvest them. If the elephants are valuable, they will look after them, maintain them, preserve them, so that they can profit from them in the future.

The case of exotic animals is slightly different. Sometimes they are introduced by farmers, sometimes to control pests. Some were introduced for sport or to begin a new industry. But what they have in common is that the people who benefit financially from the introduction usually don't pay the costs of the damage. And there is no way to make them pay, because the problem is a long term historical one. This is the only one of the three direct causes that is best served by *non-economic* solutions. Once in an environment, an exotic species is almost impossible to eliminate at any cost, so the best protection is strong border security in sensitive areas.

The third problem, loss of habitat, is the most serious problem facing all species now and in the next century. This problem is also the hardest to solve because it is the inevitable result of economic and population growth.

The problem is straightforward. Humans control virtually the entire land surface of the planet. There are few places that are out of our reach and we continually want more. This is the heart of the problem. For each piece of wilderness left on the planet, some individual or group makes a conscious decision of how that land should be used. In each case, the decision comes down to whether the land is worth more as wilderness —forest, for example—or as something else—farmland, urban land, etc. The loss of habitat we observe today is the collective result of individual people choosing 'something else'.

Sometimes environmentalists try to characterise the conflict between development and the environment as a contest between good and evil, but these aren't necessarily bad people making these decisions. Each person simply looks at their resources and their needs and makes a choice that is in their individual economic interests.

Consider also that the human population is expected to nearly double in the next half century. Now consider that most of that growth is expected to occur in the very places where most of our remaining wilderness exists, and you start to see the real picture. How can we protect this wilderness when people need that same land for their survival? How do we tell a family struggling to find food every day that they must not use their land to grow food because we want to preserve the wilderness? If we want to solve the problems their decisions cause, we must solve the problems these people face. The fundamental problem is poverty in the developing world.

And the other problem is that the vast majority of people who strongly value the continuing existence of wildlife live in the relatively wealthy industrialised nations. If the people who highly value the wilderness live in a different country than those who bear the costs of the wilderness, there is no reason for the people who bear the costs to think about the distant values.

The only solution is for the wealthy countries to pay more to the developing countries to protect their wilderness. It is usually the wealthy countries that value the wilderness—why shouldn't they pay for it? They need to make it more valuable for developing countries to keep their forests than to cut them down.

Unit 10, Unit 10.3

A: Hey Richard! Richard!

R: Alison! How're you doing? I haven't seen you for ages.

A: No, not since… what? Christmas?

R: Yeah, I guess. What've you been up to?

A: Oh, just the usual … I've had heaps of assignments this semester … feels like I've had hardly any time to catch up with people.

R: Yeah, I know the feeling. They really start piling on the work in the third year, don't they?

A: Sure do. Have you still got that café job too?

R: Mm-hm … yeah, just on Friday morning and on Sunday morning though. It's a bit of a drag, but I don't know how I'd pay the rent without it … Are you still living with your parents? Weren't you talking about moving out last time I saw you?

A: Yeah, but guess what? I'm broke!

R: Maybe next semester, huh? Got any plans for the semester break?

A: Umm, sort of … depends on whether I can get all my assignments in by the end of this semester … we thought— Jenny and I—we thought we might go across to Melbourne to see Mike and Daniella, see how it's all going with them … do you want to come?

R: It'd be great, but I can't afford to … I had my big holiday after Christmas. Remember, I was up in Thailand, backpacking around.

A: Yeah, right. How was that? Sounds really great.

R: Yeah, it was excellent … I'd love to go back and stay for a bit longer next time. Anyway, 'cause of that, I've got to work full-time in the break as well as do some assignments … won't be much of a holiday.

A: Mmm, pity … Hey look, I've got to fly, I've got a lecture in five minutes, but it'd be great to catch up properly.

R: Yeah, yeah … why don't you come round to the flat, or dinner one night next week?

A: OK, that'd be cool … I'll give you a call, yeah?

R: Right … catch you later, then.

A: Yeah, see you, Richard.

Unit 11, Listening 11.1

A: So do you think it's necessary for everyone to—to require everyone to wear a seatbelt?

B: Yeah, I certainly do, I think it's an essential … requirement really … umm, I know in some countries they don't, in the back seat anyway, but obviously it's a really basic way of protecting yourself in a car, so …

A: Mmm, I agree … and I think that if it's not made necessary by a government, y'know, the costs to a government because of more deaths and injuries are greater than … imposing the rule in the first place. People might complain about it, but in the long run, it's in their best interests.

B: … Minimum pay rates are … definitely necessary. I think that, y'know, a lot of employers … abuse particularly young workers and also elderly people.

A: Yeah, there should—there should certainly be minimum standards … I'd agree with that.

B: What about a compulsory retirement age?

A: I don't agree with that. I don't think that's necessary.

B: Why not?

A: Because I think that each person is individually able to know when they can retire, when they need to … some people need to work longer if they don't have enough savings.

B: What about people who aren't really competent any more but insist on continuing to work anyway?

A: Well then I guess they could be dealt with in the same way as other people who can't do their job properly … there's no reason to make special rules according to age, I don't think … Banning smoking in public places …

B: I don't think that's necessary.

A: I don't know, I guess it's how—what they define public places as.

B: Yes, I was going to ask that … I mean, I think that in restaurants and bars, smoking should be banned, because I hate being in either of those places when there's someone smoking near me, I find it really, really uncomfortable and unpleasant … but if you're talking about a public place as somewhere like a public square … well, I mean that's silly, I think.

A: I think you definitely need to control immigration.

B: It's a difficult thing to talk about, isn't it? A lot of politicians talk about it in such an extreme way, like there should be no immigration or something … so people feel uncomfortable talking about it, but yeah, there certainly seems to be a need for some controls.

A: It doesn't need to be controlled in a negative way, more in a positive way … y'know, trying to control the type of people we get in the country, rather than the race or the colour … y'know, you want people who can do a useful job … contribute something to the country.

B: Yeah, they've got to have something to offer, don't they … but just how you establish criteria for that is a tricky question.

A: Is it necessary to impose high taxes on alcohol? Hmmm …

B: They've already done that, haven't they?

A: Yeah, they have … and anyway, if it's to stop people drinking, it doesn't work … I mean, particularly for someone who's got problems with alcohol, it means that more money is spent on alcohol, rather than food or rent or other basic things.

B: Mmm … So should mothers be paid when they stop work to have babies?

A: Yes, I think so.

B: But they're paid anyway, aren't they … the government pays some money to mothers already.

A: But I mean, is the pay as much as they would get from their job? Do you see what I mean, it's the difference between getting a little allowance and what you would normally receive from your work … I think mothers should be paid much better in recognition that they're still really doing a job, it's just not in an office … it's pretty hard work!

B: … And of course you need a maximum speed limit.

A: Of course you do … but then why do they keep manufacturing cars and advertising them as going faster and faster? Maybe they should make cars that are mechanically restricted to a certain speed limit … but of course there has to be a maximum speed limit … speed kills, the statistics prove that.

Unit 11, Listening 11.2

Section 1

Good morning. I've been asked to talk to you today about safe driving, and particularly about *fast* driving—or better, the relationship between speed and accidents. Now I'm sure that many of you here today—and especially the young men—think that you are good drivers, that you know how to control your car, even when you're driving very fast, that nobody ever got hurt just by speeding, that traffic police only give speeding tickets because it makes them feel powerful or so that the government can raise money, that speeding isn't a real problem. Well, I'm here to tell you, you are wrong, and show you why.

This first diagram here shows how much stopping distance you need, and the speed of impact—how fast you are going when you hit someone—when a pedestrian steps onto the road about 30 metres in front of you. So you can see that if you are travelling at 50 kilometres an hour, you're able to stop just in time—the braking distance is about 28 metres, so in fact there is *no* impact. If, however, you're driving at 60 kilometres an hour, it takes 38 metres to stop and—remember the pedestrian is only about 30 metres away—and you're *still travelling at 41 kilometres an hour* at the point of impact—in other words, when you hit the pedestrian. And so on. At 70 kilometres an hour you need 50 metres to stop and the impact speed is 60. At 80 kilometres an hour the braking distance is 64 metres and you're still travelling at 75 kilometres an hour when you make impact.

So it's pretty obvious that your chances of having a serious accident increase sharply with speed. And that's what this second table illustrates. It shows the risk of casualties—where someone is injured or killed—relative to the increase in speed. If we make 60 kilometres an hour the base speed, and say that the risk is 1, then at 65 kilometres an hour the risk is 2. In other words, you are twice as likely to have a serious accident at 65 kilometres an hour as you are at 60 kilometres per hour. And so it goes on—at 70 the risk is 4.16—you are just over 4 times as likely to have a serious accident at 70 as you are at 60. At 75 the risk is 10.6, at 80 it's 31.81—these figures are all established by research, by the way,

they aren't just guesses. And at 85 kilometres per hour you are 56.55 times as likely to have a serious accident. Staggering, isn't it? In a 60 kilometres an hour speed zone, the risk of a serious accident roughly doubles with every 5 kilometres per hour of speed.

Section 2

There are three main reasons why such small differences in speed make such a big difference to the risk.

First, small differences in speed mean differences in time to impact and ability to avoid an accident. Even if a driver can't stop in time, sometimes they can avoid impact. But when they are speeding, there is less time for the driver or the pedestrian (or another driver) to:

Recognise the danger

Decide how to avoid it—braking or swerving—and

Complete the action—braking or swerving.

Second, small differences in speed—before braking begins—can mean big differences in impact speeds. We saw this in the first diagram. Consider two cars travelling side by side at a given instant, one car travelling at 50 kilometres an hour and the other overtaking at 60 kilometres per hour. Suppose that a child runs onto the road at a point just beyond that at which the car travelling at 50 kilometres an hour can stop. So the car travelling at 50 km an hour stops just in time. But the other car will still be travelling at 44 kilometres per hour at the point where the first one has stopped.

Third, small increases in impact speed make a large difference to the probability of serious injury. This is because the force of the crash varies with the square of the impact speed. For example, a crash at 70 kilometres an hour has about twice the force of a crash at 50 kilometres an hour.

So you might think you are in control of a speeding car, but the risks are just too high, and you shouldn't be doing it.

Unit 11, Listening 11.3

Section 1

I: As the problem of obesity continues to grow, one feature of our everyday lives has become a key suspect and a sensitive political issue. This morning, I'm talking to Dr Richard Wilson, head of the National Institute for Dietary Research, about advertising and obesity. Good morning, Dr Wilson.

E: Good morning, Steven.

I: To start with, how sure are you that there really is a link between food advertising and obesity?

E: Well, as any researcher will tell you, it's very difficult, or even impossible, to prove beyond any doubt that a … complex human condition like obesity has one sole cause, or even one major cause. But it's become very clear, a great deal of research has shown that the way food is advertised in our society certainly has an effect on eating habits … and when we're talking about foods with a high fat or sugar content, then you would have to conclude that advertising contributes directly to obesity.

I: Are we really so susceptible to advertising? I mean, surely the great majority of people can resist buying the products in advertisements if they want to.

E: I think you're right to some extent, but the producers and advertisers of fast food and soft drinks aren't targeting their ads at adults like you and me, they're aiming at our children. Now, as a background, we know that children as young as 3 are able to distinguish between commercials and actual programmes on television, but it's not until they're 7 or 8 that they are actually capable of understanding, uhh, that ads are trying to persuade them to do something, and that they have a choice to accept or refuse that. With that in mind, just think about this: in the United States, it's estimated that the average child sees 10,000 food advertisements a year, and that over 90% of those are for fast food, soft drinks, sweets and sugary breakfast cereals. Advertisers also link fast food and soft drinks to toys, games, movies and famous personalities—the things that have such a strong influence on children. Even at school, soft drink companies in the US have contracts with some schools to sell only their brand of drink, in exchange for sponsorship and other financial support. All this together sends a very, very powerful message to children, and it's—it's pretty hard to believe the food companies when they absolutely deny that there's any link between this flood of advertising and the increase in obesity, especially among children.

I: However, the food industry as a whole is trying to join in the fight against obesity and its effects, aren't they?

E: Yes, you're right, they are. But I'm afraid those of us facing this problem in our daily work are convinced that many food advertisers are acting out of self-interest, not really out of any—uhh, true desire to reduce obesity. On the one hand, they're campaigning for better diets and more healthy lifestyles, then on the other—on the other hand, they're continuing to produce and advertise the bad food that causes the problem in the first place. There's a lot of talk about how the food industry has watched the tobacco industry suffer in recent years because they refused to publicly accept the overwhelming medical evidence against smoking … and so the food companies are trying to avoid future problems by helping to fight obesity now, while at the same time refusing to accept their part in causing the problem, and making every effort to keep their profits high.

I: Mmm … but seeing it from their point of view, it seems like they can't do anything right. They can't win, whether they choose to help fight obesity or not.

E: Of course they can win, they can help everyone win in the long run. They just need to concentrate on the other end of the process: stop producing the fatty, sugary food that does the damage, and stop advertising it, especially to kids. We're not saying that food producers are the only cause of obesity … believe me, I know how complex the causes are … but fast food and the way it's advertised are things that are relatively easy to control, and controlling them will make it significantly—will make a significant difference to the obesity problem, so let's just do it.

I: Well, thank you for speaking to me today, Dr Wilson.

E: Thanks very much, Steven.

Section 2

The purpose of this statement is to outline the position of the Association of Food Producers and Processors with regard to recent research claiming a link between advertising and obesity.

Firstly, as obesity researchers acknowledge, there is no evidence of a direct causal link between food advertising and obesity. Among the many other factors involved in the problem of obesity, food advertising can be at most one contributing factor. There is, in fact, good evidence to suggest that levels of physical exercise have had a relatively greater and more direct effect on the rise of obesity, especially among children.

Because of this uncertainty, the Association feels that the current attempt to focus on food advertising and the activities of fast food producers, as being primarily responsible for the increase in obesity, is morally and legally unfair. Food producers and advertisers have shown their genuine desire to find a solution to the obesity problem in their generous support of research into obesity, obesity education and prevention programmes, and treatment of the conditions brought about by obesity. Also, most food producers, and especially those in the fast food sector, are introducing new products into their ranges, with an emphasis on healthy eating, as well as providing detailed information on the ingredients and nutritional content of their products. The Association sees it as important that food producers are not targeted as causes of obesity while other, equally important causes are ignored.

In addition, it is not at all clear that simply restricting fast food advertising more than it already is, and controlling the products of high-profile fast food producers will have any significant effect on the problem of obesity. Experience has shown us, in the cases of the tobacco and alcohol industries, that these kinds of artificial control have not seriously or permanently reduced consumption, and in fact, they may even have contributed to an increase in the most at-risk groups, children and adolescents. The fact is, the decision to consume or not consume food products still rests with consumers—and their parents, in the case of children. Research has clearly shown that parents, not advertising, are still the main influence on the food choices of our children.

In conclusion, the Association wishes to emphasise that its members are willing partners in the fight against obesity. Solving the obesity problem will require a change in basic attitudes to food and lifestyle by consumers. Education and an increased awareness of personal responsibility in food choices are the first and most basic steps in this fight, so this is where we should all concentrate our efforts. If further research demonstrates that increased control of food and food advertising will have a significant effect on the reduction of obesity, then food producers will be happy to comply with such controls.

Thank you very much. Are there any questions?

Section 3

R: Thanks very much for helping us with this research, Rachel.

S: No problem.

R: Now, first of all, how much effect … do you think advertising has on you?

S: Umm, I think … more than I realise … so sometimes I think— when I think about it, I realise I've bought something because of a particular ad on TV,

whatever … so, yeah I think, subconsciously, quite a strong effect.

R: Do you think it has more or less effect on *other* people? Are you different from others?

S: Umm, I don't think so, but I think … how aware you are, of the effect— maybe some people say, advertising doesn't affect me at all, but, umm, probably it does, more than they realise.

R: Mmm. What about children, in particular?

S: Definitely … because they see something on TV, and they want it, and they ask their parents for it, and … yeah, I think … a big effect, on children.

R: Do you think there is any … link between advertising and bad eating habits?

S: Umm, I think … things like advertising fast food and … I think, especially for children, umm, they see it as something cool … that they want to eat … yeah, I don't directly link it, but it has, like, planted the idea in their head.

R: Mmm, right … so, some people claim there is a link between obesity and food advertising. What do you think of that?

S: Umm, I'd agree with that, in some part … yeah, I mean it's also about discipline, and umm, keeping to a healthy diet, if you know about that, but … yeah, I think there's some kind of connection.

R: How do you think that we should tackle the obesity problem?

S: Uhh, I think education's the big one, at a younger age … as well, instead of just being told 'Don't eat this, don't eat that', umm, we need to teach them why, and … yeah, I think, education.

R: Would it be useful to actually control the advertising of fast food, and the— the kind of food that's allowed to be sold?

S: Yeah, definitely, especially—umm … what they can sell, or … just having to advertise what's the fat content in something … umm, I think that's important … I mean, you can look really hard on the box or label, but … generally, things like fast food, you don't know what the fat content is, you can only guess that … it has a high fat content.

R: Mmm … OK, thanks very much Rachel.

Unit 12, Listening 12.1

The Road Not Taken by Robert Frost

Two roads diverged in a yellow wood,
And sorry I could not travel both
And be one traveler, long I stood
And looked down one as far as I could
To where it bent in the undergrowth;
Then took the other, as just as fair,
And having perhaps the better claim,
Because it was grassy and wanted wear;
Though as for that the passing there
Had worn them really about the same,

And both that morning equally lay
In leaves no step had trodden black.
Oh, I kept the first for another day!
Yet knowing how way leads on to way,
I doubted if I should ever come back.

I shall be telling this with a sigh
Somewhere ages and ages hence:
Two roads diverged in a wood, and I
I took the one less traveled by,
And that has made all the difference.

Unit 12, Listening 12.2

Group 1

A: OK, medicine … well, the pessimistic scenario is that viruses like SARS become much more widespread and, uhh, sort of take over … there's different strains, no one's able to control them. Umm, hospitals maybe will become privatised, so operations, the price of operations will go up … and only rich people will be able to get treatment. OK, positive scenario, an optimistic scenario would be that umm, we actually find cures for our major diseases like cancer and AIDS, and umm people get to live longer and, uhh … maybe this will become cheaper as well, for the public … umm, I think probably that I'm a bit more negative than positive, myself … maybe we will find some more umm, possible ways to treat cancer and AIDS, but I doubt that an absolute cure will be found.

B: Yeah, my ideas are a little bit similar … the pessimistic scenario would probably—in my opinion would be that … umm, as we advance with medical technology, this will mean that people desire more perfect individuals, umm, and illnesses and disabilities and things like that will not be accepted …umm in our desire to have the kind of perfect body, in the same way that we do with fitness at the moment. Uhh, optimistic scenario … yes, like you said, advances in medicine will help us to prevent a range of illnesses, which will enable us to lead longer, healthier lives … umm but there's obviously drawbacks to that, like umm, increased population and so on…Umm, I would probably tend to be slightly more optimistic than pessimistic … believing that, y'know, society generally wants to steer more towards the good side rather than towards the negative.

A: Right … umm, global warming … it could be the end of the world, chaos, we die out like the dinosaurs … the optimistic scenario is that we learn how to control the effects that global warming's already had on the earth, and … people become educated and, umm … realise that we are in danger of destroying the planet if we don't do something about it now, so umm … yeah, we set up—maybe there will have to be y'know, stricter controls, more, umm, laws created and umm people will decide that it's worth protecting the planet for our grandchildren. Umm, I think that I'm probably a bit more positive than I am negative about global warming, even in my generation, people are a lot more aware … than in my parents' generation, and so I think that we will become … umm, better at protecting the planet.

B: Umm, yeah, for me, a pessimistic scenario of global warming would be that … uhh, most of the countries don't change quickly enough to—to stop the world suffering more from its effects. So there would probably be a loss of some vital species, certain animal life and plant life. Umm, optimistic … umm, yes, I mean, weather changes from global warming, I think, will ensure that the world will have to take a more sustainable environmental—a more environmentally green view … because umm, at the moment, because countries are opting—basically, some of them are choosing not to commit to reducing greenhouse gases … umm, I think that the problem is that, y'know, maybe, as you said, it will need some of the younger people to actually come into positions of power … to make some of those environmentally-friendly changes, uhh, take effect…I'm slight—I am more optimistic than … than pessimistic, but I think there's still a certain amount of damage that's going to be done before people start to realise how serious it is.

A: So now, information technology … the pessimistic scenario is that umm, we … focus more and more on what computers can do for us than on the value of human beings … umm, a lot of people might lose their jobs, umm, where they think that it's more efficient to use a computer, umm but y'know, even though humans are slower and make mistakes, computers, umm, they can bring all kinds of problems like viruses and things that we can't control that well … umm, so in that case, the world would become a lot more dehumanised, and umm…it could just become very … a kind of cold and unfriendly place to be. Optimistic scenario is that umm, information technology makes life a lot easier, uhh—travel, business, communication between different people and different countries, and uhh—this could also have umm, possible, uhh—sorry, positive effects on learning … umm, I think that the web is a great source of learning and maybe the uni—more and more universities will offer on-line courses and umm, this might make it a lot easier for different people to access education, even from remote areas … So I think, probably, more positive than negative, as long as we remember that people are important in this world as well.

B: For me, I'm going to start with the … the positive … the optimistic scenario … umm, I kind of feel that the greater freedom that IT will give to us will—and choice, will basically lead to individuals being able to take more control of their own—their own existence … umm, and by that, I mean that, for example, most people in developed countries have a … have a degree of freedom: uhh, we can choose to travel, we can choose to kind of umm…change jobs quite easily, but people in the poorer countries don't have a great deal of choice. What it will allow them to do is—being able to access IT—is that many of those people will be able to umm, create jobs for themselves; not necessarily create a lot of wealth, but they may—they might be able to sell services to—to people overseas, uhh or provide information … The negative side to that is I think … in the long run, is that governments will try to control more and more, uhh, the data that flows over the Internet … umm, and I think we can see at the moment, that uhh governments are trying to monitor information on the Internet, even though at the moment, it's obviously a free flow … I think I kind of would be somewhere in the middle, I think, y'know, both optimistic and pessimistic. I think that it *will* provide us with a lot more freedom, but that will come at a price, umm, it won't

be just, y'know, that we can exchange information on the internet without any consequences … more official control will mean that some people will actually get caught in … y'know, maybe will be arrested for sending or receiving data via the Internet.

Group 2

C: OK, GE, genetic engineering, what do you think, what are some of the negative things there … that you think might happen?

D: I think umm … the biggest negative thing is the fact that … parents in the future might be able to modify their children, select the most desirable features.

C: Designer babies … yeah right, exactly … that's a horrible thought, isn't it.

D: So you can walk down the street and see lots of … perfect kids walking along, with the same kinds of features.

C: Also, the other thing I was thinking was the spread of disease … y'know, like viruses crossing species, with genetic engineering, like … umm, like they think that some diseases might actually have come across from other animals to humans … and maybe with genetic engineering, those sorts of umm, gateways will be more common.

D: Yeah, absolutely … yeah, and also lots of genetic modification, with umm … going on in the agricultural industry … things like chickens without feathers and things.

C: Yeah right, all that sort of stuff. But it's also the economics of it, too, isn't it … like I've heard about companies developing a new kind of rice or wheat and then—and then trying to force the poorer countries to only accept that particular strain.

D: What about umm, looking at the bright side of it? Can you see anything?

C: Yeah, sure … well, we talked before about the diseases crossing species and stuff like that, but potentially, umm, genetic engineering will cure a lot of illnesses.

D: Exactly, yeah.

C: And things like—and what we were talking about before, with the designer babies, the other thing is that you can actually stop … the genetic—umm, congenital illnesses, the ones that get passed down from one generation to another … so that's a positive thing, isn't it.

D: Yeah, families will be able to see if their—if their child has any … deformities, I guess, or illness, they'll be able to fix it.

C: Yeah, yeah, take that gene out … Umm, and also, of course, with food, you can provide more, potentially … the strains that they're developing will be stronger or more productive … cheaper to produce.

D: And good business for countries that can—can develop and sell the technology to other countries.

C: Mmm, yeah … What about education?

D: Well, I've seen—in most countries, it seems that many, many students are graduating from university … and uhh, the degree you get has been devalued because so many get it … people say that the degrees are getting easier and easier … umm I know for example in my country … umm, the percentage every year increases of students getting higher grades.

C: Right, that's a good point … What I was thinking too, was that education is getting really specialised … it's often very vocational, and so there's no kind of general education any more … and I think that's to do with the fact that people need to know so much for their specific qualifications and their specific degrees, in that specific area, so they don't actually get a general education at all.

D: But on the positive side, in most places, education is becoming more available, so more people will actually be able to study.

C: True, yeah, yeah … and also it's great how students from lots of different backgrounds, different nationalities can get together and study together … I think international education will become even more popular.

D: The economy? Yeah, well, the pessimistic view is that the rich will keep getting richer and the poor will keep getting poorer.

C: Exactly, that's just what I thought … the polarisation of wealth … with most countries, there seems to be a rich group of people and a poorer group and a huge increasing gap between the two … and it doesn't look like that will change in the future.

D: And I think the other factor that may contribute to the economy in the future is the overpopulation issue … it's more—y'know, there are more people being born every year, and there's more pressure on space and resources, which leads to wars, which then under- … undermines the economies of those countries because they're…spending all their money on weapons rather than on food or education.

C: Of course, the other point is that if you are lucky enough to have money …

the … the world's your oyster, you can really do anything … and those kinds of—of possibilities will be even greater for the rich in the future ,.. that's the only optimistic side I could see.

D: But I wonder, see, there are some countries that have turned that kind of situation, y'know the wealth gap, they've turned it around a bit, and the standard of living has increased for everyone … so maybe that can happen to more countries in the future, as a positive scenario …

Unit 12, Listening 12.3

I: And what does Kaku have to say about the future of work? Will radio broadcasters like me have to find a new job?

R: Probably not. If radio is a form of entertainment, then you're safe. He says that people doing creative work, requiring a lot of common sense, and working with people, will still have jobs. Because computers aren't creative, artificial intelligence is not close to creating common sense, and computers can't really work with people. And so that includes entertainment—writers, performers, actors, and presumably it also includes media presenters, and journalists. These are jobs that will still be around in the future.

I: Great.

R: But not all jobs connected to the media will survive. The people who produce newspapers—the printers, for example—will be out of work. There are two reasons for this …

I: Screens will replace paper?

R: Yes, more or less. We won't use paper so much. But the other reason is, printing is a repetitive job, and Kaku points out that repetitive work, where people are doing the same thing again and again, is better done by computers.

I: I don't think that's too controversial—repetitive work will go. What other kinds of jobs does he think are under threat?

R: The middlemen—agents, travel agents, car dealers, sales representatives—all these people who come between the buyer and the product. Because middlemen are no longer necessary when buyers can find out far more information about what they want to buy, and much better prices, through the Internet.

I: Yes, a lot of us already book our travel on the Internet. You mentioned before entertainment, but what are some other good prospects for the future?

R: Well, Kaku lists, unsurprisingly, software developers—especially artistic software—it's much easier to teach an artist to programme than it is to teach a computer programmer to draw—but also scientists and technologists, medical and healthcare workers, biotechnologists—no surprise there, of course.

I: No. All very highly skilled.

R: Well, yes and no. Healthcare, for example, requires all levels of staff—from very highly skilled doctors, to those with quite low skill levels, like cleaners in hospitals. The point is that they need to work with people and they need to use common sense. Which is why teachers have nothing to fear; despite the spread of on-line, distance education, people still need someone to communicate with them and explain things. And he says there will be plenty of other service work as well—maids, police, lawyers, tour guides, hotel staff.

I: And did you find his arguments convincing? I don't know if you saw the recent article in *Time* magazine, but he'd disagree in a few places …

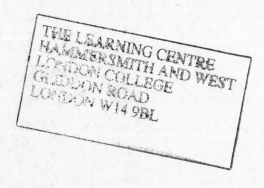